Lightning Strategies
for Innovation

Lightning Strategies for Innovation

How the World's Best Firms Create New Products

Willard I. Zangwill

University of Chicago

LEXINGTON BOOKS
An Imprint of Macmillan, Inc.
NEW YORK

Maxwell Macmillan Canada
TORONTO

Maxwell Macmillan International
NEW YORK   OXFORD   SINGAPORE   SYDNEY

Library of Congress Cataloging-in-Publication Data

Zangwill, Willard I.
Lightning strategies for innovation : how the world's best firms
create new products / Willard I. Zangwill.
p. cm.
Includes index.
ISBN 0–02–935675–X
1. New products.   2. Technological innovations.   3. Strategic
planning.   I. Title.
HF5415.153.Z36   1993
658.5′ 75—dc20   92–17542
                                                                        CIP

Lexington Books
An Imprint of Macmillan, Inc.
866 Third Avenue, New York, N.Y. 10022

Maxwell Macmillan Canada, Inc.
1200 Eglinton Avenue East
Suite 200
Don Mills, Ontario M3C 3N1

Macmillan, Inc. is part of the Maxwell Communication
Group of Companies.

Printed in the United States of America

printing number
1 2 3 4 5 6 7 8 9 10

*This book is dedicated to
the late Perry Gluckman, Ph.D.,
a scholar of profound insight.*

Contents

LSFI STEP 1

Make Innovation the Strategy

LSFI STEP 3

Eradicate Fumbles

LSFI STEP 6

Design the Product

LSFI STEP 7

Improve Continuously

20   Action Plan   *315*

List of Tables and Figures

Tables

Figures

Preface

For more than twenty years, my work has probed the characteristics that distinguish the top companies from the mediocre. Above all, one characteristic stands out: No firm stays on the top long unless it is highly innovative. That message has become even clearer with the recent rise of Japanese firms and the many high-quality products they have developed. Especially with technologically related companies, whatever their country, the companies that stay in the lead continually innovate new products that customers want.

The ability to innovate drives the economic success not only of most firms but of most nations. Because of that, I have spent the last several years studying more than fifty of the world's leading companies in order to discover how they produce new products so efficiently. I saw that compared with average firms, the top companies often produce new innovations in a fraction of the time at a fraction of the cost. This book attempts to delineate how the top firms accomplish this.

My research uncovered seven major steps in the innovation process. For each of these steps, the book provides many details that will help the reader apply the concepts to his or her own situation. Because product development involves so many parts of a firm, I have also tried to make the book comprehensive. For that reason it discusses marketing, manufacturing, quality, software, design, finance, and senior management.

This book describes some of the most advanced practices known today. It is recommended to any executive or manager who wants a comprehensive understanding of innovation, or who wants to quickly and inexpensively develop products that sell.

I want to thank the Graduate School of Business, University of Chicago, and the Alfred P. Sloan Foundation for funding part of the research that went into this book. To Arnold Berlin, Norman

Bernstein, and Joyce Orliss, I appreciate your encouragement during the difficult days when the outcome was in doubt. To my colleagues Harry Roberts, Linus Schrage, and Abbie Griffin, thank you for your insightful comments. I also want to thank Joe Williams and Moreen Alexander for helping me with the writing, and my editor Beth Anderson for her continual support, advice, and insight. To the many people I interviewed, let me thank you for your time and consideration, as you in a real sense wrote the book.

Lightning Overview

Why have so many executives suddenly become intrigued with product innovation? Because for most firms, innovation drives their success. Also, new ideas are revolutionizing innovation by slashing its cost and time up to 90 percent.

Fascinated by this revolution, I interviewed some one hundred people in more than fifty leading technological companies in the United States and abroad, including makers of autos, airplanes, computers, electronics, and even Post-it Notes. Based upon these interviews, I have synthesized the world's best practices into a seven-step strategy to stay ahead in innovation. This strategy is called the Lightning Strategy for Innovation, or LSFI. This book explains what LSFI is, why it is so effective, and how it is implemented.

Introduction to Innovation

The innovation a firm achieves today defines its tomorrow. In consumer electronics, for example, there was recently a new product onslaught. Japanese firms successfully eliminated most of their U.S. competitors, and no U.S. firm manufactures VCRs today.

But the opposite occurred in the bicycle industry, because U.S. firms innovated, and today dominate the market. Especially with the highly popular mountain bikes, U.S. firms have pioneered new features and control two-thirds of the domestic and over half of the European markets.[1] What is the secret? Michael Sinyard, innovator of the mountain bike and head of the firm Specialized, urges his employees, "Innovate or die!"[2]

If Reebok's inflatable athletic shoe, the Pump, was regarded as a separate firm, sales of the Pump alone would make it the fourth largest athletic shoe company in the United States.[3] The innovation of the Pump, state Wall Street analysts, is what fueled Reebok's impressive turnaround.[4] Compare the situation Apple Computer confronts. Its highly novel Macintosh produced top profits for many years, but that era is gone. Now, in a strategic thrust, Apple vows to reignite itself with more innovation. CEO John Sculley declares, "We want to show that Apple can be as innovative in the mid-1990s as it was (with the Macintosh) in the mid-1980s."[5]

Research unequivically confirms that innovation is vital.[6] Table 1–1 summarizes a study of more than a hundred technically related firms, conducted by Albert Page of the University of Illinois.[7] The top companies in an industry were strikingly more innovative than others, with far more of their sales from new products. Top to bottom, a firm's performance directly correlated to its ability to innovate. The conclusion is emphatic. Firms that fall behind in innovation will lose. Firms that rapidly innovate what customers want will win.

Lightning Strategy for Innovation (LSFI)

My interviews with the most successful companies revealed that they consciously follow a strategy for innovation. This strategy ties a firm's product development to its business goals and its market. That perception led me to formulate a comprehensive strategy for

TABLE 1–1

The Leading Firms Are More Innovative

Position of Firm in Its Industry	Percent of Sales from Products Introduced in Last Five Years
Leader in industry	49.1
Top third of industry	33.8
Middle third of industry	26.9
Bottom third of industry	10.7

product innovation, which I call Lightning Strategy for Innovation (LSFI).

Two Methods of Product Development

We can see how LSFI works by examining two firms with successful product development processes; 3M and the General Electric Aircraft Engines Division, which makes jet engines.

3M. 3M makes industrial, office, medical, and other products, including Post-it Notes. While many multibillion-dollar firms seek only new products with very large sales that affect the bottom line, 3M is happy with products with small sales. It follows the motto, "Make a little, sell a little." 3M knows that small sellers might grow into big ones. Post-it Notes, for example, failed their initial market test, but they are enormously successful. 3M also wants its new products to be first into a market and thereby occupy the high ground. It calls this concept FIDO—"First In, Destroy Others." In the past five years alone, 3M has launched 750 products into the market. These products were not mere extensions of existing lines but were conceptual innovations.

Since 3M accepts a low-volume product if it is profitable, it has to keep its product development costs low. Most of its new products are innovated by small teams, or even by one person with help from others. This means that anyone in the firm who comes up with a product idea can develop it—and management encourages everyone to do just this. Each worker in a technical area is allotted 15 percent of his time to tinker, to try to develop something new. 3M's management team vigorously promotes a culture of innovation, asserting that a ten-minute conversation with a janitor can produce a new product idea. To promote innovation it proclaims an eleventh commandment: "Thou shalt not destroy a new product idea."

Understanding what customers want is vital, since an innovation is useless unless it sells. Knowing this, 3M actively promotes the flow of market information through its organization. Because anyone can generate a new product idea, everyone is encouraged to visit with customers to learn about their needs. Some of 3M's business units sponsor monthly "ideation" sessions where employees and customers jointly generate product ideas.

3M also eagerly solicits ideas from outside—from the firm's public, suppliers, and customers. One of my own students phoned 3M and inquired about its product development process. When the 3M operator heard him say the words "new product," she transferred his call to a person who answered the phone with the immediate inquiry, "What is your idea?"

Not all ideas become products that get to the market, of course. 3M has a sophisticated screening process to winnow out the better ideas. But any new idea is sought, heard, and at least initially supported. In sum, 3M's product development process actively seeks new product ideas and develops many new products. Its innovation strategy thus meshes its business and marketing strategy with its process for product development.

GE JET ENGINES. The GE process is markedly different. Developing a jet engine demands billions of dollars, thousands of people, and seven years. GE's principal challenge is to manage a billion-dollar project. It must manage hundreds of thousands of interrelated tasks, ranging in size from a few thousand to millions of dollars. All of these tasks GE must coordinate and get finished on schedule and within budget.

Since performance is crucial with jet engines, many of the hundreds of thousands of tasks solve very difficult technical problems. One group develops a new nozzle, another a new high-temperature material, and another a specialized software package. To keep on schedule the groups must do detailed risk analyses, and any obstacle must be discovered quickly, have resources applied quickly, and be resolved quickly.

Even though GE operates at the raw limits of technology and even though a jet engine has thirty thousand parts, any of which could fail, quality must be essentially perfect. When I asked Sonny Pierce and Don Gregory of GE about defect measures, they almost laughed. At thirty-five thousand feet there is no such thing as allowing something to go wrong. 3M produces top quality, too, of course, but defects in Post-it Notes and Scotch Brand adhesive tape do not endanger people's lives.

The GE and 3M product development processes differ in other ways. Where 3M wants everyone to come up with new product ideas, for example, GE's product—jet engines—is fairly fixed. So instead of pondering new products, most GE employees perform specific technical tasks. Also unlike 3M, GE does not need many of its employees to meet with customers to get new product ideas. Jet engines have only a few customers—airframe manufacturers for commercial planes and governments for military planes. GE assigns a development team to each category of customer, and these teams work with the customer every step of the way.

COMPARISON. Although the 3M and GE product development processes are different, both handle innovation strategically (see table 1–2). That is what LSFI requires—different execution, depending upon the firm and its markets. LSFI is efficient precisely because it matches the product development process to the market and consciously plans the process that will most effectively develop those products.

Contrast with Mediocre Firms

By contrast, mediocre firms put out new products ad hoc, piecemeal, usually because they have to respond to the market or because someone has had an idea. Lacking a coherent strategy, mediocre firms fumble more. They lack a strategy because they suffer from a misconception so widespread that nearly everyone shares it with them: They believe that

TABLE 1–2

Comparison of 3M and GE Product Development Processes

	3M	GE Jet Engines
Number of projects at one time	Many	Few
Cost of typical project	Small	Very large
Customers	Everyone	Few
Employee involvement with customer	As many as possible	A few key groups
Management	Manage small groups of people	Manage very complex projects with many steps and uncertainties
Number of people involved	Few	Thousands

innovation is an uncontrollable phenomenon that happens by chance. Like a flash of lightning, the great idea pops into one's head, and then people produce a new product.

That belief, however, could not be further from the truth. Innovation is not spontaneous or random. Successful innovation requires that a company integrate the marketplace, the customer, the technology, and the manufacturing. As case after case attests, a failure in any one of these areas can mean a failure in innovation. What use is an idea if manufacturing cannot produce a product based on it, or if customers do not want that product? LSFI is designed to prevent failure. Just as lightning rods focus natural lightning bolts on the highest buildings, LSFI focuses the lightning of ideas on marketplace success. LSFI focuses and manages the lightning of new product ideas.

Results of LSFI

The results one can expect from LSFI are many. It can considerably cut the cost and time of product development, and some innovations come out lightning fast and lightning cheap. Here are the results that some top firms have had.

Dan Russell, who directs semiconductor applications at Motorola, notes that compared with a few years ago, Motorola is now developing new products in half the time, sometimes in one-fifth the time. General Electric vice-president Bill Sheeran states that a reasonable five-year goal is to cut product development time by at least 75 percent. At Xerox, despite reductions in development time, some Japanese competitors are still faster, according to Walt Sargent, manager of advanced manufacturing, and Xerox is now chopping its development time by another 50 percent.

The automobile industry is charging ahead too. As Al Jordan, head of General Motors' Phase Zero Launch Center, notes, GM did not start cutting its product development time until 1987. But in only three years, it slashed its development time from sixty months to forty-five. GM developed some products like the Buick Park Avenue and the Chevrolet Caprice even faster, bringing them in at a little over three years. GM's goal now is to get high-quality models out in twenty-four months or less, with corresponding reductions in cost. John Hauser of MIT comments that Toyota has decreased its product development time by 40 percent and its cost by 60 percent.[8]

Which auto firm's product development process is the fastest? Many observers believe Honda leads the race. It expects to reduce its current three-year development time to two, according to Dave Nelson, vice-president of Honda of America. Nelson's voice rises in excitement when he recalls the period in the early 1980s when Honda was in a fight with Yamaha over which of them would dominate the motorcycle market. When Yamaha announced to the world its intention to grab the number-one position from Honda, Honda was incensed by what it considered a personal affront. Honda vowed to fight back and retain its preeminence. It proclaimed *"Yamaha wo tsubusu!"* or, "We will crush, squash, and slaughter Yamaha!" With the battle under way, Honda counterattacked by launching a flurry of product development. During the eighteen-month fray, Honda came out with a new motorcycle model almost every week. Stunned by the onslaught and unable to keep up, Yamaha publicly admitted defeat, retrenched, and accepted a smaller share of the market.

If Honda were forced to wage a similar contest over automobiles, Nelson believes it could originate a new car model yearly. Honda clearly understands how to get products out quickly and effectively.

Success stories in product innovation have occurred in diverse industries. As reported by Preston Smith and Donald Reinertsen, the following reductions were made in product development time[9]:

- Hewlett-Packard computer printer—54 months cut to 22
- Honeywell thermostat—48 months cut to 12
- IBM personal computer—48 months cut to 13
- Ingersoll-Rand air-powered grinder—40 months cut to 15
- Warner Electric clutch-brake—36 months cut to 10.

Costs have dropped and product quality has gone up in other firms, as displayed in table 1–3.[10] The conclusion seems clear: LSFI can strikingly improve the efficiency of product innovation.

The Seven Steps of LSFI

This book presents the seven steps of LSFI (see figure 1–1). Steps 1 through 5 ensure that when a product is developed, it is done quickly, efficiently, and correctly. Note, the product is not actually

TABLE 1–3

Improvements Achieved by Several Firms

Firm	Cost Reduction (percent)	Product Development Time Reduction (percent)	Quality
AT&T (Circuit pack)	40	46	Defects reduced 30% to 87%
Deere	30	60	Cut inspectors by two-thirds
Hewlett-Packard	42	35	Field failure rate cut 60%

developed until Step 6, because LSFI does not throw products out, ad hoc or piecemeal. Rather, it follows a strategy.

Step 1: Make Innovation the Strategy

Product innovation has always been part of business strategy. The novel aspect of LSFI, however, is that it makes innovation so efficient that it changes business strategy itself, overthrowing traditional concepts of marketing, cost structures, and even acquisitions.

Step 2: Establish Foundations

Whatever products are developed, they can be developed more quickly and cheaply if top management first establishes foundation competencies in the firm. Waiting until a product is under development to fashion these competencies is too late. Because innovation is impossible without knowledge and technology, two competencies should be in place from the outset: the expertise of the staff, and the technological base. Other foundation competencies include creating the corporate culture, planning, and instituting the best practices (benchmarking).

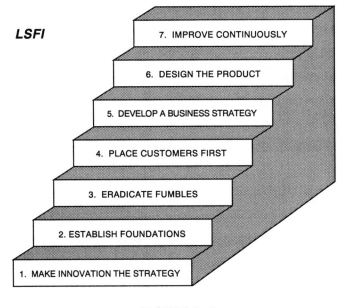

LSFI

7. IMPROVE CONTINUOUSLY

6. DESIGN THE PRODUCT

5. DEVELOP A BUSINESS STRATEGY

4. PLACE CUSTOMERS FIRST

3. ERADICATE FUMBLES

2. ESTABLISH FOUNDATIONS

1. MAKE INNOVATION THE STRATEGY

FIGURE 1–1
The Seven Steps of LSFI

Step 3: Eradicate Fumbles

Most product development processes are riddled with "fumbles," such as rework, changes, and delays. For instance, bottlenecks jam up projects, administrative delays occur, and approvals must be awaited. Since fumbles are usually hidden, management is often amazed to learn how extensive they are. Step 3 helps management find and eliminate fumbles. It alone has more than halved product development time and cost.

Step 4: Place Customers First

Once the foundations are set and fumbles have been eliminated, the firm can think about developing a particular product. The most crucial input here is to determine what the customer will buy. Many new products fail, despite the best efforts, for one overwhelming reason: The customer does not want them. To anticipate what products customers will like, firms should employ new techniques such as quality function deployment, conjoint analysis, cultural anthropology, and kansei analysis. In certain circumstances, this new thinking overturns previous beliefs. For instance, sometimes the best strategy skips customer research altogether, as in the case of the Sony Walkman.

Step 5: Develop Business Strategy

For a product to be a hit, a company needs more than the right technology and the right marketing, as business concerns are also crucial. Step 5 evaluates corporate strategy, finance, distribution, government regulation, and other big-picture factors to conceive the right business strategy for the product. The innovation must make sense from a total business perspective.

Step 6: Design the Actual Product (Concurrent Engineering)

Only after a firm has taken the first five steps should it develop the actual product. Product development is a complex, interconnected process involving marketing, engineering, and manufacturing. Many delays are caused by the "walls" separating these different groups, as each often operates independently of and even in conflict with the others. Engineering, for example, may throw a design to manufacturing, who throws it back, claiming they cannot make it, and the tosses often go back and forth, wasting money.

Step 6 discusses how to get these groups to cooperate and to produce a fast, effective product development process. Further, it explains top management issues, how to conduct the phases of a project in parallel, how to manage and schedule, and a variety of other techniques. All are targeted to get that new product out quickly, inexpensively, and correctly.

Step 7: Improve Continuously

In innovation especially, the only constant is change. When a firm systematically and continuously improves the innovation process, it uses the knowledge gained in making one product to improve the development of the next. When a firm does not systematically analyze what went wrong and what went right in a project, it will repeat the same mistakes over and over again.

Case Studies: Time and Cost Efficiencies

In cutting the time and cost of product development, a firm has to match its techniques with the product and the market. Most ladies' fashions, for example, require six to eight months from their introduction in the salons of Paris or New York to reach the retail stores. Vowing to be first in fashion, The Limited has slashed that period to a few weeks. It spies the new fashions as they emerge in the salons, and in a few hours, it makes drawings of them, using a computer-aided design system. The drawings are then transmitted electronically to its East Asian suppliers, who manufacture the clothes. In a few weeks one of The Limited's chartered 747s, which leave four times a week from Hong Kong, flies the finished goods to the United States.

The Limited slashed the time so impressively by unleashing modern computer electronic imaging to rapidly create and transfer information. To further enhance this capability, together with Sony, it is using high-density television to develop three-dimensional computer drawings. In addition, with its new organization, complete with airplanes, The Limited has eliminated the layers of contractors and middlemen that previously took months to transfer drawings and materials among the countries involved.

A quite different but no less dramatic case is that of the air grinder developed by Ingersoll-Rand. As reported in *The New York Times,* many Ingersoll-Rand products were taking four years to develop.[11] As one executive joked, "World War II was over faster than we can develop a product." The firm was losing business, and a major customer finally gave it an ultimatum. The customer declared that if Ingersoll-Rand did not have a new grinder at next year's distributors' conference—about one year away—he would buy from a competitor. Ingersoll-Rand accepted the challenge.

Determined to meet the deadline, James Stryker, head of business development, knew he had to overcome a problem. The marketing, engineering, and manufacturing groups would toss the design back and forth, and each would blame the others for the problems that emerged. Some of the milder remarks the groups made about each other were, "Did some lunatic dream this up?" and, "The engineers have really been hitting the bottle." To avoid this confusion for the new air grinder, Stryker formed a team of sales, marketing, engineering, and manufacturing representatives to work on the design in unison. This was a different approach for the firm, and with it the usual design-tossing ceased. As one team member put it, "Everyone would play in the same sandbox. We were going to share our pails and shovels."

For the product to succeed in the marketplace, the team knew it had to discover exactly what the customer wanted. So they traveled around the country holding focus sessions with people who use air grinders all day on their jobs. They learned that air grinders stall and that people develop hand pain. The team went to work, committed to developing an air grinder superior to anything that previously existed.

Stryker also realized that projects had mostly been developed haphazardly, on a play-it-by-ear basis, so that unforeseen delays were common. He devised a road map to structure the work and thereby avoid many problems. Despite the careful planning, some crises still did erupt. One was the question of what material should be used for the housing; aluminum, steel, or a plastic composite? To test the materials, someone had an ingenious idea. They made a model from each potential material, then dragged the models around a parking lot from the bumper of a car. The aluminum was hopelessly dented, and the steel was badly scratched. The plastic composite emerged in almost perfect shape, however, and although other tests were conducted as well, this composite became the choice. Worried about meeting the deadline, the team cut additional time by initiating a new practice in the firm: it designed and manufactured simultaneously. It started to produce some of the parts before the final product had been completely designed.

The dash toward the end was furious, but the team met its goal of a one-year development period. Even more important, the product was a clear hit in the market.

Both The Limited and Ingersoll-Rand thought strategically about their product development, by determining what the customer wanted, the business strategy, and how to develop the product efficiently. Their two examples also illustrate specific techniques for

TABLE 1–4
Summary of LSFI Steps

Step 1:   *Make Innovation the Strategy.* Get top management involved, as major changes cannot occur without their commitment.

Step 2:   *Establish Foundations.* Get the risky research and invention done first, preventing delays during the development.

Step 3:   *Eradicate Fumbles.* Target for elimination the innumerable fumbles—delays, changes, rework, and unnecessary work—that plague most development projects.

Step 4:   *Place Customers First.* Get more accurate information about what customers want. Managers will be less likely to change their minds about what will sell and make costly changes in the middle of the project.

Step 5:   *Develop a Business Strategy.* Get the business issues right, preventing later revisions and delays.

Step 6:   *Design the Actual Product.* Stop the "throwing over the wall" syndrome, and plan the project carefully to prevent problems, delays, and bottlenecks before they start.

Step 7:   *Improve Continuously.* Ensure that the knowledge gained doing one project is not lost but is used to make the next project even more efficient.

cutting the time and cost of innovation, techniques this book will examine in detail.

Summary

Product development time can be cut by as much as 90 percent, with corresponding reductions in cost. The key is to think about product development strategically. The seven steps of LSFI do this by providing a framework for designing a product and making tradeoff decisions (see table 1–4). It is crucial to determine what the market wants, and what is the best product development process for that market. Only after determining those factors should a firm design the actual product.

Putting products out as needed does not work anymore. LSFI provides the strategic thinking that makes product development efficient and creates a competitive advantage.

Make Innovation
the Strategy

2

Strategic Impact

Step 1 in LSFI makes innovation fundamental to a firm's business strategy. Senior management that views innovation as merely an operational task delegates it. But top management can no longer dodge the issue—it must stand erect and take personal responsibility for innovation. We will scrutinize how LSFI changes a firm's strategy, beginning with marketing.

Impact On Marketing

As we have seen, LSFI produces impressive reductions in time and cost in product development, causing market success (see table 2–1). Consider the markets in which Japanese firms have thrived: cameras, fax machines, computers, semiconductor memory chips, automobiles, VCRs, stereos, Walkman radios, and camcorders. For virtually all these products, the Japanese have shorter product development times than Western firms. And most of the U.S. firms that have remained competitive in these markets have very fast new product development times as well. Sun Microsystems, according to the *Wall Street Journal,* produced eight generations of computers in its nine and a half years of existence.[1]

As product development times decline, the length of time a model is on the market, its life cycle, also declines. New models quickly make current ones obsolete. The life cycle of a fax machine model is a matter of months, as are those of many semiconductors, small computers, software packages, small copiers, and communications equipment. Mar-

TABLE 2–1

LSFI Cuts the Time and Cost of Product Development

- Short product life cycles
- Considerable market segmentation
- Markets unpredictable
- Competition based more on speed to market

keting is like competing in a game of children's leapfrog, but with much higher stakes because new innovations are doing the leaping.

Since a model remains on the market only briefly before it is superseded, the sales volume of a given model will generally be smaller. But fewer sales will generate less money to pay for the model's development. Since today's winners are gone tomorrow, development must be not only quick but low cost.

Market Segments

This new marketing game has many implications. Market segmentation will burgeon, and quite small, even tiny groups of customers will get products designed for them. Mazda devised its highly successful Miata sports car to be profitable with annual sales of only about 40,000. According to *The New York Times,* Detroit is having difficulty making a profit on models with sales under 200,000.[2] The new GM Saturn originally had to sell 500,000 units annually to break even, although by opening one plant instead of two, break-even was cut to about 250,000.[3] Detroit, as presently constructed, cannot attack these small markets and must turn itself around. The prospects for the future are for continuing segmentation. By the year 2000, the cost of creating a new automobile model will probably drop, so that it should be profitable to produce a model with sales of only 5,000 to 10,000. Segmentation into tiny markets will occur in many industries. It will be a niche-marketer's nirvana, and the more product development time and costs drop, the closer that nirvana will come.

Top Management Strategy

LSFI forces top management to reorient its thinking. Ralph Gomory, president of the Alfred P. Sloan Foundation, states the message succinctly and unequivocally: Do not fall behind in speed of product development.[4]

Not heeding that message can be devastating. The *Wall Street Journal* recently discussed the "woes" and "pressure" facing Hewlett-Packard's CEO John Young.[5] "Some customers also aren't sure," the article stated, that "Hewlett-Packard is up for the intense game of technical leapfrog that defines the work- station business today." One customer who purchased machines from Silicon Graphics instead of HP explained that Hewlett-Packard had been "too late" with technology in the 3-D graphics field.

CEO Young himself laments Hewlett-Packard's "tiny presence in PC's." "It's the problem of being too late," he insists. "You've got to displace someone else and that's hard to do." The *Wall Street Journal* article did not mention that HP had already taken steps to reverse the situation. Nevertheless, the message to top management is unmistakable: Any firm with a product development cycle longer than that of its competitors has a profound handicap. It is like starting a 100-meter race from 20 meters behind the starting line.

Impact on Acquisitions

It may come as a surprise, but acquisitions, the realm of the financier and Wall Street, is also influenced by LSFI. To see how this is so, let us enter the office of a vice-president for acquisitions. Behind his mahogany desk, he is seated at his PC crunching some numbers. Bingo, goes the computer, about a particular firm. The financials look great, and the firm is number one in its markets. The vice-president acquires the firm.

Looking again two years later, we observe that the acquisition has turned sour. Its market share has dropped almost out of sight. What happened? The new acquisition, it turns out, was slow to innovate. Its competition innovated new products and grabbed the market. With its financials falling through the floor, the vice-president is now looking to divest that acquisition.

The perspective behind this story is that at present, many firms follow a portfolio strategy of acquisition and divestiture. A division is bought or sold largely on its prospects in the industry or market. Certain markets are deemed to have greater potential than others and thus to be better for the firm to be involved in. Sophisticated market-matrix planning approaches assist in analyzing these potentials.

But this approach may be fundamentally flawed. As the time and cost of product development drop, predicting how a market will evolve becomes increasingly difficult. New products that eclipse the older ones will come out, and still newer ones will quickly render the less new obsolete. Rebecca Henderson of MIT discovered that when a new generation of product is introduced, the leaders in its market often change.[6] In industries like photolithography, which involves machines to make semiconductors, the top firms one year might totally disappear from the market a few years later.

To acquire a firm based upon its market position today may therefore be naive, as future products introduced by competitors may very well upset that market position. A firm's ability to introduce new products will shape its future, and innovation will become a primary consideration in acquisition or divestiture strategy.

If you are a Wall Street warrior battling in the trenches of acquisitions and divestitures, considerations about innovation can help you make your decisions. For any given firm, determine the product development times and the length of the product life cycles. If they are long—as for, say, refrigerators—then the old market-analysis approach is still fairly good, because new products are not likely to enter the market quickly and market shares are likely less turbulent.

But if development time and life cycle are short, then watch out. New products will hit the market, and the market shares may shift quickly. Carefully examine the product development processes of a firm. Expect a firm with a really good process to move to the head of the pack. Obviously, many other factors also enter into an acquisition or divestiture decision, but it is worth considering that short product life cycles mean turbulence ahead.

Rethinking "Mature" Markets

Not only can LSFI change markets, it can instill them with new life. As Fujio Mitari, president of Canon USA, has noted, "Saturated markets don't matter because innovation can break through to new markets."[7] Companies can use innovation to blast open new markets, and old notions that markets are "mature" or "in decline" will fade.

The General Electric Busway project illustrates this concept. The ceilings of many factories are cluttered with big electrical power cables that carry the enormous current needed to run the giant machines. Whenever a machine is moved or a new machine is put in, electricians must climb up to the ceiling, move power cables around, and create new electrical circuits. It is a costly and cumbersome undertaking. But GE conceived an innovative solution. It created a plug-in system, akin to the electrical strips in homes that have plugs every few inches. The plugs it created little resemble the home variety, of course—they are often as big as a footlocker. But with them, there is no need to rewire. All the electricians have to do is move the plug. This innovation transformed a market that was practically asleep into a growth industry for GE.

Many markets that were once declared to be "mature," "declining," or on their death beds, have been similarly revitalized through innovation. The market for radios has long been called mature, but it keeps evolving with products with new sizes and features, not to speak of the Walkman. The market for home irons to press clothes was moribund until Black and Decker revitalized it with an iron that shuts itself off. In personal computers, many U.S. firms were complaining about a market slowdown, but at the same time, Japanese firms kept up growth by innovating in portable, laptop, palmtop, and notebook-size computers.[8] (Many such products put out by U.S. firms contain key components from abroad. Apple Computer's Newton product, for example, is manufactured by Sharp.)

Some markets do become mature and die, to be sure. But far more are declared dead when they are not. Even worse, asserting that a market is mature might be harmful. If senior management declare that the market for their firm's product is declining, that declaration will discourage people in the firm from striving to be innovative. Although it is an overstatement, the following notion may contain a germ of truth: There are no saturated and mature markets—only saturated and immature minds. The issue is often brain death more than market death.

Scotch Brand cellophane tape is a prime example of a product whose market was erroneously declared dead. The tape was originally sold on a roll, requiring the annoying job of picking the tape off the roll. That frustrated customers, and the market became flat. An enterprising business manager, John Borden, eager to boost his revenue, conceived of the dispenser with the serrated cutting edge. Once the dispenser was developed and marketed, tape sales soared.[9]

The message here is clear: Too many markets are said to be on their death bed and dying, when what they really need is a lightning bolt of innovation.

Design Determines Cost

Most people believe that the manufacturing process governs manufacturing cost—that cost is determined by the machines and personnel in the factory. But that is false. Nearly always, it is engineering design that determines most of the manufacturing cost. The crucial cost determinations are whether a part will be plastic or metal, stamped or molded, and how many parts will be needed. As Karl Ulrich and Charles Fine have reported, particularly in discrete-goods manufacturing, decisions made in design specify up to 85 percent of the manufacturing cost.[10] According to Dan Dimancescu, product design accounts for 70 to 80 percent of costs.[11]

Few people think of screws and other individual parts as strategic, but as Ulrich and Fine note, eliminating a few screws in its 2760 model cash register saved NCR $12,000 per screw over the life of the product. Ralph Gomory has described how IBM reaped an enormous saving in the manufacture of its Proprinter by cutting the number of parts in it from 150 to just 62.[12] In one instance, 20 parts were replaced by a single plastic frame. The front bumper of a Cadillac now has only 139 parts instead of the 249 it had before, and it is now attached with two bolts instead of eight.[13] Reducing the number of parts in a product generally spawns a significant cost reduction—not just in the cost of the parts themselves, but in the costs of storage, dealing with suppliers, invoicing, accounting, and shipment.

An entire field called design for manufacturing is now devoted to studying how good design can significantly cut the cost of a manufactured product. Geoffrey Boothroyd and Peter Dewhurst have conducted much excellent research for that field.[14] Let us take a quick glance at it here. (For more details, see chapter 18.)

Suppose that while an item is being assembled, it must be turned over several times. How many times is determined by choices that were made during engineering design. The best number of times is usually zero. Now consider another issue. Can one combined part be substituted for two parts? If the two parts need not move independently of each other, and if they need not be made out of different materials, perhaps one part can be designed to replace both of them. Systematic application of principles like these can often slash product cost.

Cost Strategy

These considerations immediately apply to top management strategy. Top management frequently pursue cost reduction by telling manufacturing to cut costs. Certainly an inefficient production system adds unnecessary costs, and just-in-time techniques can often slice manufacturing costs substantially. But manufacturing can usually attack only part of the cost problem. The real solution to cost reduction is typically a new design. Siemens, for example, redesigned its automobile fuel injectors, thereby cutting the manufacturing labor time from thirteen minutes to one minute and twenty seconds. General Motors struggled for years to get its costs down but made little progress until it changed its development process to emphasize making a design producible at low cost. As Mary Ann Keller, an automotive analyst at Furman Selz, emphasizes, "The costs weren't in labor or manufacturing. They were in the way GM developed its cars."[15]

Time versus Cost

The new concepts of LSFI can shrink both the time and the cost of product development. Time, however, is most often a more crucial factor than cost. Hewlett-Packard, for example, studied a typical high-growth market.[16] If a product is shipped six months late, that can cause a 33 percent loss in after-tax profits. But if the firm overruns the cost by 50 percent but ships the product on time, then the loss is only 3.5 percent. In other words, being six months late is far more expensive than incurring a big cost overrun to get the product finished on time.

Getting the product out late starves a firm's profits because the competition eats up much of the market and the firm is served only leftovers. In purchasing parts and choosing suppliers, for example, firms very often opt for the cheapest. But even if it costs a fair amount more, they would be well advised to go for the fastest. Most experts agree—"Spend money to save time."

How Late Is Late?

Here is a quick way to estimate the potential damage if a product is late to the market. Determine the length of the product's life cycle. If the product will be late for more than 10 percent of that cycle, beware. Suppose the life cycle of a vacuum cleaner is twenty years. If the vacuum cleaner is one year late to the market, it misses only 5 percent of its life cycle, so few sales are lost. But suppose the life cycle of a product is two years. If it is six months late to market, 25 percent of the total sales are lost (see figure 2–1). That is courting disaster, and a sizable expenditure to get the product to the market on time is warranted.

Since most of the products considered in this book have short life cycles, the rule is simple and imperative: Do not let that market window shut on your fingers.

Is Lateness Ever Permissible?

Despite the above discussion about speed, speed is not always advantageous. Sometimes being late is the right strategy. One acceptable reason for lateness is when the delay permits the firm to develop a product that is distinctly superior to that of its competition. If the technology is rapidly evolving, the firms that launch early are employing a technology that is quickly superseded. Waiting can then help them clarify what technology is better for the market. Delaying might also help if the extra time lets the firm develop a product whose features (including cost features) are unquestionably superior to those of products launched earlier.

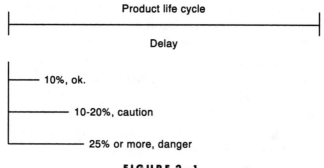

FIGURE 2–1
How Late Is Too Late?

But in neither of these instances is the company launching a product similar to the others. Rather, the product is distinctly superior. It is opening a new market window, and within that new product generation, it is not late, but first. Within an established product generation, by contrast, being late is rarely advantageous and is often disastrous.

A Caveat

A warning is in order here. Often a firm is slow getting into the market, but justifies the delay by stating that it is developing features superior to the competition. Although the product being developed usually does have some features that are improvements, from the customer's perspective—which the firm rarely examines carefully—these improvements are minor. Nevertheless, the firm uses these improvements to rationalize and excuse its delay. It fails to confront the truth that its innovation process is too cumbersome and too long.

Top Management's Role

Since innovation can propel a firm's business strategy, top management has much to do to enhance innovation. Their exact role will depend upon the nature of the company. In a small firm the CEO might do product development, while in a giant one the CEO might be involved only in strategic issues. Wayne Casper, vice-president for product development for Sargento Cheese, humorously suggests that the best thing a CEO can do is to "walk down the halls with his arm around the VP of development." More seriously, Casper strongly recommends that top management set a goal for the percent of sales that are to come from newly introduced products. That will unmistakably signal to general managers that developing successful new products is a major strategic objective. But Casper discourages setting a "batting average" goal of how many new products are to be successes. This will encourage only minor improvements and will serve to deter more innovative but riskier products. Minor improvements are useful and can provide "quick hits and quick profits," Casper says, but needed also are innovative "home run"–type products that might open new markets.

Casper suggests that CEOs actively reward and recognize product innovation. 3M, for example, financially rewards senior management in

TABLE 2–2
Summary of LSFI's Strategic Implications

LSFI cuts product life cycles:
• Navigates turbulent markets
• Helps segment markets
• Invalidates traditional acquisition strategies

LSFI rejuvenates "mature" or "dead" markets

LSFI cuts manufacturing cost, since most of manufacturing cost is determined by the design

LSFI creates speed to market, providing a clear competitive advantage

LSFI allows delayed market entry if
• the technology is rapidly changing. (Introduction too early might mean adoption of a technology that is quickly superseded.)
• the product under development has a clear and demonstrable competitive advantage. (Avoid rationalization to justify a delay, when the real cause is a slow development process.)

LSFI requires top management to
• be involved in the overall guidance of innovation
• reward, recognize, and publicize innovation
• set financial and market share goals for innovation
• have a goal for the percent of sales from newly introduced products

a division for the sales of new products. Further, CEOs should publicize a firm's innovations in their speeches, in discussions with employees, and on Wall Street. Companies should have a written policy and strategic mission for innovation, and CEOs should participate in the new product development steering committee. Moreover, the CEO should oversee the implementation of the LSFI steps.

Summary

LSFI not only changes product development, it revises corporate strategy (see table 2–2). Product life cycles are generally getting shorter, and firms that fall behind risk being left behind. Innovation, in itself, becomes a strategy. It will alter acquisition and divestiture activities and even the concept of a "mature" market. Since design greatly determines cost, cost becomes a strategic element. Innovation, propels strategy, and is the responsibility of senior management.

Establish Foundations

3

Expertise and Technological Foundations

LSFI is strategic since it changes life cycles, markets, costs, acquisitions and divestitures, and overturns traditional marketing and finance. This leaves no alternative—senior management must be personally involved in innovation. As its first task, senior management should build the solid foundations that underpin successful innovation. Doing that constitutes Step 2 of LSFI.

The most important foundation that management should provide is the quality and expertise of the staff, since staff decisions determine the outcome of innovation efforts. Intimately related is a strong technological and research foundation, as any lack there might make new product development impossible. These two foundations— expertise and technology—are presented in this chapter, while the subsequent four chapters address the foundation capabilities of the corporate culture, management, and planning. All these foundations should be in place prior to the start of product development, because establishing them after product development begins is too costly, too late, and too risky.

Building staff expertise and a technological and research base has two prime purposes:

1. *To permit a wider range of products to be developed.*
   Exactly what products will be needed in the future is usually uncertain. But solid expertise and technical foundations make it easier to launch whatever product the market will need.

2. *To speed the development of a particular product.*
Difficult technical problems often arise in product
development. Good foundations will help solve them and
avoid delays.

We begin by considering staff expertise.

Staff Expertise Foundation

People—their knowledge, experience, and commitment—are the
most important issue in product development. However trite and
obvious that statement is, an unusual twist exists: The quality of
designers and engineers is not at all uniform, but the range is enormous. In software development, for example, a programmer at the
ninetieth percentile is three to five times more productive than a
programmer at the fifteenth percentile.[1] Some programmers are ten
to twenty times more productive.[2] Consider that out of all the engineers and scientists in the world, only a small percent ever have
a patent issued to their name. Simply recall Beethoven, Mozart,
Shakespeare, Michelangelo, or Frank Lloyd Wright to see that the
same extraordinary range of capabilities seems to exist not just in
engineering and design, but throughout all creative fields.

People who are far ahead of others in inventiveness do the most
important part of product development—they conceptualize the
overall design, the architecture of a new product or software program. Joel Birnbaum, vice-president of Hewlett-Packard, recalls
that although IBM had a team of engineers struggle for months,
they failed to come up with an ink-jet printer. A single person at
HP reconceptualized the problem and solved it in a week. After
Xerox and a joint Du Pont–IBM team had failed to develop a machine to quickly give photo labs color proofs, 3M succeeded.

Alasdar Malarney of CACI stresses the importance of having a
design team leader who knows what is doable and not doable and
who has a global conception of the product. Leading companies
like Texas Instruments, Hewlett-Packard, Apple, and IBM have
special designations for their top experts, such as senior technical
staff, fellow, or architect. Although they are few in number, these
are the people who drive innovation forward.

One example is Gordon Bell. Now a venture capitalist, Bell

spearheaded the development of the highly successful Vax computer for Digital Equipment Corporation. He asserts that expertise is "everything." To conceive the Vax, Bell recalls, "I knew about all of the research going on anywhere." He had taught at Carnegie-Mellon, and he knew the history of computers. "I understood the different levels of computer integration," he says, "from transistor to circuits all the way up to applications." He talked to the top technical experts and to the leading customers, and he put a team of the "best and brightest" together to develop the Vax. Without this exceptional level of knowledge and expertise, he is convinced that the project would have failed.

When Kim Clark of Harvard studied these people in the automobile industry, he found that the most successful projects have a "heavyweight" director who manages the people and the project. These people are rarely in their offices, Clark says, but are nearly always out talking and checking on the incredible number of details that constitute a development project. They have excellent knowledge of the project in order to balance the tradeoffs in suggestions that would enhance one aspect of the project while harming others.

Characteristics of Top People

From these observations, we can draw several general conclusions about the characteristics of these top people.

1. They understand not just the technology but the market and the competition. People involved solely in the technical aspects of a product might not comprehend the market and competition. The individual directing an innovation project, however, should know the business issues as well as the technical ones.

2. They understand the many levels of a project simultaneously. Many projects fail because although they have a brilliant strategy, the technical details cannot be executed. Conversely, the technical capability may be excellent, but the strategic goals faulty. Most people have difficulty fully understanding even one of these levels. The top people perceive how the different levels interact and must reinforce each other for the project to be successful.

3. Especially for project leaders, they possess the leadership to manage a team of co-workers. Similarly, they have the ability to garner that support of the many groups in an organization that are needed to make an innovation a success.

Salary of Top People

The suggestion about to be made will give some readers apoplexy. But top people should be paid in proportion to their contribution. That means perhaps ten times more than the average professional employee. Such a person might be paid millions of dollars over time. This suggestion is not outrageous, and some firms already do it. Bill Gates, head of the vigorous software firm Microsoft, encourages loyalty among his technical wizards, in part, through financial rewards. A decade at Microsoft made Charles Simonyi, a Microsoft executive, "independently wealthy."[3]

Few firms are likely to pay enormous salaries to their top people just on this suggestion. But a more formidable power, the competitive market, may succeed in persuading them. Japanese firms now opening laboratories in the United States are planning to lure talent by paying new Ph.D.s about $70,000 and senior researchers more than $250,000.[4]

Management of Staff Expertise

Since the top talent ignite the development process, management is well advised to nurture and develop them. But the same concept applies to all employees, top or not, as a firm should develop all of its engineers and scientists as fully as possible. Innovation requires many people to solve technical problems. Yet solving a technical problem requires a person with the proper technical expertise. Differential equations cannot be solved without the proper training. A circuit that an expert can design in his or her sleep might take a novice months to design. Moreover, as the level of a firm's knowledge advances, the level of expertise required correspondingly rises.

The price of not creating and managing staff expertise is high. Lance Ealey and Leif Soderberg report that in one automotive supplier, 40 percent of the troublesome design problems that came up had already been solved in prior programs.[5] Thirty percent of the design time was wasted in repeating what had been learned before. The company had not taken the effort to retain its knowledge, and it paid the price (see table 3–1). Most firms are similar, Ealey and Soderberg believe, unwittingly squandering perhaps a third of their development time due to lack of expertise. Jim Dubay, an EG&G executive, agrees; "We are always solving the same problem."

Perhaps the easiest solution to this problem is to have some of the team members of one project participate in the next project. Intel, for example, does that to maintain its expertise. Still, people forget and new team members are inexperienced. To combat this issue, Mentor Graphics has an individual who asks people, at the end of each phase of a product's development, what problems they confronted. He enters that information into a database repository. In the future, whenever a problem comes up, someone can quickly check the database and learn what might be done or who might help. Similarly, Xerox and Digital Equipment also maintain databases of past problems and solutions.

Despite the import of these techniques, nothing can substitute for a systematic approach to developing the expertise of the individual designers and engineers. IBM, according to vice-president Bob Friesen, evaluates what skills will be needed and makes plans to have those skills available when they are needed. IBM directs training, experience development, and promotion toward providing employees with those talents.

Even with these efforts, however, fate dealt IBM an unfortunate blow. The firm encountered expensive delays in getting its top-of-the-line mainframe to market.[6] The problems were caused by the

TABLE 3–1

Resolving Old Problems Again

When firms fail to build up expertise, design teams resolve problems that were solved previously by earlier design teams.

Problems solved that were solved previously	Problems solved that were genuinely new problems

| 0% | 40% | 100% |

fact that to cut costs, IBM had instituted an early-retirement program and lost many of its most experienced people. One financial analyst commented about the situation, "When you run into a problem, you may not have available all the expertise you used to have."

Agreeing, Xerox vice-president for research Bill Spencer says that a corporation requires "memory," or a storehouse of people who are knowledgeable in the key technical areas. Xerox maintains a battery of experts in such fields as photoreceptors, design issues, and paper-handling systems. This "memory" should not be limited to the technical level but should extend into the suites of top management. A case in point is Motorola, whose software development costs were approaching half of the cost of developing new products. Most of Motorola's senior managers had been educated before software became essential, however, so they were making major decisions ignorant of half of the problem. Motorola thereupon launched an extensive training program to bring its senior managers up to date.

Not all firms develop their employees' expertise in such an exemplary fashion. When Karl Ulrich of MIT visited a Japanese auto manufacturer, he saw that the people who designed tailgates had about a dozen years of experience. The comparable people in a U.S. firm usually had only two to three years. At Xerox, Walt Sargent comments that the design team gains a great deal of important knowledge while it is designing the product, but when the project is over, that knowledge is often lost because the people are dispersed, transferred, or promoted.

At many firms management is so busy fighting fires that they pay little attention to building up the expertise that would have prevented the fires in the first place. The cost of developing expertise is typically small, especially compared with the sizable cost of being late to the market.

Ensuring Training Is Used

Any program to develop expertise must have training at its core. At least with classroom training, however, this is a widespread dilemma. Classroom training is often wasted because people use little of what was taught on their jobs. When Matsushita was confronted with that issue, according to Xerox executive Richard Greene, it conceived a novel solution. Six months after an employee attends a training course, an expert examines whether the employee used the techniques learned on the job and used them properly. If the employee passes this test, the employee's boss is reimbursed for the cost of the training course. If the employee fails the test, the boss is not reimbursed, which gets the boss very upset.

Expertise Strategy

Training, provides only part of the solution to furnishing the right expertise. Tellabs implements an entire strategy. It starts by determining the firm's corporate objectives three to five years ahead. To achieve those objectives Tellabs delineates the specific skills that will be needed, not just in technical fields but in all its managerial and professional competencies. It then evaluates each employee's personal skill base. This evaluation, interestingly, is done not just by the employee and his or her boss but by co-workers and subordinates as well. The evaluations are quite detailed. Leadership, for example, might be divided in several skills: ability to delegate, goal-setting ability, quality of guidance and feedback to subordinates, and ability to motivate. Using a 0 to 7 scale for each skill, the firm obtains a quantitative profile of each individual's skills, which is displayed on a graph.

Tellabs then sits down with each employee to find out his or her career objectives. Jointly, they create a career plan to develop the skills the person needs not only to achieve his or her personal objectives but to meet the firm's strategic requirements. A quick glance at a person's graph indicates exactly what expertise that person needs. Other graphs summarize the firm's aggregate data, and a quick glance at them reveals the firm's overall expertise level.

Tellabs previously relied on training, but it now prefers this more detailed and personalized approach. Most important, employees like it because it reduces the politicking and subjectivity in the evaluation/promotion process and helps them identify key areas for improvement. As one employee states, "I know where I'm headed with this company, and I feel my manager actually wants me to get there."

More specifics on developing expertise are presented at the end of this chapter. But now we must consider the technological and research foundations, as they interact very closely with the expertise of the staff.

Technological and Research Foundations

A firm's research base is an essential foundation. Research differs from product development in that research explores the unknown. Suppose a new material has excellent strength and weight properties but gets brittle at low temperatures. The firm wants to know if the material's use can be extended to a lower temperature. This is a research question, since no one knows the duration or cost of the investigation, or even if it will succeed in providing an answer.

Product development differs from research in that it is not aimed at examining new technical ideas. Rather, development takes a technology that is already well understood and transforms it into a salable product. Also, unlike research, where time and cost are somewhat loosely budgeted, product development has clear time and budget constraints. Despite these differences, however, the distinction between development and research is not precise.

Top firms handle the interface between the two in various ways. At Honda, according to Dave Nelson, vice-president, the research arm of the firm experiments with new concepts and new products, such as four-wheel steering, air bags, and aluminum bodies. Not only does the research group conduct basic research, it examines far-out and risky projects. Although a screening process is used to decide on funding, Honda does want to explore wild ideas. According to Nelson, for new ideas it expects a 99 percent failure rate. Honda encourages a high failure rate in order to promote breakthroughs.

A different part of Honda, the design arm, actually designs the car. Moreover, it operates quite differently from the research arm. Its failure rate is supposed to be only one percent. This one percent seems very low compared with the 99 percent allowed the research group. But design is able to adhere to it because Honda ensures that glitches, bugs, and problems are all worked out in the research lab. The design group utilizes only parts and concepts that have already been proven workable by the research people.

A very important task of the research group is to ensure that a new part or design can be manufactured. With advanced technologies, manufacturability is a complex issue. For its NSX sports model, marketed as the Acura in the United States, Honda had to meet the challenge of welding aluminum. It is one thing to make a few items in a research lab with Ph.D.s. It is quite another to mass-produce thousands of them in a factory. At Honda, the research lab eliminates the manufacturing bugs before design utilizes the new item.

When the design team starts to create a new car, according to Nelson, they "go shopping." They visit the research labs and see what new items have been developed that are ready to be used in a car. They might visit the headlight group, Nelson suggests, and select from perhaps five designs of headlights. The designers, he says, sort of "pick items off a shelf."

Assembly

With the parts well tested and manufacturable, the designer then assembles the parts. Designing a car is very complex: Style must be decided, dies and tools must be made, metal must be bent, and myriad parts must be made to work together. All of this is a sizable undertaking. But the designers do not bear the considerable additional burden of creating the parts to begin with. Honda eliminates difficult technical problems before it begins product development.

The U.S. Approach

By comparison, consider an approach where, in the midst of product development, the product designers try to invent and research new engineering advances. Imagine that during development a serious problem arises with an engine concept. If the problem had been discovered when the engine concept was still back in the research lab, a few people would have been merely inconvenienced. But if the problem was not uncovered until product development, scores of people are help up at great expense. If the product misses its scheduled market-entry date, it might even precipitate a sizable financial loss.

Unfortunately, according to Phil Barkan of Stanford University, U.S. firms tend to take this latter approach and do not fund research adequately. They usually wait until a specific product has been decided upon, then furiously do the research and "push" the technology. Almost always, Barkan notes, costly delays ensue. Typically, says Leonard Marx of Northrop, an aspect of the development project that was expected to take 10 percent of the resources balloons and consumes 25 percent. This is because when the designers are asked to conduct research, Marx states, no one really knows how long the research will take or how costly it will be.

Edith Wilson, a Hewlett-Packard executive, explains how such unfortunate events happen. As part of product innovation, let us say, a new adhesive that will bond material A to material B must be developed. To accomplish this, the product development schedule allots two weeks. Two weeks are allotted because that is all the time that is available if the product is to be finished and hit the market window on time. But no one has ever bonded material A to material B before, and no one really knows if developing the adhesive will take two weeks, two months, or two years.

The issue is that the time needed to accomplish a research problem is highly uncertain. But the time allotted for it is determined by the date marketing needs to release the product. It's no wonder problems ensue.

Strongly corroborating this view is Bill George, vice-president of Motorola, who has interacted on a joint project with Toshiba. When Toshiba innovates a product, it uses whatever technologies are already fully developed. Toshiba, George observes, develops technologies four or five years in advance of when they will be needed. The U.S. approach is the opposite: First a firm decides upon the product, then it develops the technologies. But if any of the necessary technologies do not work, George says, the project will likely fail.

Motorola made such a mistake in 1983, when it tried to develop a 256K dynamic RAM memory chip. "We were committed to a design," George recalls, "that required a low resistance layer of tungsten silicide." Despite heroic efforts on the part of the people involved, that technology could not be made viable, and the entire project crashed. Motorola learned an important lesson, and it now develops its technological foundations in advance.

Solid Foundations Required

The technological and research foundations should be complete, moreover, because the lack of any crucial technology can devastate a project. An executive at one leading scientific firm recalls that the firm conceived a major advance in the design of a particular part. But the new design's development was held up due to a lack of test equipment. Although the part itself was relatively cheap, it was to be used in a very expensive piece of equipment, and if the part failed, this piece of equipment might be damaged. The customer quite understandably refused to use the part until it had been thoroughly and exhaustively tested. But the test equipment was not ready. While the basic technology was being devised and before the actual part development started, the test equipment should have been under development. But this was not done, and a one-year delay was the result.

Delays Are Common

Despite the risks involved, "pushing" a technology during the product development phase is very common. A firm often feels it has no choice because its research base is inadequate and the market is highly competitive. To beat the competition, management exerts great pressure on the engineers to create a technically superior product to beat the competition. The engineers must then strive to gain a technical edge by reaching beyond the firm's weak research base. That effort nearly always causes delays, however, which holds up the product's entry into the market. To make matters worse, during that delay, its competitors' technology has advanced. So the engineers have to push the technology still further ahead. This spawns still more delays, and a vicious cycle of delays and costs spins into motion.

Not all problems can be found during research, of course, but building the research foundation avoids many expensive difficulties later. Indeed, a firm's research foundation can determine its future. Intel is often cited as a world leader in microprocessors because, according to an analysis by T. R. Reid and Brit Hume, it made "the long term investment that we tend to associate with Japanese industry these days."[7] On the other hand, U.S. construction firms are now losing market share to Japanese firms because the Japanese firms have spent heavily on research and development.[8] They have developed special tunneling techniques, cut the number of workers needed on many projects, and even designed such futuristic devices as construction robots. Specific suggestions for creating technological foundations can be found at the end of this chapter.

Case Studies

Here are some actual examples of foundation competencies that leading firms have instituted. Sony has a corporate strategy of building smaller and lighter portable products, and has heavily invested in establishing the technological foundation of miniaturization. It has strongly emphasized developing technologies such as batteries no bigger than sticks of chewing gum, very flat motors, circuit boards that fit into tiny spaces, and light headphones. Sony, it should be noted, developed these foundations with no particular product in mind, merely in the knowledge that they would be useful for future products. That has certainly turned out to be true, as the Walkman, the Data Discman, and camcorders illustrate.

Sony was once asked by Apple to help build Apple's notebook computer. Apple had tried to make the computer with its own manufacturing facilities but had failed. Apple had not invested in the foundation technologies needed for miniaturization and had to turn to Sony.

3M and Canon have also been exemplary in building foundations, as C. K. Prahalad and Gary Hamel cite.[9] 3M's array of different products is quite large. It has hundreds of products in many diverse businesses, including Post-it Notes, magnetic tapes, coated abrasives, Scotch tapes, photographic films, and others. But all of these products resulted from the exploitation of only a very few core competencies in substrates, coatings, and adhesives.

Canon, too, has only a few foundation competencies: precision mechanisms, fine optics, and microelectronics. On these foundations, however, Canon launched its impressive range of products, including basic cameras, electronic cameras, laser printers, bubble-jet printers, basic fax machines, laser fax machines, color copiers, and mask aligners.

To implement foundation competencies, a firm must sometimes alter the way it conducts its business. Charles Fine of MIT mentions the case of GM's accounting procedures. The GM accountants had required that the task of developing any new component be tied to a particular car project. Every development project had to be tagged in with a product whose sale would pay for it. A brake might be developed for, say, a Buick Skylark, and Skylark sales would then pay for the brake development.

GM has since ceased this practice and is now creating foundation capabilities. Components are now designed for a class of cars, without knowing exactly what cars GM will make in that class. This new approach permits GM to have only five brake assemblies instead of the present thirteen.

It is absolutely crucial, Prahalad and Hamel suggest,[10] for top management to invest in and create these underlying foundations and competencies. Further, they argue, in the 1990s firms will be judged on their "ability to identify, cultivate, and exploit the core competencies." They believe that this will force people to "rethink the concept of the corporation itself."

Prahalad and Hamel also suggest that the concept of foundation competencies will change the idea of market share.[11] A firm should seek market share not in a product, they reason, but in an underlying competency. They note that many U.S. and European firms—like GE, Motorola, GTE, Thorn, and GEC—believed some years ago that the color television market was mature, and they divested those divisions. In doing so, these firms failed to distinguish between a particular market—color television—and its underlying competency—namely, video. As a result, U.S. firms today find themselves lagging behind in developing large-screen TVs, flat television displays, and many industrial uses of video.

Even if a particular product line is not highly profitable for a firm, staying in it could further the underlying competency and permit success in the next generation of that technology. To accomplish this, however, top management should shift its thinking from products to foundation competencies. They should calculate market share, cost, and profitability not just for a product line but for the foundation capability.

Transform Research into Marketplace Success

Although building foundations is extremely important, merely having them does not guarantee that they will lead to new products. Researchers at Fairchild Semiconductor and Xerox PARC, for example, pioneered many ideas that the parent firms did not develop. The researchers' ideas were nevertheless excellent and were successfully commercialized later by other firms; and often by the original researchers, who, frustrated with the lack of support, left and went to the other firms. Researchers at Xerox PARC conceived at least a dozen ideas that other firms made into hits. The most famous example is the personal computer, and other examples are modern chip-making technology, silicon compilers for chip design, portable computing, mouse and icon computing, laser printers, drawing tablets, graphics computing, and computer animation.[12]

Sometimes outstanding research is ignored because the research is out of sync with the corporate strategy. In the case of Xerox, it perceived itself as a copier firm and had little notion of the commercial need for PARC's computer-related ideas. Xerox has since changed its attitude toward research and integrated PARC closely with the rest of the firm.

Robert Schaffer identifies another impediment to transforming research results into marketplace success. In a company he studied, the marketing manager told him, "Our project work is not very glamorous, and so it's hard [for us] to get R&D's attention. They prefer to concentrate on exciting technologies."[13] In the same firm, an R&D scientist commented to marketing: "You don't get us the information clearly, and the messages keep changing, so we concentrate on other work. If you would tell us specifically what you really need, we could design the product." Clearly, in this firm marketing and R&D had little understanding of each other.

Technological Road Map

To capitalize on their research foundations and successfully integrate them with the rest of the corporation, top firms use a technological road map. At Motorola, according to Paul Noakes, vice-president, the map helps assess the future of the firm's core technologies. The map evaluates not only the technological trends but competitive factors such as the likely changes in the market, products that might be developed, and actions of the competition. To summarize the analysis, it uses a color-coded chart to portray Motorola's preparation in the foundation technologies. The green code for a given technology indicates that Motorola is well prepared—that good plans are in place, they are well staffed, and they expect to be operationally and organizationally excellent in that technology. Yellow signifies a technology in which Motorola is only fair. Red indicates a technology in which Motorola is inadequate.

To keep the important technologies green, states Neil Hagglund, vice-president of technology planning, Motorola not only wants its internal expertise strong, it scours the world to identify top researchers, then interacts with them. It also creates strategic alliances with firms that are tops in an important technology.

Although road maps generally cover at least the next five years, Motorola plots crucial technologies—such as gallium arsenide, the replacement for silicon in certain high speed semiconductors—for ten to fifteen years ahead. After the firm does the annual technological road maps, the CEO personally reviews them. The CEO's input is especially relevant if additional funding is required or if several parts of the firm need to cooperate on a particular product or foundation.

Technological road maps are "very useful" and have saved his firm from "many problems," proclaims Amit Datta, EG&G executive. His operation makes dynamic seals that act as barriers to prevent the transmission of fluids. An example is the seal on a jet-engine rotor, which keeps oil separate from air. The difficult aspect of the product development is that the seals must be able to withstand extremes of temperature, pressure, and speed. Datta's team does a technological road map for several years in advance. First they forecast the speeds, pressures, and temperatures that the seal is likely to confront. Then they make sure the necessary technologies are ready. To withstand the high temperatures, special materials such as ceramics might have to be developed. They might also have to pioneer advanced computer-aided design systems that solve complex fluid mechanical equations and help them design the actual seals.

Steps for Developing the Foundations

Although the technological road map plays a central role, it alone is not sufficient to establish foundation capability. Rather, an entire organizational commitment is required. Recall that the establishment of foundations has two primary goals. One is to permit a wider range of products to be developed. The examples of Sony, 3M, and Canon show that it is often not known in advance what product will be developed, but good foundations facilitate the development of many innovations. The second goal of these foundations is to avoid problems and delays during the development of a particular product. Honda and other top firms achieve this by using only proven technologies, "off the shelf," in their product development.

Given these two goals, the following general plan can help a firm more fully develop and utilize its foundation competencies.

1. Identify the firm's major strategic objectives.
   For the years ahead, identify:
   • What markets is the firm likely to be in?
   • What products might be developed?
   • What are the major technological trends?
2. Identify key foundation capabilities that will foster the firm's strategic objectives. These capabilities should serve as a base to launch a wide variety of products.

   The foundations should be complete, with all the crucial technologies subsumed, so that development of a product is not held up by the unavailability of a needed expertise or technology. Optoelectronics, for example, the marriage of light and electrons, promises vastly improved processing of information. According to Robert Galvin, retired chairman of Motorola, a firm must build up competencies in six basic areas to be successful in that market, and these must be planned years ahead.

   This analysis can be facilitated by the technological road map.
3. Decide which foundations the firm will maintain itself, and which it will obtain through partnerships with other firms.

   Product development requires a diverse array of

technologies, most likely too many for a single firm. So partnerships with other firms are generally required. Establish these partnerships early. Letting a contract out to a supplier shortly before the development of a product is too late, especially if any sophisticated technology is required. It generally requires years for two firms to learn about each other and form a synergistic relationship.

4. Install and maintain the foundation competencies. Evaluate market share and profitability not only for products but for foundation competencies as well.

5. Identify in detail what expertise will be needed to support the foundations, and train staff in those areas.
   - Establish systems to ensure that people are not solving the same problems all over again, but that the knowledge gained in developing one product helps in developing the next product.
   - Identify what expertise the company will need in the future, and establish procedures to ensure that staff is trained and experienced in those areas.

6. Install personnel policies to retain staff in the key competencies. Training "the best and brightest" has little value if they do not remain with the firm.
   - Continually monitor and survey employees and reevaluate company policies to minimize departures.
   - Layoffs create fear in employees, so avoid them. It is the best people who are most likely to leave, since they can get other jobs more easily. Even *in extremis,* top firms like Hewlett-Packard, Tellabs, and Lincoln Electric will cut salaries, shorten work weeks, transfer people, and use creative cost-cutting techniques before they resort to layoffs.
   - Create an environment where people can stay enthused. Joseph R. "Rod" Canion, founder and former president of Compaq Computer, suggests that getting people to work hard is not a firm's biggest problem—people want to accomplish.[14] The problem, he says, is to remove whatever gets in the way of people's accomplishment. What upsets people most are the politics and attacks,

and the unnecessary burdens of attending useless meetings, waiting for approvals, and filling out forms.
- Make work "fun and exciting," suggests Wayne Casper, vice- president of Sargento, not just to reduce turnover but to enhance innovation. "Find something to celebrate," is the way Jack Stack, president of Springfield Remanufacturing states it. After a milestone is passed, have a pizza or beer party. Top firms strive to make work not work, but fun.

7. Ensure that technology transfer between the researchers and the product developers is excellent.
   - Have the research arm and the development arm plan jointly.
   - Transfer people back and forth between the two arms to promote communication and interaction.
   - Assign marketing people to the research labs, as Xerox has done.[15]
   - Suggest that researchers spend 15 percent of their time with operating people and design engineers, as they do at General Electric and General Motors.
   - Encourage interaction. GE researchers are routinely informed of the needs of the operational divisions and have joint beer-and-pretzel sessions with product designers.
   - Blend research and marketing. After a period of unsuccessful product introductions, Du Pont created "Centers of Excellence," where researchers work alongside product managers. This team approach has helped focus R&D on customers and on current product lines, and it has significantly enhanced Du Pont's product successes.[16]

8. Establish incentives for researchers whose ideas are used. At GE's research labs, a researcher says, "I also have to be entrepreneurial."[17] GE researchers are given rewards and faster promotions if their ideas are picked up by the operational units of the firm.

   3M encourages researchers to "champion" a new product. That means that the researcher who conceives an idea is subsequently placed in charge of the team that

TABLE 3–2

Summary of Expertise and Technological Foundations

Major Goals for Foundation Capabilities

I. To enable a wide range of products to be developed

II. For any particular product, prior to the start of development, as fully as possible:
   - to ensure the required expertise is in place;
   - to ensure the difficult technical, research, and manufacturing problems are solved.

The Implementation Steps

1. Identify the firm's strategic objectives.
2. Identify the foundations what will help achieve the strategic objectives.
   - Use the technological road map.
   - Ensure that all the crucial technologies are included.
3. Identify which foundations to develop internally and which with partners. Establish partnerships early.
4. Establish foundations. Evaluate the profitability, cost, and market share not just of products but of the foundations.
5. Identify the expertise needed, and ensure staff is trained.
6. Establish personnel policies to retain expertise.
7. Ensure excellent technological transfer by
   - joint planning by the researchers and the developers
   - exchange of personnel between the two arms
   - joint meetings
   - assigning marketing people to the labs
   - giving researchers 15 percent of their time to interact with operating people
   - blending research and marketing.
8. Create incentives for researchers to commercialize their ideas. Have researchers "champion" their own ideas and bring the product to market.
9. Monitor and revise as necessary. Check:
   - if development projects are being delayed due to lack of expertise or last-minute inventions;
   - if technological transfer is effective.
10. Conduct integrated planning of product development and foundations.
    - The foundations that are needed to develop a product should be in place prior to the product's development.
    - The foundations should produce as many products as possible.

develops the product and gets it to market. Not all researchers choose to do this, but many do, and if the product is successful, they are handsomely rewarded.

9. Monitor the situation, and make changes as needed.
   - Conduct a study to identify any lapses due to lack of expertise, like the study conducted by Ealey and Soderberg.[18]
   - Check to see if product development is delayed due to trying to invent during development.
   - Check which foundations are being transferred easily into product development and which are not.
10. Continually do integrated planning of the foundations and the products.
    - For the products that are likely to be developed, ensure that the expertise and foundations will be ready.
    - For the foundations, ensure that the maximum number of products are being developed from them.

Summary

Product development is inherently risky and costly, and unless the proper foundations are in place, it is even riskier and more costly. Two of the most essential foundations are staff expertise and the technological base (see table 3–2). If these are in place, a firm should be able to develop more products and develop them faster. If a firm waits until a product is under development to build these foundations, that is too late.

4

Cultural Foundations

The previous chapter elaborated on the expertise and technological foundations, and this chapter portrays another essential foundation—corporate culture. This foundation signals to the entire firm the commitment of top management to making innovation succeed.

The Innovative Corporate Culture

A corporate culture of innovation may well be the foundation capability that is most difficult to establish. Culture comprises the complex web of interactions, goals, incentives, and basic assumptions that guide our activities and thinking. We are explicitly aware of some cultural issues, while others are hidden or implicit, yet no less powerful. If a firm is to be propelled by innovation, the corporate culture must actively support innovation—indeed, innovation should drive that culture.

Innovation as CEO

Put on the shoes of a typical employee, and ponder how you respond to your firm's CEO. If you should get a call to go to the CEO's office, you jump up and charge right over there. Suppose the CEO asks you to undertake a project and to complete it as quickly as possible. You immediately drop everything and get the CEO's project done.

Now make a cultural switch and pretend that innovation itself is the "CEO," and that the people in product innovation are "CEO's" as well. If someone in product development wants to speak to you, you will charge right over there since that person is a "CEO." If that person asks you to handle a project quickly, you will give it urgent priority.

Taking this "innovation as CEO" notion to an extreme, the firm's actual CEO also "reports" to innovation. Let's say the actual CEO is dashing to the airport because she must meet with New York investment bankers in a few hours to discuss an upcoming stock offering. Just as she steps out of the cab at the airport, her cellular phone rings. Innovation is calling—a problem has arisen about a product under development. Immediately, she turns around, climbs back into the cab, and returns to her office to work out the innovation problem. Her secretary calls New York to delay the meeting with the investment bankers because the wishes of innovation, the "CEO," come first.

Although this story is fanciful, it illustrates how corporate culture would change if innovation were the "CEO." How much faster and more efficient product development would be if it were treated as "CEO" and were not involved in politics, or delays, or if it did not have to play second fiddle to financial, marketing, or legal activities. When innovation needed something, innovation would receive it fast—even from the firm's real CEO. Consider your own firm. When a problem related to innovation comes up, with what urgency does the CEO personally attend to it? That level of priority signals to everyone else how they themselves should treat innovation.

Eliminate Blame, Fear, and Distrust

Unfortunately, in too many firms the corporate culture does not support innovation. Indeed, a negative culture often exists that harms it.

By its very nature, innovation demands risk taking. Many unforeseen problems arise that must be quickly solved. Management aid must be sought to avoid allowing the problems to delay the project. The culture in many firms, however, hampers interaction between management and employees (see table 4–1). Employees frequently are afraid to admit that an error or a problem exists, fearing that the "messenger" will "be shot." Management likes to

TABLE 4–1

How Culture Thwarts Innovation

- CEO pays little attention to innovation, but is wrapped up in other issues like financing or marketing.
- Little trust or mutual respect exists among colleagues.
- Managers are involved in politics and game playing.
- Communications and discussion are not open.
- Executives and managers advance themselves at the price of others.
- Blame and finger pointing are allowed.

hear about good results, not problems, and employees with problems do not get promoted. When I interviewed people in different companies, I was surprised to find how often they mentioned these concerns.

Watts Humphrey, head of the Software Engineering Institute at Carnegie-Mellon University, suggests that many management reviews, procedures, and measures end up being used to assign blame. What that often does, he notes, is foster a series of lies. A project is having problems and incurring delays, but fearing blame, no one mentions this to management, and everyone lies, pretending that everything is fine. Eventually, the situation gets so bad that someone is forced to admit to management that a serious problem exists.

A Solution

Honda takes an interesting approach to this issue. When a problem arises, Honda wants it to be revealed quickly. According to one senior Japanese executive, "If I get mad at or embarrass someone for bringing me bad news, they would hesitate in the future. But I need to know about any difficulty immediately." Honda gives two reasons for wanting this openness. One, it allows a problem to be shared so others can help solve it and share the burden—people should not have to face such responsibilities alone. The second reason is that sharing a problem informs others and helps them avoid similar problems in the future.

According to Dave Nelson, a vice-president, Honda assumes that things will go wrong, that "people will rise to new challenges and occasionally go off the deep end." In particular, Honda expects

1. No hiding of errors. All errors should be revealed right away.
2. No blame or finger pointing.
3. Active support and mutual assistance when errors or problems arise.

Trust

A related problem is insufficient trust on the part of management and insufficient trustworthiness on the part of staff. Suppose engineering requests that top management approve the budget and schedule for a project. In many firms, the senior people have little trust and simply assume that the engineers have given themselves a 20 to 25 percent cushion. So top management proceeds to lop 25 percent off of the request. The engineers, being bright people, quickly learn to tack on the amount they expect to be lopped off next time. Top management must then cut double—once for the cushion, and once for the additional amount tacked on. In this situation, no one will ever be able to figure out who is to blame. Are the engineers trustworthy or not? Is top management trustworthy or not? No one will ever know. The only thing we do know is that the lack of trust and honesty creates a vicious cycle.

Although this story is exaggerated for the sake of clarity—it is not far from the truth. Perry Gluckman, president of Process Plus, a consulting firm, recalls that when he was consulting for one company, he knew, because he had personally worked with the engineers, that the cost and time figures for a project were as accurate as humanly possible. When the project was submitted to top management, however, management would not approve the numbers and cut them back. Since he had been hired by top management, Gluckman informed them that the numbers were correct. He said that the schedule that top management demanded was unrealistic and would almost surely be missed. Factory capacity would then be wasted, suppliers and customers would be upset, and many additional costs would be incurred. But management insisted that the engineers could do the project faster. Unfortunately, top management was wrong. Significant expensive overtime was incurred, and after the product was delivered the engineers had to repair and fix problems on the site of the customers.

What to Do

As one of its fundamental precepts, Motorola requires honesty and trustworthiness. Anyone violating this precept finds severe consequences. Jack Stack, president of Springfield Remanufacturing, pointedly corrects anyone whom he feels is not totally open or not fully cooperating with and helping others. He has a cardinal rule; "Do not destroy the firm internally." Disagreements arise frequently in innovation. But these disagreements should be honest and forthright, not efforts at personal aggrandizement or gain at the expense of others.

The important point here is that top management will get only the amount of trust and honesty that they expect and demand. If top management permit people to juggle numbers, inflate estimates, and "play games," the trust problem will spread like a weed. But if they insist on honesty and trustworthiness, that is what they will get.

Specific Cultural Issues

To follow through on these issues, consider several specific points that help establish a culture that supports innovation.

A Fair Hearing

Ensure that ideas are given a fair hearing. If a person is not getting a fair hearing for an idea, the most common culprit is the person's boss. In most firms, if the boss does not like an idea, the idea is dead. Think of your own experience. Even a small number of negative bosses can devastate innovation in a firm.

A number of things can be done to rectify this situation. At 3M, if a boss does not like an employee's idea, the employee can go to anyone else in the firm for approval and funding. They do not even have to be working for that specific person to get funding from him or her. Texas Instruments, Frito-Lay, and other firms have established special funds to support "orphan" ideas. People who cannot get their idea approved elsewhere can apply to these special funds.

The basic concept, however, is simple: Do not let one person kill a new idea. Provide mechanisms so that a new idea has multiple chances for funding approval.

One vice-president of a large firm offers another intriguing approach. If an employee makes a suggestion to one of this vice-president's subordinates, the suggestion is to be forwarded to him only if the suggestion is not (that is correct—*not*) approved by the subordinate. His managers have quickly learned it is easier to approve ideas than to explain to a vice-president why they were not approved.

Clear Incentives

Clear incentives for product innovation should be established. At 3M, a person's advancement and promotion—especially promotion to senior level—are heavily influenced by whether the person has innovated a successful product. The compensation of 3M's senior management in the divisions is partially dependent upon sales of newly introduced products. Many other firms give awards to individuals and design teams for developing new products as well.

Not long ago, I attended a meeting at a company that was having severe problems with innovation. Several of its projects were two years behind schedule. I asked senior management if being the leader of a product development project helped a person's career. They responded, "Not really." This firm clearly had some work to do in improving its incentives for innovation.

Cooperation and Communication

Ensure that the different groups involved in product development cooperate and communicate. Deborah Dougherty and Trudy Heller note that people who work in different departments are usually in different thought worlds, and they tend not to cooperate.[1] Marketing fights with engineering, while engineering fights with manufacturing. They quote a salesperson discussing his ongoing battle with research: "The big issue is when I tell research people what I need in the marketplace, they don't believe it," he said. "I had to take Fred and Bob out and introduce them to customers. Suddenly, everything I've been saying, they now say we need." By taking the research people out to see for themselves, this salesperson settled his conflict. Most conflicts, unfortunately, are not so easily resolved. Often top management accept conflict, politics, and game-playing as part of life. But such behavior hurts product development. A superior approach is for top management to stop conflict between groups and to encourage and reward groups that help each other.

Making Better Decisions

Corporate culture can also influence a firm's decision-making processes. Senior management should ensure that decisions are made using the best possible consideration and evidence. Honda has a rule that in making technical decisions, a person's rank does not count—only their technical competence. No matter what the person's level, that person's statements are to be evaluated based upon his or her expertise. When the issue is a technical one, even the lowest-level factory worker can tell a Honda CEO what to do.

Honda also goes a step further, according to Dave Nelson. It utilizes a *waigaya,* which Nelson loosely translates as a "controlled yelling session." If a person has a complaint, he or she can go to any level of the firm, including the president, and ask to have a *waigaya.* During it, the person is allowed to state his or her opinion without any fear of punishment, no matter what it is. Often everyone involved in the particular problem raised is called into the discussion. Nelson says that people come to him a few times a week for a *waigaya,* and although most of these sessions are brief, others last for hours until all the issues are resolved.

The essential aspect of a *waigaya* is the absence of fear of retribution, even for complaints or disagreements with the highest levels of the firm. This is the only way to ensure free and open discussion. One can only wonder if the disastrous blowup of the NASA Space Shuttle *Challenger* would have occurred had people felt free to strongly object. Some of the engineers had warned that the "O-rings" on the shuttle could not withstand cold weather, but they were overruled. Out of fear of retribution, they did not feel they could strongly object. The O-ring error produced one of the most catastrophic technical failures in history.

In a similar vein, Bill Sheeran, vice-president of General Electric, recognizes that fear of retribution may have contributed to the $400 million disaster that GE experienced with refrigerators. Two million rotary compressors had to be replaced in refrigerators in homes across the country. It was one of the biggest industrial mistakes ever made, and given the size of the loss, few firms other than GE would have been able to back their commitment to their customers. According to Sheeran, some of the technical people had previously had reservations about the long-term reliability of the compressors, but they had been reluctant to be fully candid. They feared the "shoot the messenger" syndrome, Sheeran suggests.

Sheeran himself now ensures that all employees are freely heard in making major and risky decisions. It took a while for them to get over their fear of speaking out, he notes, but the result is that GE now makes more informed decisions. He recounts a meeting he once held about a major decision. He involved everyone who worked in the project, including the sales and shop floor people. The people raised ninety questions, and a second meeting had to be held to answer them. Finally, at the end of the second meeting, he asked if everyone in the room now supported the decision. Two people objected. One person's objection was really a misunderstanding and was immediately cleared up. The other concern had been examined previously and was quickly allayed.

Even with these procedures, the final decision, being risky, still might be wrong. Not all objections to a decision can be accommodated, and sometimes the final decision must overrule some objectors. But because these approaches eliminate fear and allow people to speak more freely, they can increase the percent of good decisions.

Keep the Customer in the Decision

Reducing fear and allowing greater participation are only part of the decision-making process. Compaq relies upon a powerful maxim to facilitate its decision-making: Keep the customer in mind. That goal sounds obvious, yet without constant reiteration from management, it is neglected. Although innovation and new ideas are keenly desirable, innovation beyond what the customers want— or will pay for—is not. In the midst of product development, many people have "great" ideas and want to change the product and "improve" it. But people should not be allowed to add their ideas to a product willy-nilly. The question must always be asked: Will the change please the customer and benefit sales?

While this approach is definitely helpful, it is certainly neither perfect nor a panacea. Compaq made some severe misjudgments about laptop computer customers relative to pricing and to the importance of the product, and the firm took big hits on its profits. Making the customer the top priority does not guarantee that the customer's needs will always be properly evaluated, but at least it ensures they will be carefully considered.

Survey Staff Opinion

The most serious impediment to creating a culture that promotes innovation is top management's blindness to what is really going on at the operating levels. Time and time again, senior management misjudges what the working-level staff really thinks. One of the best ways to probe that information is by conducting a confidential survey. Confidentiality is usually best assured by having an outside, independent firm conduct the survey.

Here are some sample questions that might be asked in a survey of the staff involved in innovation. Each question could be answered on a scale of one to five:

Strongly disagree	Moderately disagree	Neutral	Moderately agree	Strongly agree
1	2	3	4	5

Sample questions could include:

1. Top management strongly supports innovation in this company.
2. Management listens to my suggestions to improve innovation.
3. When I have a problem getting my work done, management helps me solve it.
4. When I need a decision made from management, it is made quickly.

5. There is a lot of politics around here.
6. Management seems more interested in advancing their own careers than in promoting product innovation.
7. I am given good resources and support in getting my work done.

Just as important as the survey itself, management should estimate how they think the staff will answer these questions. Management should answer each question the way they think the typical staff member would. Doing this provides information on how in touch management is with the real culture of innovation. The results often are flabbergasting to management. In one case, management guessed that 85 percent of the staff would agree with the statement that top management strongly supports innovation. In fact, most of the staff disagreed and felt that management did not support innovation. Investigation of why that discrepancy had occurred led to some major changes. In many firms management has quite distorted opinions about what the staff really thinks, and such a survey can help change that.

TABLE 4–2

Create a Culture That Supports Innovation

Many firms have negative cultures that harm innovation and that discourage ideas and free discussion. To create a culture that supports innovation:

1. Make innovation the "CEO."
2. Eliminate politics and self-serving behaviors, and replace them with trust and honesty
3. Eliminate blame and fear of retribution, and replace them with mutual support.
4. Encourage open creative discussions and *waigaya*.
5. Ensure that ideas get a fair hearing and are not blocked by an employee's boss.
   • Require ideas that are *not* approved to be forwarded.
   • Create funding for "orphan" ideas.
6. Foster creative cooperation among groups.
7. Keep what the customer wants in mind.
8. Conduct a survey to find out what the innovation staff really thinks about the culture. Management should estimate how they think the staff will answer the survey questions.

Summary

An encouraging, helpful corporate culture is an essential foundation of Step 2 of LSFI (see table 4–2). Negative attitudes of blame and distrust must be replaced by cooperation, open-mindedness, and support. Innovative ideas should be encouraged at all levels of management, and all employees should have the opportunity to voice criticisms and suggestions. Innovation should be treated almost as if it were the CEO. Developing the right culture is a subtle process but absolutely necessary to successful innovation.

5

Managerial Foundations: Competitive Benchmarking

The corporate culture must support not only innovation, but the best management practices. A powerful competence for achieving those practices is known as benchmarking. Benchmarking is a way of assuring that every person, every group, and every department in the company follows the best possible practices. It involves identifying the best practices wherever in the world they can be found, learning about them, and implementing them in the firm. Then, benchmarking dictates, the firm starts to exceed the best existing practices elsewhere and becomes best itself.

In its drive to become the best, Matsushita's goals is "Every employee should strive to become the world's number-one expert in what he does." Think for a moment what would happen if a firm could implement that goal even reasonably well. Certainly, that firm would be an extremely exciting place to work, and it would be almost unstoppable in the market. Benchmarking is a path to that goal.

The Emergence of Benchmarking

The pioneer in competitive benchmarking was Xerox, which initiated the practice near the end of the 1970s. At that time, formidable competition from Japanese firms had put Xerox in serious trouble. The Japanese were manufacturing copiers at half of Xerox's manufacturing cost and were even selling them at less than Xerox's manufacturing cost. Xerox's market share was plunging, as were its profits. After years of disregarding its Japanese competition, Xerox decided it had to confront the truth.

Xerox counterattacked and successfully boosted its profits and market shares. Although it launched several programs to do this, the most crucial was competitive benchmarking. The benchmarking required every group in Xerox to determine what the best practices were in its field. Typically, the best practices could be found in other companies. The Xerox people had to learn these best practices from those other companies, implement them internally, and in time surpass them and become the best themselves.

Benchmarking is an outgrowth of traditional competitor analysis, which requires that a firm carefully identify what its competitors are doing, then ensure that its own product is superior to that of the competitor (see table 5–1). But Xerox contributed a couple of ingenious additions to competitor analysis. It first questioned limiting the comparison to the product alone. Instead, it compared all aspects of the firm, even those aspects that had nothing to do with manufacturing. This made sense because a major percentage of costs is not in direct manufacturing expense but in overhead. Xerox required all groups in the firm—be it the mail room, the accounting department, or the sales team—to benchmark.

Next, Xerox questioned limiting the comparison to competitors. Instead, each group had to compare itself to the best operation of that nature wherever it was—even if it was not in a competitor. For instance, many copiers have sheet metal frames. To compare Xerox's frame with a competitor's frame might not yield much information, because no copier manufacturer might be really good at making frames. Rather, it makes more sense to seek out the best

TABLE 5–1

Benchmarking versus Competitor Analysis

- Competitor analysis attempts to put out a product superior to the that of competition.
- Benchmarking
  - seeks the best practices in any firm in the world, not just in the competition;
  - requires all areas of firm, not just those directly related to the product, to strive to be the best.

sheet metal frames in the world, then compare oneself to their man-ufacturer. Going outside one's industry may actually be easier, be-cause direct competitors are less likely to share information. Many competitors' overall performance measures—such as revenue per employee, inventory turns, investment, market share, and length of time to develop products—are available in their annual reports and in the open literature. Based upon such insights Xerox designed its competitive benchmarking program.

Implementation of Benchmarking

Executive John Kelsch says that Xerox benchmarks on two levels—the strategic and the operational. The strategic level benchmarks overall performance goals. American Express's billing-error rate is 1.6 percent, for example, which is a better rate than Xerox's. That rate then becomes the goal for Xerox.

The strategic level specifies targets for improvement, but it does not delineate how to achieve those targets. That is the purpose of benchmarking at the operational level. To match American Ex-press's performance in billing, Xerox studies the details of Ameri-can Express's process to learn how to reduce its billing errors.

As another example, suppose a firm wishes to improve its prod-uct development. First it identifies a benchmark firm, and that firm's level of efficiency becomes the strategic target. Then the oper-ational level probes the benchmark firm's procedures to discover how to improve. Relative to product development, Cuneyt Oge suggests investigating three aspects: time to develop a product, quality, and cost.[1] By getting at the details of these aspects, the operational level yields the really interesting insights.

Xerox implements benchmarking as part of its annual planning process. For each area of the company, management uses strategic benchmarking to establish performance goals. Then it employs op-erational benchmarking to learn how to achieve these goals.

Most managers believe that given the resources they are allotted and pressure that is on them, they are doing a good (if not excellent) job. Yet they have no real evidence to justify this belief; nor can they state what constitutes the best performance. Benchmarking adds objectivity to this situation and is a systematic means to becoming the best.

Benchmarking Procedure: Ten Steps

The following ten steps for implementing benchmarking were adapted from *Industry Week*,[2] the book *Benchmarking* by Robert C. Camp, and from interviews. Because of its generality, benchmarking, as presented, is applicable not solely to innovation but to almost all parts of the firm.

1. *Identify the firm's key success factors and benchmark areas relevant to them first.*

A unit or group in the firm should identify the areas most essential to its success, and benchmark these areas first. To identify the crucial areas, the following questions might be answered:

- What is most crucial to business success?
- What problems are causing the most trouble?
- What factors are responsible for customer satisfaction?
- Where are competitive pressures being felt?
- What are major cost components?

The best answers to these questions are often obtained by asking customers of the process (which may be another department in the same company) what they want the process to do for them. The group should also evaluate what competitors are doing.

2. *Assemble a team to conduct the benchmarking.*

This team should include the people who will be needed to implement the findings. If these people are not included now, there is a frequent tendency for them to object later, deny the findings of the team, and derail the entire benchmarking effort. Some of the team members might be worker-level individuals who are expert in the process being benchmarked. Depending upon the team's experience in benchmarking, an outside facilitator who is knowledgeable in the benchmarking process itself could be included.

OBTAIN APPROVAL FROM TOP MANAGEMENT FOR AREA TO BE BENCHMARKED. Since some of the team's findings may be critical and create antagonisms, prior senior management approval is helpful.

Also, if major changes will be required, senior management support will be needed to implement the findings.

3. Benchmark the unit's process.

The team should study its own function in depth and measure the process carefully. It should determine what steps are required, the cost and time of each step, the manpower needed at each step, the materials used, the quality, the scrap and the machines. This detailed collection of data on the team's own process is very important. It provides the baseline data. And usually this data collection itself uncovers ways to improve.

OBTAIN NUMEROUS PERFORMANCE MEASURES OF THE PROCESS. Some of the metrics could include:

- unit cost, by product and by line
- measures of customer satisfaction with time delivery and returns
- quality—defects per unit, warranty costs
- cycle time—time of response, time of delivery

The summary measures from logistics, for example, might be:

- unit cost-per piece, line item, or order
- service level-percent fill rate from first echelon
- inventory level—inventory turns, months' forward supply
- number of distribution centers
- location of distribution centers
- operations performed

Transportation might assess measures of:

- delivery service to customers
- consolidation and redistribution practices
- returns, removals, and disposal

ANALYZE AND DOCUMENT THE UNIT'S PROCESS. Create a flow diagram, step by step, of the process. For an order entry unit, this diagram might include:

1. order acceptance
2. order editing

3. customer data
4. inventory status
5. pricing
6. credit checking
7. reserve inventory for customer
8. emergency or rush orders
9. returns

An invoicing unit diagram could include:

1. frequency
2. invoice accuracy
3. invoice data
4. invoice inquiries
5. payment terms
6. collections
7. bad debt writeoff

For each step in the process analyze the time it takes the unit to do the step, its cost, and the quality of the step as it is performed now. At the same time, identify where the problems lie, including delays, errors, rework, and missing information.

4. Identify the sources of information on procedures, especially those of the best-in-class, or benchmark, companies in that function.

Many sources of information are publicly available, such as libraries, databases, industry journals, annual reports, professional associations, and articles in trade magazines. Suppliers and customers are also excellent sources of information.

Then contact the companies that look best. The initial contact is often made by a phone call. If the firm contacted is interested, conduct an initial screening to find out if the firm is truly world class in the function the team wishes to benchmark. For the screening, develop a questionnaire that can be answered over the phone or through the mail. The questionnaire should be brief and take less than an hour to complete. It should also be pretested. Note that designing the questionnaire forces the team to do careful thinking about the process.

5. Visit the firms that seem most promising from the screening. (Sometimes phone conversations can substitute.)

The team should obtain as much data as it can before making the visit. Prepare an outline of topics to cover, and prepare questions in two major areas: best practices and the metrics developed in Step 3.

At the visit, the team should emphasize its interest in finding best practices, on a professional-to-professional basis, and collect quantitative data using the metrics. Identify the key success factors as well as any management approaches that help. Take detailed notes, and make diagrams and flow charts of processes.

Before leaving, extend an offer for a reciprocal visit and to share the findings. Thank the people for their time and help. The findings of the visit should be documented in a written report.

6. Analyze and compare the data. Set performance targets to close any gap.

Identify any gaps between the home team's performance and the benchmark team's performance, and set performance targets for improvement. If the home team is already the best, establish metrics to create further improvement.

7. Present the findings to senior management and others.

Share the information with others, and get their input and feedback. Gain their involvement and commitment to the benchmarking process.

8. Create an action plan for achieving the goals.

The action plan should close the gaps identified in Step 6 and implement the best practices found. The plan usually consists of two phases. First, improving those aspects that do not require major changes or capital investment. Second, undertaking the larger changes.

The action plan should include objectives to be accomplished, assignments of responsibilities, a funding schedule, and time points at which progress will be reviewed by higher management.

9. Monitor progress.

Establish milestones and goals for progress and improvement. Collect data to ensure that these progress goals are being met, and make adjustments and revisions as necessary.

10. Repeat the process every year and recalibrate the benchmarks.

Recalibrate the benchmarks annually. Check with the best-in-class firm to validate progress and changes made. Revise the process as necessary.

These ten steps, first and foremost, clarify the distinction between simply visiting another firm and benchmarking. Benchmarking is an organized approach to becoming the best, using goals, steps, and action plans. It is not just another educational visit to a different company.

The ten steps listed above need not be followed precisely, but benchmarking always requires a systematic approach. The most essential step is number three, benchmarking your own process. Careful analysis of your own process can itself yield important insights. Further, understanding every aspect of your own process is pivotal. Often the differences between companies lie in subtle details that superficial analysis does not reveal.

Be careful also of the phenomenon that William Smith, vice-president of Motorola, points out. "Most companies benchmark their strongest function against the best-in-class company," Smith says. "That is not the most productive approach, though. It's much more beneficial to make major improvements to your weakest functions rather than making smaller improvements to the areas in which you are already strong."[3]

Top Management Provides Leadership

Successfully implementing the benchmarking procedure, according to Rolf Soderstrom, vice-president of Motorola University, requires leadership on the part of top management. The leadership should compare the factors critical to the organization's success against its present competencies. The gap between the two suggests what to benchmark. Further, the benchmark performance is a moving target, so that the longer a firm waits to implement a benchmarking program, the more the gap widens. To close the gap, Soderstrom suggests that management estimate how fast the top firms are improving. Their firm must improve faster.

Case Studies

Ford's Benchmarking

An excellent example of benchmarking is the design of the Taurus and Sable at Ford, which assiduously strove to develop the top cars in the price class.[4] First, Ford had to determine what was best, so it examined fifty vehicles from its major competitors to identify their specific best features. Ford discovered that:

- the best accelerator pedal feel was that of the Audi 5000;
- the best fuel-gauge accuracy was on the Toyota Supra; and
- the best tire and jack storage was on the BMW 528E.

Then it identified the major categories in which it would strive to beat the competition:

- ride
- performance
- steering
- ease of driving
- brakes
- power transmission
- operational comfort
- power transmission smoothness
- seat performance
- body chassis
- climate control.

Ford's analyses of these categories revealed thousands of opportunities for improvement—too many to work on. So the group narrowed these down to the four hundred that were most crucial to the customer and to sales. Teams were then set up to tackle these four hundred items.

Immediately, the teams came up against the problem of how they would know when they had really equaled or exceeded the competition in a given item. To determine this, they developed measures. For example, a heating system would be judged superior if it reached a specified level of heat within a given time. A superior trunk storage would be higher, as measured in inches. The superior hood would provide good accessibility, as measured by the angle of opening.

The teams visited other facilities and gathered detailed information about the processes they found there. Factory line workers were also involved and their inputs utilized.

In these ways, Ford systematically strove to develop cars that were clearly superior to the competition in their class, and in most of the four hundred items, it actually achieved this. Ford's accomplishment would be impressive for any single car model, and judging from the sales of Taurus and Sable, customers agreed.

Share Information with Competitors

It is often easier to share information with firms that are not competitors, but many competitors share as well. An especially refreshing attitude is that of Bob Galvin, retired chairman of Motorola. Galvin welcomes it when competitors benchmark against Motorola. Making Motorola's competitors better, he feels, will make Motorola better.

Xerox and IBM implement a similar idea, according to Xerox executive John Kelsch and IBM executive Michael Brady. Although the two firms compete with each other in high-end printers and other equipment, they routinely exchange information. The West Coast vice-president of Xerox sits down regularly with his counterpart from IBM to benchmark. They do not trade confidential or proprietary data, but they share information on the efficiency of their processes. They feel that doing this makes them both stronger and, if not more competitive against each other, at least more competitive against their mutual adversaries.

The General Electric Approach

GE's guiding philosophy dovetails with benchmarking, although it is somewhat different. GE requires each of its divisions to be number one or number two in market share in its markets. Market share is a good criterion of success, GE feels—perhaps a better criterion than profits, which fluctuate with changing economic conditions. If for some compelling reason a division is not number one or two, it must have an excellent plan, and it will be given some time to gain that position. But the rule is clear and it is enforced. GE has repeatedly divested divisions that did not meet the rule's standards. The rule puts great pressure on the divisions to improve and strive to be best.

Through this rule, GE enforces a type of benchmarking. It differs from formal benchmarking in that it focuses only on the division level, not on every section of the firm. Moreover, GE stresses market share, while benchmarking measures depend on the task being studied. The GE concept is thus more useful when a central corporate office seeks to manage various divisions. Benchmarking, by contrast, is helpful on any level of the company. The GE approach and competitive benchmarking reinforce and supplement each other.

Not Invented Here (NIH)

A plague of product development and of many operations generally is known as NIH, to wit; "If we are not doing it," or "If we did not think of it, it cannot be any good." Many people are convinced that they alone are on the right path. They do not want to learn what others are doing, and they do not want to incorporate the ideas of others. They believe they are unique and that their situation is different from all others and that nothing else really applies.

NIH holds not only between different firms but within a single firm where obtaining information is comparatively easy. The innovative practices of one division do not seem to spread to other divisions. General Motors conceived the excellent idea of a joint venture with Toyota at the NUMMI plant, in order to learn Toyota's advanced manufacturing and quality practices. It took years for the NUMMI concepts to spread around GM, however, because most of the other GM plants paid little attention. GM is not being criticized here, but its case merely illustrates that the NIH disease is more rampant than the common cold and afflicts all firms.

Under a program of competitive benchmarking, NIH is not permissible. People are required to identify and install innovations and best practices no matter where they occur. Motorola succeeded in avoiding NIH when it was developing its Bandit pager.[5] Management knew that if it allowed NIH, it would kill them. According to Russ Strobel, Bandit engineering director, "We wanted to foster the idea of building on past successes and previous designs." For the Bandit pager to be the best, the Bandit project had to learn what was best everywhere else and do even better. Strobel continues, "We have a sign outside the lab that says it all: 'Please don't leave this area without leaving us a good idea.' We needed ideas from anywhere we could get them to prevent reinventing the product. That's why we called it Bandit."

To be best, one has to know what is best. Bandit, in effect, enlisted everyone in benchmarking, bringing in the best ideas from everywhere, even from people who walked in the door.

Benchmarking Culture

For most firms benchmarking is not at all easy to implement. Some managers may argue that they are already doing a good job. Others may object that other firms are different, with different products, customers, and levels of computerization or capital investment, so they are not realistic examples for comparison. Xerox, although it was a pioneer, was no exception. Xerox found that many managers perceived the process as threatening and denied its value. People repeatedly gave rationalizations and justifications for not benchmarking: "The Japanese have a different culture." "They get government support." "Their school system is better." Psychological denial that anyone else could be doing a better job than Xerox was rampant, and that was the biggest problem the company had to overcome.

Establishing an effective benchmarking program requires, in many companies, a change in corporate culture. Here the last chapter's discussion about creating a supportive culture comes in. A supportive culture will declare that although it is temporarily acceptable not to be the best, it is not acceptable not to *strive* to be the best. Nor is it acceptable to cover up or deny problems. In a corporate culture that is open and free, employees will feel more open and free to adopt the best ideas from anywhere.

Some employees may also be apprehensive about approaching

TABLE 5–2
Summary of Benchmarking

1. Benchmark all areas of the firm.
2. Benchmark not just against competitors but against the best in the world in that area.
3. Benchmark on two levels:
   • strategic to establish performance targets.
   • operational, to uncover ways to achieve those targets.
4. Implement the following key steps in benchmarking:
   • Benchmark a process that is very important to the area's success.
   • Use a team of people who will later do the implementation.
   • Benchmark the firm's process in detail. This is very important and itself yields valuable insights.
   • Identify what firms to benchmark, and visit those firms.
   • Close any gap, using an action plan.
5. Do not accept NIH. Get the best ideas from anywhere.
6. Establish partnerships, even with competitors, to benchmark.
7. Handle psychological issues that might block benchmarking, as people are often defensive.

other firms to benchmark. But this issue should cause no concern. Bernie Sergesketter, vice-president of AT&T, was surprised that firms were very hospitable to them. Ron Davis, a Caterpillar executive, similarly comments that very few firms turned down their requests for information. Most firms are quite flattered to be asked, and as long as proprietary data are not involved, firms tend to share information freely.

Still, the psychological impediments to benchmarking are very real as most people are naturally defensive. To overcome that and implement benchmarking successfully requires the right culture, training, and incentives. Most important, it requires leadership from the highest level—a CEO who knows that world-class success cannot be achieved in a second-class operation. Benchmarking requires a leader who will help employees face the often cruel fact that they are not the best and must improve—and who will accept nothing less than relentless pursuit of being best.

Summary

Benchmarking is one of the most powerful general procedures for management (see table 5–2). It is almost universally applicable and sets into motion procedures by which all pats of a firm can improve and ultimately the become best. In innovation especially, striving to be second best is a prescription for disaster. Benchmarking provides an organized approach to help a firm excel and be number one.

The Planning Foundation and Risk Management

The previous three chapters emphasized the foundations of staff expertise, research and technology, corporate culture, and benchmarking. Another foundation competency is planning, because a company must plan how it will conduct its overall innovation effort.

Planning for innovation, however, is markedly different from traditional corporate planning. The primary reason is that the future is so unpredictable. Designing a car can take at least three years, but who knows what people are going to want three years hence? Just because the future is uncertain, however, does not mean that planning cannot be valuable. Throughout the planning process, top management structures how it will tame an unruly future. Central to this effort is the management of risk, in which risks are transformed into opportunities. This chapter overviews the planning process, while the next chapter delves into what distinguishes a good planning process from a mediocre one.

Planning in the Face of Uncertainty

Most traditional corporate planning approaches are based on forecasts. From forecasts about future market demand, technology, competition, and the economy, management draws up specific plans. What many executives are now realizing, however, is that forecasts are often in error and the traditional planning methods faulty. Tom West, vice-president of Data General, says that rigid top-down planning does not work because the future never turns out as people expect. Many other firms have abandoned the old corporate planning systems as well. Xerox, Tom Mika says, simply threw its away.

The problem with traditional planning is the presumption that forecasts of the future are accurate. Interest rates are predicted to rise, but instead they fall. The market for a product is supposed to grow, but it becomes stagnant. One study of economic forecasters found that during nineteen economic periods, the forecasters were wrong fourteen times on the direction of Treasury bond rates and eleven times on bill rates.[1] Predictions of corporate earnings were similarly deficient. The future does not obey the forecasters' orders.

Does this mean the future cannot be managed? Should we throw up our hands in despair and give up? Absolutely not. Just because something is unknown does not mean it cannot be managed. We can deal with risk and uncertainty quite successfully. As Richard E. Rainwater, whose assets are estimated at over $300 million, declares, "Each industry seems to have its own cycle of good times and bad times. You make money on the risk."[2]

It is crucial to realize and accept that forecasts will contain errors—then use that insight to advantage. Error, even though we may not like it, can actually help us. Risk management begins by estimating what the error might be, stating a forecast as "quite accurate," "reasonably accurate," or "not very accurate." A firm that is planning what the size of the market will be for a certain product three years in the future might consider a forecast of $20 million, plus or minus 10 percent, to be very accurate. A forecast of $20 million, plus or minus 50 percent, however, might be considered not very accurate.

Next, utilize this estimate of accuracy in the planning process. Suppose a firm is working with a forecast that is not very accurate. Then the ideal, according to Tom West, is to create the ability to "zig and zag." In the face of high uncertainty, the optimum approach is high flexibility. On the other hand, sometimes people have a profound insight that makes the future relatively clear to them. Then the best approach might be to charge straight ahead at full speed. For example, a "bet the company" approach led to such significant innovations as the IBM 360 and Digital Equipment's Vax. Those firms created products so impressive that customers could not help but buy them. Determining what approach is best will depend upon the particular circumstances.

Profits Despite Risk

In spite of this discussion, some readers may still worry about uncertainty. If a forecast has a high degree of uncertainty, they may fear a great deal of risk to the firm. But they should not confuse future uncertainty with risk to the firm. Despite future uncertainty, top management can actually lower the risk to the firm.

An analogy may help here. Suppose you must take an extended two-week trip to visit a number of your firm's facilities in different cities. But you will not know which cities you will be visiting during the second week until the end of the first week. You do know that some of the second-week cities might be in hot climates, while others might be in cold locations. The uncertainty of the weather on your trip is therefore high. But does that mean you have to suffer? No—by packing clothes for both warm weather and cold, you are prepared for both. If you throw in a swimsuit and ski pants, ski underwear, and gloves, you might even be able to swim in the warm climates and to enjoy the slopes in the cold ones.

The great uncertainty in the weather does not prevent you from having fun, and the same is true with forecasts. There is nothing bad about a forecast that has a high expected uncertainty, as long as there are also plans for turning that uncertainty into opportunities (see table 6–1).

How does this risk-management approach work in practice? Shell used it to surpass Exxon to become the world's largest and most profitable oil company. A *Fortune* magazine article about it was called "Shell Gets Rich by Beating Risk," and the subtitle said that Shell got that way by "preparing for anything."[3] An industry in which oil prices can fluctuate from $4 to $40 per barrel is very uncertain, and a single accidental spill can cost billions to clean up. Shell manages risk by thinking through virtually all aspects of the future and being well prepared. In 1990, when the Gulf war severed hundreds of thousands of barrels of oil supply, Shell was prepared.

TABLE 6–1
Planning with Risk Management

- Traditional planning fails because it assumes that the future can be predicted or forecast.
- LSFI plans by managing risk.
- Aspects of the future should be categorized as quite certain, reasonably certain or uncertain.
- Flexibility and responsiveness must be planned for those aspects that are more uncertain.
- Risk can be profitable when it is managed.

According to its chairman, Lodewijk van Wachem, "I don't think we missed a beat."

If the appropriate foundations and flexibility are in place, an uncertain future can be planned for and can be just as profitable as a certain future. Risk management is the fundamental issue in planning. It reduces risk wherever possible, and it turns risks into opportunities.

Anticipation, the Planning Ideal

Within this perspective on planning, the perfect approach is anticipation, as articulated by Bob Galvin, retired chairman and CEO of Motorola. If a firm could only anticipate what will happen in the future, it would know the correct actions to take. Obviously, that is impossible. Nevertheless, anticipation can guide the planning process and help manage risks (see table 6–2).

The basic idea that Galvin advocates is this: Enumerate the products that have a good chance of being successful in the future. Fund the development of as many of these as possible. Indeed, Galvin strongly urges that the firm commit the funds to develop all of these

TABLE 6–2
Anticipation as Part of the Planning Process

1. Anticipate future events
2. Monitor what actually happens
3. Learn how to anticipate better

products. Ultimately, these products are likely to be hits, and if the firm does not develop them, a competitor will likely do so, stealing market share and profits.

Next, follow what happens over time, and keep score, like a baseball batting average. What percent of the successful products did your firm anticipate? What percent of successful products did your firm come out with? If a competitor's product was a hit, was that product on your list of likely prospects?

Now answer this key question: How can your firm's average be improved? If a successful product was not on your list, perhaps your market studies were weak and must be improved. Or perhaps your firm lacked the foundations needed to develop a product, requiring your firm to do more funding of the foundations in the future.

The anticipation concept forces people to think very carefully about which products have a reasonable chance of success. This in itself will improve a firm's ability to innovate. Finally, by keeping data and a systematic analysis of data, it leads to improved planning and risk management. The anticipation concept is fundamental to innovation.

Culture and Management Issues in Planning

Let us now delve into specifics about planning in the face of uncertainty. The first issue is clearly distinct from traditional planning approaches. As Jerry Dehner, director of strategic manufacturing at Northern Telecom, states, a firm must just create the right culture. Similarly, Nancy Farr, director of strategic planning at Apple, says that a firm must first understand that relationships are more important than plans. Specific plans are important, but since the future is uncertain, specific plans are likely to go awry and be changed. Therefore, a firm must just establish a culture that facilitates rapid changes, revision, and flexibility.

In practice, flexibility usually involves the extensive use of teams. If an unexpected event occurs, firms often bring together the strengths and experiences of many people into cross-functional or interdisciplinary teams to meet the new challenge. Jeff Jue, an Apple executive, notes that he is typically assigned to several different teams a year, depending upon what problems must be solved.

With its culture of flexibility, Apple can physically shift fifty to one hundred people into new groupings in only a few hours.

In a culture of distrust and conflict, however, such fast changes are virtually impossible because people resist cooperating with each other. When people are quickly thrown together in a new situation, trust, mutual support, and mutual respect are essential. In planning, therefore, the first step is to implement the ideas of chapter 4 and establish a culture of trust and respect.

Processes That Promote Innovation

The next step in planning is to establish the processes, systems, and procedures that promote innovation despite uncertainty. The key to that is benchmarking. Chapter 5 outlined how to benchmark the top firms on their product development processes. For each step of the process, determine how the top firms do it, what the cost is, and how long it takes them.

General Electric did this, according to Bill Sheeran, a GE vice-president, not just for product development but for all its operations. It started with 250 companies and winnowed them down to nine that had impressive growth records or that had revitalized themselves. Teams of ten to fifteen GE people then visited these top nine firms. The teams presented their findings directly to the chairman, Jack Welsh, and according to Sheeran, it changed the way top management thought. Previously, top management had stressed the "home run" type of innovation, in which the new product has to be a major improvement over existing products. But home runs, the GE benchmarking revealed, can take a long time to develop, and always swinging for the fences can lead to a lot of strike-outs. "Singles," or minor improvements in the product that can be done quickly are often preferable. Also, a sequence of small improvements can add up to a very large improvement.

GE presented the lessons it learned from its benchmarking in a novel fashion. It implemented a cascade-down process, in which the findings went first to the chairman, then to the CEO, and then to the corporate executive council. To carry the message far and wide, GE conducted an extensive training program for all management.

Benchmarking should, therefore, be part of planning, and many top firms implement procedures for it annually.

Selecting Which Products to Develop

With the corporate culture and benchmarking foundations in place, planning for innovation can consider what products to develop. But a dilemma immediately arises: Most firms have far too many products under development. Perry Gluckman, president of Process Plus, notes that most firms have five to ten times the number of projects under development as R&D can handle. Similarly, as Steven Wheelwright and Kim Clark report, when senior management is asked to total up the resources needed by development projects, they are often amazed by the result, since R&D's capacity is overloaded by several times.[4] Mike Bischoff of Hillenbrand, for instance, notes that their R&D had five times the projects it could handle. With R&D jammed up, projects inch out at a snail's pace.

Adding to the dilemma, many projects are started independently, with little regard for the other development projects. Too many projects may be targeted for one area, while another area might have not enough—a situation that often occurs when an executive uses political clout to get his or her pet project funded.

To attack this dilemma, planning should provide priorities for funding. Top firms accomplish this with a portfolio approach, selecting development projects that balance the overall portfolio. To select projects, these firms usually employ a series of screens. The criteria vary from firm to firm, but Sealed Air executive Abe Reichenthal employs the following criteria to initially screen projects. A potential project

1. must meet a customer need,
2. must provide a market leadership position,
3. must offer strategic advantages,
4. must fit the business's strategic objectives, and
5. must be expected to achieve reasonable sales and profit goals.[5]

Balancing Market and Technical Risk

A project that passes the initial screening should be checked to see how well it fits into the overall portfolio. Robert W. Hallman, vice-president of Polychrome, suggests examining the portfolio's market and technical risk.[6] Specifically, for each product currently under development, determine the product's market risk and its technological risk, and plot its position in a table like table 6–3. A low-market-risk and low-technology-risk product might be a slight adaption of an existing product. Line extensions and flanker products would generally be low or medium in both market and technical risk.

When a firm plots the locations of its products in such a table, Hallman says, it may well find that they are clustered together. Most may be low or medium risk, or most may be high risk. Balance is much better, Hallman suggests. Indeed, when Thomas D. Kuczmarski, president of Kuczmarski and Associates, conducted a study of twenty-seven firms, he found that the more successful firms had a better balance. For instance, Kuczmarski learned that the less successful firms tended to develop less risky products. The more successful firms, however, had twice the percentage of products with new technologies as the less successful firms. Although the risk is greater with a new technology, so is the potential reward, since the new concept might significantly expand the customer base. The better firms, thus, did not skimp on the riskier projects but balanced the risk.[7]

For a different way to balance the portfolio, Wheelwright and Clark evaluate both process risk and technology risk.[8] Breakthrough projects are those that have both new technology and a

TABLE 6–3

Classification of Market Risk and Technical Risk

Market Risk	Technical Risk		
	Low—known to firm	Medium—new to firm	High—new to world
High—new to world	New market, existing technology	New market, extend technology	New market, new technology
Medium—new to firm	Extend market existing technology	Extend market extend technology	Extend market, new technology
Low—known to firm	Existing market, existing technology	Existing market, extend technology	Existing market, new technology

new process. Derivative projects are those that are less risky and that include minor extension and cost-reduction efforts. In between are platform projects, in which a basic technology is used to launch a number of products. Again, a balance among these is suggested.

Timing

Also important to the portfolio is to balance the timing of new product development projects. When a firm's various products are due to hit the market can be plotted on a time line, like that in figure 6–1. If the target dates are poorly spaced, remedial action might be considered.

Resources

The portfolio approach, as mentioned, should ensure that each project under development is allocated adequate resources. This can be done by plotting over time the resources required by all projects. A convenient matrix approach for this is presented in Chapter 7.

These screening processes can quickly eliminate many of the less promising projects, but Hallman suggests a final filter in addition. A cross-functional senior management team would determine criteria similar to those below and weight each criterion for its importance. The team would then score each project on a scale of one to ten for each criterion. The top-rated projects get funded.

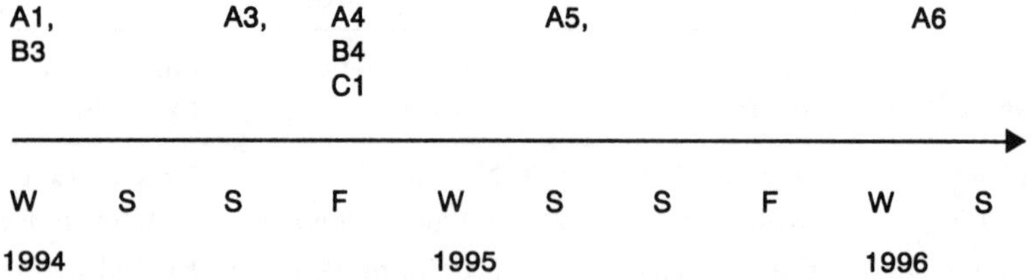

A1, B3		A3,	A4 B4 C1		A5,			A6	

$\longrightarrow$

W	S	S	F	W	S	S	F	W	S
1994				1995				1996	

FIGURE 6–1

Time Line: Completion Schedule for Development Projects. Product A1 Is Due to Enter the Market Early 1994

Hallman's suggested criteria for evaluating projects (which should be altered to fit the specific company) are:

I. Business attractiveness of the project
   1. Sales and profit potential
   2. Expected grow rate of sales per year
   3. Competitive situation and competitor's likely response
   4. Risk of technology
   5. Opportunity to restructure industry
   6. Special features (ecological, international, intellectual property)

II. Company strengths for the project
   1. Capital requirements and availability
   2. Marketing capabilities
   3. Manufacturing capability
   4. Technology base
   5. Raw materials available
   6. Skills available (existence of strong advocate or champion, technical, legal)

A CAVEAT. In screening projects for funding, be careful of projected profit and sales estimates. These are notoriously in error. When Albert Page of the University of Illinois examined more than a hundred firms, he found little correlation between the initial guesses of profits and sales and the final success of a product.[9]

Although portfolios can help provide overall balance and adequate resources, specific competitive analyses must still be undertaken. To help conceptualize that aspect of planning, an excellent technique is functional maps.

Using Functional Maps

During planning, management must consider the market, the competition, and what new products are likely to be successful. A powerful aid to that analysis, recommended by Wheelwright and Clark, is a functional map.[10] A functional map is any graph, chart, or diagram that visually depicts the driving variables of the competitive process. It may portray interactions, time trends, and competitive issues, and it can identify both risks and opportunities.

Suppose that Amalgamated Widgets wants to become more aggressive. To launch its planning process, it decides to determine the sales of its various products in its markets. To assist that analysis it creates a functional map, shown in table 6–4, which shows Amalgamated's market share compared with that of its competition. The table reveals the unpleasant fact that, relative to its competition, Amalgamated's market penetration figures are low.

Annoyed with this situation, Amalgamated tries to find out why it lags in market share. It decides to compare its products' price and performance against those of its competitor. In the functional map shown in figure 6–2, products C1 through C3 are those of the competition, while the Amalgamated products are the A100 and A101, the A102 series, and the A200 and A201 series. The graph reveals that the competition beats Amalgamated by providing more performance per dollar.

To correct the situation Amalgamated decides to attack. It plans to develop a new high-performance series, the A300 series, quickly. The functional map in figure 6–3 shows that model A300 is scheduled to be launched in the third quarter of next year. Models A301 and A302, derivative products with only minor feature changes, will be launched shortly thereafter. The competitor is not asleep, however, and is expected to bring out its own new series, indicated by C100 and C101, by the first quarter of the following year. Still, if no delays occur in the development of the A300, Amalgamated will have a six-month lead on its competitor.

Because the development of this new A300 series is so important, senior management compares its product development time with that of the competition. The functional map in figure 6–4, a time

TABLE 6–4

Functional Map for Market Share

Product	Department Stores	Private Label	Discount Stores	Catalogue Mail Order
A100	20%/22%	20%/18%		15%/18%
A101		8%/10%		5%/8%
A102		10%/12%	8%/6%	
A200	15%/20%	15%/18%		
A201	18%/25%		5%/10%	10%/12%
Totals	18%/23%	12%/15%	6%/8%	10%/12%

Note: The first number given is Amalgamated's market share, and the second is that of its major competitor.

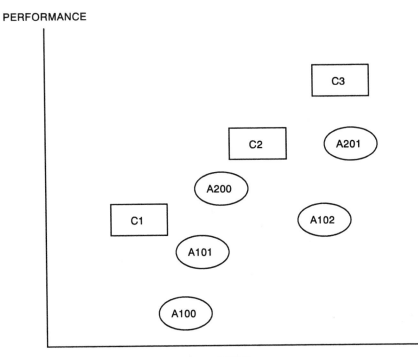

PERFORMANCE

PRICE

FIGURE 6–2

Price/Performance Functional Map

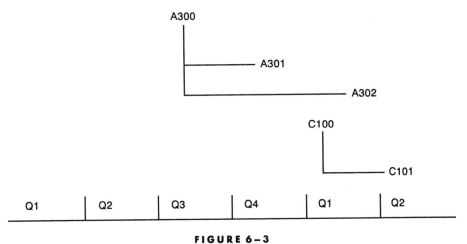

FIGURE 6–3

Product Introduction Functional Map

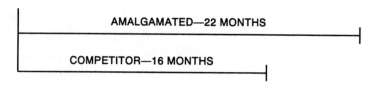

FIGURE 6–4

Speed of Product Development Functional Map

line, graphically shows that Amalgamated is considerably slower than the competition on its existing schedule. That lays bear the danger that the new A300 series may not be developed on schedule, and then lose its six-month lead on the competitor. Fearful about this risk, Amalgamated management declares it has procrastinated too long in cutting its product development time and must quickly implement the concepts of LSFI.

Forms of Functional Maps

Functional maps are visual depictions of the competitive issues that top management confronts, and as the Amalgamated Widget example shows, they can take almost any form. Functional maps can be made by plotting almost any two strategic variables for example, almost any two variables from the following list.

- market share
- location of markets
- costs
- profits
- time of product development
- time of market entry
- production capability
- performance characteristics
- profits
- investment
- budget allocations
- type of technology
- competitor behavior
- competitive products

- marketing channel
- amount of research and development.

Planning for Product Families

Functional maps help a firm determine what products it wants to develop, but then it must plan the details of that development. The firm will likely develop most products not singly but as part of a product family, and often will plan several generations of the family. For example, Philips introduced the first practical VCR in 1972, and in 1979 marketed its V2000 model, which even Japanese manufacturers admitted had a substantial technical edge. The Japanese manufacturers, however, planned ahead for three generations of product. Despite its initial lead, Philips was soon eclipsed by the Japanese, who introduced better and better features generation after generation. Philips, however, had learned its lesson well. For its compact disc player, it planned four generations ahead, letting it focus its research more precisely and getting the future generations out faster.

To plan the generations of a product, a firm might use a table like table 6–5, which depicts three product generations; alpha, bravo, and charlie. It specifies the technological and design improvements going into each generation and shows when new technologies must be ready.

Each generation of the product also requires detailed planning, as illustrated by figure 6–5. In January 1994, the firm expects to introduce the A200, the first model of the alpha generation. Since it is targeted at the middle of the market, which is highly competitive, the firm wants a new entry there quickly. Improvements to the A200 model will be made in April, with the A201 model. The firm also needs to rapidly penetrate the lower-price segment and will strip the A200 of some features to create the A100 model. To hit the high-price segment, the firm will launch its A300 model in October, a fully featured enhancement of the basic A200 series design. Figure 6–5 shows that the A200 model is the platform for several models. Thus, the design team should make the A200 design flexible, permitting easy inclusion of the features for the A100 and the A300.

TABLE 6–5

Specifications of Future Product Generations

	1994	1995	1996
Model	Alpha	Bravo	Charlie
New technology	graphics software	ceramic base	multimedia software
Number of components	600	400	350
• Different motors	5	4	2
• PC board	30	20	15
Defects per million units	300	100	30
Expected sales volume	1,000	1,500	1,800
Weight (in pounds)	10	8	7
Production cost, in dollars	100	80	70
• Labor content	15	12	10
• Material	50	42	40
• Overhead	35	20	20

Source: Adapted from Steven C. Wheelwright and Kim B. Clark, "Creating Project Plans to Focus Product Development," *Harvard Business Review* (March–April 1992), pp. 70–82.

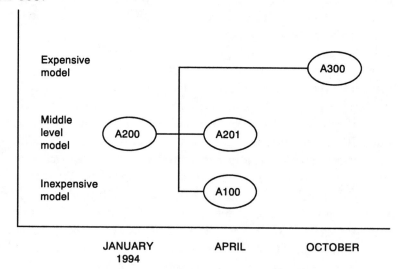

FIGURE 6–5

Market Position of New Product Introductions

The Innovation Plan

Although the techniques just presented are highly beneficial, no ideal approach to planning exists since depending upon its products and market, each company has its own planning methodology. Nevertheless, experience suggests that the following steps are valid across a wide spectrum of companies.

1. Estimate the risks and opportunities ahead. Careful analyses should be conducted of how the market, technology, and other relevant factors are likely to evolve in the years ahead. Based on these analyses, graphic plots should be constructed as follows:
   - Using a technological road map, plot the likely evolution over time of the relevant technologies, including possible new technologies. This should display how the technologies will influence future products in terms of type of product, size, performance, features, and cost.
   - Another plot should show how the market is likely to evolve in the years ahead. Likely competitor actions, market share trends, and possible market opportunities should be portrayed. Special attention should be paid to what products might be successful.
   - As appropriate, the firm should also analyze governmental and regulatory issues, economic and political trends, and international issues.
2. Establish strategic goals such as what markets to enter and what profits and sales should be. Management usually does this for a reasonable planning horizon.
3. Consider what products the firm should design that will further its business strategy. Use various screens and portfolio analysis to create a balanced portfolio. Most project proposals should be evaluated on a number of criteria including:
   - technical risk
   - market risk
   - other risks, such as regulatory, environmental, and intellectual property

TABLE 6–6

Summary of the Planning Process

In innovation especially, the future is difficult to predict. Planning therefore should incorporate risk management.

1. Anticipate future events, especially new product introductions. By observing what events actually occur, learn how to anticipate better.
2. Create a culture of trust, honor, and respect that can handle risk.
3. Benchmark, to ensure that the best practices are followed.
4. Functional maps, by graphically displaying strategic variables, can facilitate planning and risk management. Using almost any two strategic variables, a functional map can be created.
   - Strive to develop a balanced portfolio of R&D projects.
   - Before formal planning starts, conduct detailed analyses of the likely evolution of the technologies, market, and other relevant factors.
5. Ensure R&D is not overloaded with too many projects, and re-check this quarterly.

Specific plans for innovation might use the following steps:

1. Consider the risks and opportunities ahead.
2. Specify strategic goals.
3. Indicate specific products to be innovated.
4. Organize the products into families.
5. Plan each product family in detail.
6. Specify the resources needed to develop the products.

- fit with strategy of firm
- likely financial return
- effect on competitive position
- effect on furthering technical base
- availability of resources
- development cost
- time of development
- investment in equipment and marketing required

  Be careful not to overcommit resources. Management should also use the technique of anticipation here.

4. Organize the products to be developed into families. Using product families permits modular design and produces cost savings.

5. Determine the general specifications for the products in each family. Helpful here are targets for time of market entry and design specifications, as laid out in table 6–5.

6. Specify the major resources, staffing, and development activities needed to complete the products on schedule.

Most companies should do detailed planning only for the short term—six months to a year. For the longer term, they should emphasize risk management and developing foundation capabilities. Functional maps often aid this analysis.

Summary

Planning for innovation should stress risk management (see table 6–6). Ideally, planning should anticipate the future, but even if that is not successful, the practice of anticipation can lead to insights that should improve planning. Responding to an unpredictable future requires a culture and incentives that permit quick and flexible adaptation to unexpected events. Functional maps provide a useful planning technique by graphically displaying competitive threats and trends. Moreover, since most firms have far too many projects under development, a portfolio approach can provide a more balanced set of projects.

7

Creating a Good Plan

Based upon the previous chapter's overview of planning, this chapter probes the particulars. Good plans do have some common themes, and research into the top companies indicates that most good plans:

- avoid overloading the resources
- budget wisely
- integrate activities
- evaluate uncertainty using computerized planning models
- do competitor analysis
- provide market windows of opportunity
- have vision.

This chapter investigates each of these characteristics.

Allocate Resources and People

One widespread problem in planning is that senior management often asks development for too many new products. It is not uncommon, as we have seen, for development to have several times the number of projects it can handle. As Bernard Walsh, president of Vistakon, notes, "There is always pressure to develop one more product." Yet when product development is overloaded, it jams up, bogging down the development of almost all products.

Resource Allocation Matrices

To avoid such jamming, allocate the key resources using matrices. Table 7–1 depicts a matrix that shows the expected number of

TABLE 7–1

Resource Allocation by Matrix: Expected Need for Plastics Engineers (in people-hours) by Project

	Jan.	Feb.	Mar.	Apr.	May	Jun.
Project 100	200	150	100			
Project 101		150	150	50	50	
Project 102			50	50	50	50
Project 1000		200	250	200	150	150
Maintenance of past projects	300	300	300	300	300	300
Totals	500	800	850	600	550	500

people-hours of plastics engineers that each project is expected to require for six months. The totals reveal an unevenness in the expected demand, with severe problems in February and March. Since overloading can occur in almost any area, similar matrices should be developed for all important resources, including engineering time by specialty, factory capacity, and the capacity of the model-making shop. Even include the allocation of certain essential individuals.

Allocate People to One Project

Time Fuller, a consultant and lecturer at the University of Chicago, takes this reasoning one step farther. A company was developing two products, and its engineers were working on both products simultaneously. Both products would take about the same amount of effort, and in a year both would be completed.

Fuller suggested the firm stop splitting its resources. Instead, it should concentrate all its resources to get one product out, and only after that should it work on the second. Under Fuller's plan, the first product would get out in six months, and the second six months after that. The first product thus would be out six months earlier than with the old approach.

The second product would likely be out earlier, too. When two projects are being worked on at the same time, the developers switch back and forth between the two, wasting time getting reacquainted with each project.

Interestingly, Fuller's idea—to concentrate the developers' time on one project—reversed the managers' previous thinking. Before, engineers had been assigned several projects in order to make sure they were busy. Management wanted to squeeze every last penny out of the engineering budget, but they did not realize that in doing so they were jamming up the system, creating delays, and causing extra work.

Budget Wisely

Allocating adequate resources invariably involves budgeting. If budgets are not handled wisely, they can roadblock innovation. Kim Clark of Harvard has recounted a half-billion-dollar project that was six months late to market. The cause of the delay was the lack of two process engineers. The engineering group did not hire them because it would have cost $200,000 out of their budget. The firm ended up losing $10 million from being late to the market because one group did not have $200,000 in its budget.

The problem here was a lack of incentive. The performance of the head of this particular engineering group was to be evaluated relative to his own budget. He had no incentive to worry about the project as a whole.

Unfortunately, this situation is by no mean unique. Often a few extra dollars spent in research can greatly simplify the manufacture of a product. But if the research group has a separate budget, it has little incentive to help the manufacturing group.

Time to Break Even

Hewlett-Packard has pioneered an approach to overcome this incentive dilemma. It previously evaluated marketing according to sales, engineering according to innovation, and manufacturing according to cost—all different and often conflicting incentives. For a product development project to be successful, it realized these departments had to pull together. HP therefore instituted a new criterion to evaluate all groups participating in an innovation project: "time to break even."

"Time to break even" is the length of time it takes before the profits from the sales of a product equal the expenditures on that product. All expenditures on a product are added up, including marketing, design, development, and manufacturing. The time until those expenditures are offset by the incoming profit stream from sales is the time to break even. HP wants that time to be as short as possible.

Many firms use a different criterion: "time to market." Under this criterion, a team is evaluated on how fast it can get a product into the market. The team then pushes to get the product to market as quickly as possible. HP does not like this latter approach. Under the time-to-market system, HP fears a team will rush a product to market before it is fully ready, or skip features that a customer might like. HP wants the development team to think about sales and factors that influence sales, such as production and distribution, in addition to getting the product to the market fast. Because it stresses both profits and speed, time to break even is often a better criterion for evaluating innovation projects.

Quarterly Profits

Concerning budgeting, quarterly profit goals can devastate innovation if they are not properly handled. The problem is this: To reach quarterly profit goals, some managers cut back on development activities. This action slices expenses for the quarter and boosts their profit numbers, making them look good to top management. And since the products under development will not hit the market for a couple of years, the repercussions of the cutting are years away. By that time, these people will likely be in new positions, and someone else will be left holding the responsibility for the underfunded innovation.

Such budget reduction practices disrupt product innovation and cannot be tolerated. To prevent this situation, companies like Texas Instruments and Motorola have a separate and distinct budget for innovation. Except by special permission of the top management, this budget cannot be changed.

Integrate Activities

Most good plans integrate the many diverse functions in a company. In developing an innovation, marketing, engineering design, and manufacturing will certainly need to carefully coordinate. Engineering, manufacturing, and quality will need to devise new manufacturing techniques. Accounting will have to provide cost information, and purchasing will play a major role by interacting with suppliers.

Regrettably, in many firms the different departments communicate poorly and fight amongst themselves. Conflicting memos fly back and forth as each group advances its own agenda. It makes no sense to waste time battling when the real job is to get the new innovation developed. Many experts believe that the success of Japanese firms is partially because they easily integrate among different departments, as if the firm were seamless. A coordinated and integrated approach is faster and cheaper.

Policy Deployment Matrix

A policy deployment matrix is a technique to promote interdepartmental cooperation. The one in table 7–2 shows the objectives of the different departments in relation to the overall goals of the firm. These overall goals are to increase the return on investment by two percent, increase the market share in market A by five percent, start a new product line, produce no defects, and cut costs by five percent.

TABLE 7–2
Policy Deployment Matrix

Overall Corporate Goal	Finance: Low-Cost Loan	Sales: Train Sales Staff	Sales: Install Computer	Manufacturing: Flexible Assembly	R&D: Install New Lab Equipment
Increase ROI 2%	XX	XX	X	XX	
Increase Market A share 5%		X	XX	X	X
Market B: Start a new product line	X	X	X	XX	XX
Zero defects	XX			XX	XX
Cut costs 5%	X			XX	X

To achieve these goals, different departments work to accomplish certain objectives. The finance department, for example, works to arrange low-cost financing to help customers purchase products more easily. The manufacturing objective is to adopt a flexible production system. (One "X" indicates that the objective is important to the success of that corporate goal, while an "XX" indicates that the objective is very important to that goal.)

The importance of the policy deployment matrix emerges in its application. Usually it is developed in a meeting of the executives from all relevant departments. This meeting can take hours as the executives assess where the firm is going and how to get there. Often the executives repeatedly change and revise the goals and objectives until they finally determine the right ones. Indeed, much of the policy deployment matrix's value is that creating it forces cross-departmental discussion.

Changing the row and column designations gives the matrix multiple uses. The matrix in table 7–3 relates the objectives of each department to the success of different product lines. Research has two objectives—to develop a new compressor and to write a particular software program. The objectives of the different departments are designed to enhance the sales of the various product lines. Again, the relevant managers should jointly create this matrix, because that forces them to coordinate.

A policy deployment matrix can also help a firm plan its basic foundation capabilities. The matrix in table 7–4 shows how different expertises, like capability to fabricate titanium and microelec-

TABLE 7–3

Policy Deployment Applied to Product Lines

Product Line	Research Objective: New Compressor	Research Objective: Software Program	Manufacturing Objective: Robot Assembly	Marketing Objective: Increase Share 5%
1	X	XX		
2		X	X	X
3	X	X	X	XX

TABLE 7–4

Policy Deployment Applied to Foundations

	Product Line			
Expertise	1	2	3	4
Titanium	XX			XX
Plastics		X	X	X
Microelectronics	X	X	XX	XX
Software	XX		X	X

tronics, can enhance different product lines. Here, the titanium capability contributes to only two product lines, while microelectronics is essential to all four lines.

The policy deployment matrix promotes cooperation because it is visual. By placing it on a blackboard or flip chart, all participants can simultaneously look at it, revise it, and jointly develop it.

In actual practice, matrices are much more detailed, often having thirty columns and rows. Florida Power and Light employs them for strategic planning and feels they were a major factor in helping it win the W. Edwards Deming Award.

Evaluate Uncertainty Using Computerized Planning Models

Another feature of excellent planning processes is the sophisticated estimation of forecasting error. The forecasts of some data, it turns out, are surprisingly accurate. For example, with computer main memory and Winchester storage memory, the price performance ratio has declined rather steadily, at nearly 25 percent per year. This drop represents the improvement from one generation to the next. Similarly, military fighter and attack aircraft performance increases at about five percent per year, while tank performance increases by four percent per year. At the same time, the cost of the equipment rises by eight percent per year.[1] All of these percentages, moreover, have been fairly consistent over a number of years. With many products, forecasts of cost and performance data have been highly accurate.

Regrettably, predictions are not this precise for all phenomena. It is much harder to divine what features the customer will want. Nancy Farr, an executive at Apple Computer, notes that during the late 1980s Apple concentrated on the high end of its line and was quite successful. But markets rarely behave as companies would like, and that market stagnated. Apple had to reverse itself and quickly develop an innovative low-end model, which incidentally, sold extremely well. In short, while forecasts of particular customer desires are not very accurate, forecasts of performance and cost are frequently quite accurate.

Computerized Planning Models

The forecasts of performance and cost are often input into computerized planning models. Computerized planning models estimate how the technology and the market will evolve, and can forecast sales, plant capacities, market changes, and technology trends. Like financial analysis models, they often employ a spreadsheet format and allow "what if" analyses, letting planners examine many possible scenarios.

What makes computer models distinctive is that they can be systematically improved. Past errors can be analyzed and the model revised and corrected. Motorola, according to Jim Page, has built computer models to help forecast the sales of its pagers. Originally the model did better in forecasting U.S. sales than sales in foreign markets. That, they discovered, was because their assumptions about foreign markets had been strongly colored by their American background. After some revisions, the model did a very good job of predicting foreign market sales as well.

Years ago, Motorola considered the pager market to be one market. But after years of working with the model and improving it, Motorola knows that there are many little markets: lawyers, real estate agents, medical professionals. Moreover, the computer model lets management analyze all the markets at once, including how many people will lose their pagers and have to buy new ones. Further, the model helps Motorola make production and distribution plans.

Quantum is a firm that makes mass storage memory for computers. Under its director of planning, Bob Peyton, Quantum developed a very sophisticated model. The computer market has several major price segments, with a low end of $2,000 to 4,000. Customers spend 15 to 20 percent of a computer's retail price on primary mass memory storage, then buy the most storage they can for their money. For low-end computers in particular, customers spend $300 to 400 for a single disk with the largest possible storage. To Peyton, this means that when the cost of a given-size disk drops below $400, it can be placed in a low-end computer and sold.

The cost of storage drops about 25 percent per year, Peyton says. Knowing the present price of storage lets him estimate when a given size of storage will drop below $400 and be able to go into a low-end computer. If a given size of storage presently costs about $500, in one year its cost will drop below $400. By estimating the sales of those computers, which he gets from the computer manufacturers and vendors, Peyton estimates how many storage devices of that size Quantum will sell. He can then tell development to be sure to have that size of storage ready by a given date, and he can also apprise manufacturing and suppliers.

Quantum's model is quite sophisticated. It also forecasts the life cycle of a product, how fast a market for a new product will increase, and how fast it will decline. The fact that the model can help specify what has to be done by what date makes it very valuable.

Strengths and Limitations

Many executives are skeptical about the output of computer models. And until a model has been fine-tuned and proven itself, their suspicions are well founded. Quantum followed its model because, Peyton says, it was right on the money three times, and after that the executives believed it.

Certainly models are not always right. To paraphrase Bill Weisz, retired vice-chairman of Motorola, no matter how brilliantly a model had analyzed the market for candles, it would never have predicted the electric light. People are still best at that type of planning. Nevertheless, as Frank Trotta of Rolm and Haas comments, most human decisions are made by "tribal wisdom." Models, because they can be systematically improved, can often do better than that. Computerized planning models are an invaluable adjust to human analysis.

Do a Competitor Analysis

Most top firms conduct careful analyses of their competitors in order to forecast what they are likely to do. Gathering intelligence on competitors suggests cloak-and-dagger activities by spies in trench coats, but these images are fantasy. A surprising amount of information about competitors is public. Computer databases available at most libraries, such as Dialog and Nexus, track an incredible amount of information on patents and trademarks, detailed financial numbers, reports by security analysts, and market and technical trends. Many trade associations also bulge with data. As Leslie Cole, vice-president of Burrell, notes, at many companies an entire staff of information-management specialists searches for such intelligence.

Some firms use ingenious means to obtain competitor intelligence. Komatsu scrutinized the trash behind the service centers of its major U.S. competitor, Caterpillar, to find parts that had failed and had had to be replaced. On the basis of this, Komatsu designed new models that were considerably more durable than its U.S. competition.

The most crucial role of competitor analysis may be to forecast what products competitors will come out with and when. For this purpose, analysts often integrate intelligence data with market data by carefully evaluating competitors' product development activities, capital purchases, and plant tooling. For instance, Motorola noticed a pattern in the purchasing of capital equipment by Japanese firms, which tipped the firm off that the Japanese were planning a major move in Europe. A couple of years later, when a half-dozen Japanese firms started selling consumer electronics equipment in Europe, Motorola was prepared for it and retained most of its market share.[2]

As another instance, a competitor of Coors Brewing Company was sued by another firm, and a court fight resulted. Coors gobbled up the information revealed in the court documents. On the basis of that information, Coors pieced together a mathematical model of how much beer the competitor shipped. The model was accurate to within one percent.

Smaller companies may fear that such intelligence-gathering activity is too expensive. But small firms can rely on market information companies, which have detailed information broken down by market segment, product, region, and firm. They also answer specific questions for their client firms. Further, market intelligence companies often adjust their fees for small firms.

Any size firm, however, should gather intelligence from its salespeople, suppliers, distributors, and customers. Being on the front lines, these people often hear about a competitor's move first. Many firms also have hotlines so that anyone with competitive information can immediately report it. Competitor intelligence provides a foundation for good planning.

Provide Market Windows of Opportunity

By integrating competitor intelligence with other information, top firms identify market windows of opportunity—the interval of time during which a particular type of product can be profitably sold. The window closes when the competition tops the firm's product or the market otherwise shifts.

Market windows are important because they provide indisputable targets and goals. Bob Peyton emphasizes that point, and he uses his model at Quantum to identify these windows. Gordon Bell, who developed the Vax computer for Digital Equipment, agrees that engineers need market windows as deadlines. These market windows must be based upon solid believable data. Then they provide definite and credible deadlines that a firm cannot miss without experiencing serious consequences.

Deadlines that are arbitrarily set by executive declarations are less effective. Instead, they should be driven by the external realities of the market and competition. When Roger Schmenner of Indiana University and his colleagues studies the factors that influence quick product development, they found that competitive pressures are the most important factor in creating speed.[3] The unmistakable threat of the competition coming out with an excellent product by a certain date is a mighty motivator.

Market windows thus provide both motivation and credible deadlines, and determining these windows should be part of the planning process.

Have Vision

The most difficult, almost ineffable aspect of good planning is to have vision and sense the way markets and technologies are moving (see table 7–5). The most important ingredient of vision is expertise. Some people are on top of situations, keep in contact with the key people who are making things happen, and have a special intuition for trends and events. Unfortunately, those people are rare and more formal systems are usually required.

Early Warning Teams

Quantum obtains vision, according to Peyton, from special teams—early warning teams—that monitor the major segments of its markets. Quantum has them for PCs, laptops, work stations, and large computers. The early warning teams keep in touch with important customers and monitor competitors and technology. Who is buying what and why? Are customers using computers for different applications than before? Are competitors making headway? These are some of the issues the teams keep track of.

The teams identify what aspects are driving the market, and they monitor how these change over time. Especially important, the teams plot curves that show trends in features, performance, and cost. Watching trends can give early indications about changes in market share and profits.

Profits Blind Vision

On this issue, Peyton notes that firms like Compaq and Apple started out with moderately priced models but over time went to the higher-end, more expensive models. Expensive machines have larger markups and thus generate more profit per unit. It is easy for a firm to give up sales of lower-end products to competitors and

TABLE 7–5

Steps to Clearer Vision

Assign people to stay on top of the situation and keep in touch with the market and leaders in the field.

Use models to predict changes.

Assign early warning teams to monitor key market segments and technologies.

Beware of profit hypnosis. Profits are a very poor predictor of the future.

still make substantial profits from sales of the high-end machines. But this tendency is dangerous. The competitors who are the lower-ends often start biting away the higher-ends as well. Both Apple and Compaq, Peyton feels, suffered that fate.

Good profits excuse many sins, and when profits remain high, firms tend to overlook potential problems. But eventually, when the high-end slips away, too, the profits vanish. In cases like this, early warning teams monitoring the low-end might have been able to sound the alarm of possible danger ahead.

The moral to this story is that although senior management tends to be hypnotized by profits, profits are a late and poor portent of future trends. Sometimes they hide more than they reveal. Early warning teams can help provide a much clearer signal of what is ahead.

Summary

Planning for innovation means not only planning for specific events, as in traditional planning, but preparing to manage risk. Leading firms use various approaches in their planning processes. By building solid foundations and the processes to handle future uncertainty, risk can not only be managed but become profitable.

Eradicate Fumbles

The Cost of Fumbles

Now that the general foundations are in place—expertise, technology, culture, benchmarking, and planning—we must probe the product innovation process itself. The first challenge is to get rid of unnecessary delays and costs. This is done by eliminating "fumbles"—bottlenecks, changes, rework, and unnecessary work. Implementing LSFI Step 3 will help find and eradicate the fumbles, and often produces savings in cost and time of 50 percent or more.

Causes of Fumbles

Sometimes, in order to get more products out faster and cheaper, senior management increases product development's budget and asks it to develop more products. Although that sounds reasonable, innovation is not something that one can bring about just by throwing money at it. Quite perversely, these seemingly reasonable actions can actually obstruct new product innovation.

Bottlenecks

Perry Gluckman, president of Process Plus, has frequently seen how innovation is not improved by additional funding. The product development process is extremely complex, with many stages and steps. Despite additions of funds and staff, this complex system will still be plagued by bottlenecks. Bottlenecks are steps that handle work more slowly than the rest of a system. When the system gets moderately full, projects have to stop and wait for the bottlenecks to clear up.

The more work the bottlenecks get, the more work piles up in front of them and waits. Placing more and more projects into the system makes the waits longer and longer. The startling conclusion is that—since projects wait longer—adding projects actually increases the total time it takes to get a project through the system.

If the projects take longer, they are late to market. Either sales are lost, or products have to be scrapped because their market opportunity is gone. Additional funding can create harm because it rarely goes to ease the bottlenecks but instead generates more projects, which jam up the system more. The more we put into this system, paradoxically, the less comes out.

Locating Bottlenecks

Almost any activity can be the location of a bottleneck—making models, obtaining design specs from marketing, getting information from a supplier, designing test equipment, or getting purchase orders approved. Perry Gluckman recounts one firm that had a hidden bottleneck at the CAD machine. Unknown to management, the engineers were wasting time in frequent meetings just to schedule time on those machines. Roger Bohn of the University of California identified a bottleneck for many firms in obtaining sheet metal parts. One might think that these low-tech and rather simple parts would be quickly obtained, but they usually come from undependable Ma and Pa suppliers.

Due to the delays, management gets frustrated. To expedite a few important projects, it takes engineers off some projects and puts them onto rush jobs. As Edith Wilson, an executive at Hewlett-Packard, explains, expediting is very costly in time and money and can severely harm the system. If project A is late to market, engineers are switched from project B to get project A finished. But that makes B late. Engineers from project C are then shifted to help B. After a while, almost like musical chairs, shifting people becomes a way of life.

Shifting staff is expensive and time consuming. After being transferred to a project, people must be trained and brought up to speed. Doing that training, however, takes effort away from getting the project done and can delay the project even further. Frederick Brooks immortalized this insight as Brooks's Law: Adding manpower to a late software project makes it later.[1] Brooks's Law applies just as strongly to almost any innovation project.

The Hidden Weak Link

Management cannot expect that adding money and staff to a complex system will make it perform at a higher level. The hidden weak links in the system will frequently snap, impairing the system's performance. Bruce Coleman, CEO and president of Information Science, recounts the experience of a firm that made computer peripherals. To improve its production efficiencies, it tried to cut costs by moving plants overseas to Mexico and Singapore. But because of coordination problems and the longer shipping distances, its inventories grew to an astounding 40 percent of revenues. Its lead time in obtaining a product stretched to ninety days, while the customers wanted a twenty-day response. After that failure, the firm sought a technological solution by adding new equipment, new testers, milling equipment, robots, and automation. That did not work, either. Coleman says the company tried all the things mentioned in the well-known management texts, but nothing helped.

Finally, management analyzed the production process in detail. It pinpointed the bottlenecks, delays, and inefficiencies. Fixing them worked. Looking back, Coleman realizes that improving manufacturing efficiency by throwing money at it had only made things worse. Nothing helped until the underlying process was analyzed step by step.

General Motors had a similar experience when it spent $50 billion to install flexible automated factories.[2] The factories that it "improved" ended up operating less efficiently than the older "unimproved" ones. It was a costly lesson, but GM determined that complex processes have subtle features that must be understood before improvements can be made. Michael Hammer makes a similar point about information technology.[3] He notes that heavy investments often deliver disappointing results. Instead, he suggests, a firm should "reengineer" its process—that is, look at the little steps in the process and creatively revise and reorganize them.

The basic message is clear: Throwing money into innovation might help, but it may also harm. If bottlenecks are not eased, adding projects to a system may make things worse. The constant pressure to do just one more project, as Bernie Walsh, CEO of Vistakon, notes, must be avoided. Product development has many subtle and hidden features, and to improve it, it must be understood at a detailed level.

The Ideal: No Fumbles

To begin improving an innovation system, it is helpful to have an abstract notion of what an ideal process of product development would be. No real process comes close to it, but the ideal helps guide our thinking. Any aspect of the real process can be compared to the ideal and, hopefully, improved in the direction of the ideal.

The ideal, as Jerry Dehner of Northern Telecom says, is "one cycle design." Everything is done right the first time. This means that there are no fumbles: no changes, no work redone, no waits for information or materials, no delays for approvals, no bottlenecks, and no unnecessary work. It would be like an uncongested superhighway that would speedily lead to the development of the new product.

No such highway exists, of course. New product development is really more like chopping a path through a dense uncharted jungle with a machete and a broken compass. Nevertheless, being mindful of the ideal of no fumbles—no delays, no changes, no rework, no unnecessary work—can help.

The Reality: Abundant Fumbles

Reality is usually far off the superhighway because fumbles and bottlenecks are rampant, and in many projects they can double or even quadruple the cost and time of the product development.

Consider a fascinating study that David Sartorius of MIT conducted of a company that makes electromechanical consumer products.[4] The firm employed many good product development techniques, including cross-functional engineering and marketing teams. It also integrated manufacturing needs into design decisions, had robotic assembly lines, and employed other sophisticated approaches. The firm was by no means backward—it was quite knowledgeable in advanced techniques.

But the time it took to develop new products was long, four to five years. A major reason was what Sartorius calls "false starts." After a project was well under way, questions arose as to whether the product was right for the market. Management would put the program on hold for several months while it conducted further marketing surveys and engineering analyses. "This has happened not only once," Sartorius notes, but "repeatedly on some of these programs." A couple years into development of a major project, in fact, management cancelled it and started over.

But false starts was only one of the problems Sartorius discovered. To increase communications between engineering and marketing, the firm had created a joint product development team. Having marketing and engineering representatives sit together to enhance communication is a widely recommended technique. Because the marketing manager constantly put him on other assignments, however, the marketing person was rarely at his desk. With no marketing person to talk to, a key link in the communication chain shattered, defeating the entire purpose of the joint team.

Still more changes and delays resulted from scheduling difficulties. Certain important production tools, for example, had long lead times. Due to poor coordination, they were not ready until very late, close to the start of scheduled production. As luck would have it, the tools had problems, and to fix them pushed back the production startup further.

Curiously, management's actions created a vicious cycle. Management would make a change in the product's conception, causing a delay. During the delay the market would shift, forcing management to again change the product conception. This would launch a new delay, during which time the market would again shift, and the cycle of changes and delays would start all over again.

Unfortunately, this firm is by no means unique. George Stalk, Jr., and Thomas M. Hout discuss a firm whose competitors were introducing twelve and a half times as many products and had more than ten times the output per engineer.[5] The firm had a "chain reaction" of delays: Development of the product was slow to begin with, and during that period the market price for the product would decline. To meet the new price, management had to stop and redesign the product. That delay would then cause the firm to miss its assigned slot in the manufacturing plant and to wait several months for the next open slot. But they would not make that slot either, since other delays occurred in nearly all aspects of the project. In fact, the various delays took so long that almost all the members on the design team were transferred to new jobs. This was not unusual, as the firm normally rotated people. Nevertheless, the previous experience was lost to the project, and additional delays ensued as new people were brought up to speed.

Fumbles Are Often Hidden

This firm could have dramatically reduced its product development time and cost, but management was unaware of the extent of fumbles. And this situation is by no means unusual. Tim Fuller, lecturer at the University of Chicago and an international consultant, mentions a firm that was developing software. He asked management what percent of the firm's activities were being completed on schedule. Management did not know, but confidently thought it the majority. Fuller prevailed upon them to collect some data. Only 12 percent of the activities, it was discovered, were completed on time. Nearly always, when one collects hard data, fumbles turn out to be far more frequent than management presumes.

How Much Improvement Is Possible?

Most development projects are very far from the ideal because fumbles are typically epidemic. As this book has suggested, improvements of 50 percent, 75 percent, or even 90 percent—in time and correspondingly in cost—are often possible. More than one reader likely scratched his or her head in disbelief at that suggestion. But these examples, showing how time consuming and costly fumbles can be, may make the logic behind this suggestion somewhat clearer.

Let us pin this down by considering the following penetrating case provided by Perry Gluckman, president of Process Plus, about product development in a chemical firm. Knowing that management's perceptions about problems and delays are often wrong, Gluckman collected some data. First he determined how the senior researchers were spending their time. It turned out that meetings consumed 70 percent of their time, 20 percent was spent on safety and disposal activities, and 5 percent was devoted to miscellaneous activities. Astonishingly, only 5 percent of their time was spent doing actual product research.

Gluckman then probed what went on during that 5 percent research time. The researchers did chemical experiments. But 90 percent of the experiments were rescheduled because of an equipment problem or because something was not ready. Of the experiments that were actually conducted, nearly 38 percent had been done previously. But no one knew this since the library records were so poorly kept. The previous experiments had obtained the same results, of course, since the people were good scientists.

How could so many experiments have been done previously without anyone knowing? Although this is purely speculation, perhaps a previous CEO issued a cost-reduction order. Management might have said, "Do we really need a full-time librarian? No, a part-timer will do." Soon the library records were in disarray.

With Gluckman's data, the firm was able to quickly improve its product development. Meeting attendance by researchers was reduced considerably. To be sure, meetings were still held. When a customer such as Ford came for a visit, for example, scientists still had to meet with them. Previously, however, *all* the senior scientists had had to attend the meeting. Now, instead, they asked Ford in advance what topic it wanted to discuss, and only the scientists involved in that topic would go to the meeting. The firm eliminated other meetings, too, and individual meeting attendance time was cut from 70 percent to 50 percent. With these and other improvements, the amount of time the scientists could spend on research tripled, from 5 percent to 15 percent. Tripling the research time cut the time and cost of developing new products by more than half.

Notice that no additional resources were required to achieve this cut. It was simply a matter of getting rid of some of the fumbled time and reallocating it along the no-fumbles superhighway.

Value-Added Work

The concept of value-added work is basic to how LSFI obtains very large improvements. Value-added work is the work that moves us along the superhighway. Value-added work means design work that is really used in the final product design.

Everything else—such as setting up equipment, checking, inspection, transportation, waiting for approvals, meetings, delays, and changes—is nonvalue-added work. None of this work is actually part of the superhighway. It may seem to be useful at first blush, but it is not directly used in the final product design. "Nonvalue-added work" is a technical term for fumbles.

In the chemical firm, the value-added work was less than 5 percent, because that is the percent of time when the scientists were working on product development and actually moving forward on the highway. A value added of only 5 percent might seem unusually low, but the time that engineers actually spend on design activities is low in most firms. Until management conducts a careful data analysis, it is often not aware of the full extent of the delays, wastes, changes, and omissions that constitute the nonvalue-added work. Indeed, most operations spend only a small portion of their time moving forward on the superhighway.

Tim Fuller mentions that when most people study the amount of value-added work in firms, they initially get a figure close to 40 percent, because people are actually working on something that percent of the time. But when one examines on what they are working, that figure drops dramatically. Why? Much of that effort is spent redoing work that has already been done—perhaps because of a technical change or a change in the market. That effort does not count toward value-added work, since doing things again is rework. It means that someone made a mistake or misjudgment to begin with and had people working on the wrong thing.

Fuller's studies also found that a lot of working time was spent on overhead activities, on support of previously designed products that did not work properly, or at computer terminals waiting for a response. None of that is value-added work, however. "What happens when you eliminate all these other activities?" Fuller rhetorically asks. The initial figure of 40 percent value-added work drops to 5 or 10 percent.

In one software firm, people were very busy, but they were not getting product out. Fuller collected some data and found that every task assigned had to be changed an average of 1.3 times. People were doing more changing, revising, and shifting than they were doing the job correctly to begin with. The value-added work was almost negligible.

Consultant John Guaspari of Rath and Strom believes nonvalue-added work is rampant, with only 10 percent of engineers' time actually spent on product design. Little things are the big time-wasters, he says, such as "taking three days to get management approval on a decision." A. Blanton Godfrey, chairman of the Juran Institute, says that design engineers rarely spend 20 percent of their day on design.[6] Boeing executives say that one out of three engineers just fixes the mistakes made by the other two.[7] Graham Haddock of Motorola estimates that engineers spend 15 to 25 percent of their time engineering and 75 to 85 percent of their time chasing paper.

The harder one searches for value-added work, the less of it there seems to be. Nick Siriani of Westinghouse considers the value-added figure to be about 5 percent, and he feels that most engineers' days are filled with wastes of time. An engineer, Siriani notes, will start on something and find out that the information he needs is not all there. He calls up someone to get the information, but that person is not in his office. He goes to a meeting that starts late and is inconclusive, so he must attend a follow-up meeting later. Even in research, Siriani suggests, a lot of time is wasted setting up and working on the lab equipment or on support activities and relatively little time on active research. Stalk and Hout believe that only 5 percent of all work is value-added, as does Joseph D. Blackburn.[8]

Obtaining the Improvement

But now the fun starts. If the value-added work is 15 percent (which might be high), that means that 85 percent of staff time is spent on other activities—typically on delays, wastes, changes, and rework. If those other activities can be cut to 70 percent, the time spent on active product development doubles to 30 percent (see figure 8–1). The percent of time moving forward on the highway would be doubled. Although the number might differ somewhat in practice, the time to complete the project should fall in half.

This point is very important. In most projects the proportion of nonvalue-added work is so large that a small reduction in it can double or triple the proportion of value-added work. When the

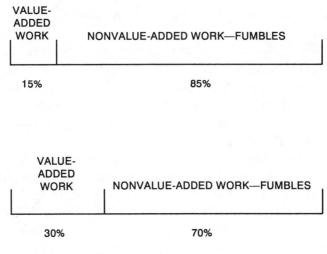

FIGURE 8–1

The Leverage of Value-Added Work

amount of effective and useful work on a project per day doubles or triples, it can chop the cost and time to complete the project in half or more.

So much time is lost due to fumbles that many product development projects contain an enormous potential for time and cost reduction. Moreover, this requires no big allocation of funds or people but an identification and elimination of fumbles.

Summary

In many companies innovation is considerably slower and more costly than need be. Throwing money at a problem may not help, either. Instead, to move toward the ideal superhighway of fast product innovation, fumbles need to be eradicated. The fumbles—delays, changes, or any nonvalue-added work—must be uncovered. How long does it take to get an approval for a purchase order? How long does it take a supplier to make an item? How many items on the schedule get completed on time? How many changes and revisions are made in the plans? Sandhi Bhidi of Mentor Graphics interviews the key people in a project at the end of each milestone. He says his job is to "find out what works and what does not work." Armed with that information he takes steps to improve the situation.

How to Get Rid of Fumbles

Chapter 8 posited a conceptual approach for improving product development based upon the idea of eradicating fumbles (nonvalue-added work). Since fumbles are rampant in most product development activities, reducing them slashes the cost and time of product development. But can fumbles really be reduced? If so, how should it be done? Answering those questions is the mission of this chapter.

Case Studies

Canon's Fumble Elimination

In 1982, during a visit to Canon's head offices in the skyscrapered Shinjuku section of Tokyo, I first learned about this phenomenon. Canon had recently had a team of top experts conduct a thorough study of how it could cut its time to develop products. The team's approach was to examine where the time was being spent. First it discovered that of the total engineering time, about 25 percent was spent on administrative activities. Each individual activity might be small, such as filling out a form or getting an approval, but their cumulative impact was sizable.

When the team examined the other 75 percent of the engineering time, they were not happy about that, either. One big fumble they discovered was that marketing and engineering continually argued about what the specifications for a new product should be. Marketing would want one thing, engineering would say they could not make that, and around it would go for months. Still another very large delay was in manufacturing startup. When beginning to manufacture a new product, it seemed to take forever to get the production line operating smoothly.

Armed with these findings, Canon attacked these wastes on all fronts by launching a program called TS ½, or "time savings one-half," aimed at cutting the time of product development in half within three years. To begin, it greatly simplified its administrative tasks. Next, it tackled the way engineering and marketing decided product specifications. Whenever a new product had to be innovated, a special team of key people was created to go off, isolate themselves, and work out the specifications. As for the manufacturing problems, Canon made design responsible for starting up the manufacturing, thereby forcing the designers to carefully consider the needs of manufacturing.

TS ½ succeeded—in three years it reduced product development time by half. Moreover, the principle Canon used was the one this book has been articulating. First, it identified the fumbles—in its case, the delays due to administrative work, deciding specifications, and starting up manufacturing. Then it eliminated them.

Hewlett-Packard's Fumble Elimination

To further illustrate the approach, Mike Galane of Hewlett-Packard recounts the development of a computer terminal at HP. The development team, proud of their accomplishment, invited Bill Hewlett, the firm's co-founder, to see their work. They spread the parts of the terminal out onto two tables and asked Hewlett to assemble it. This he did in about twenty minutes.

Then actual production started, and the team forgot about the project. A student from Stanford was brought in for the summer, and just to give her something to do, the team asked her to study the production of the terminal. In her report at the end of the summer, she mentioned that assembly took four and a half hours. Someone recalled that Hewlett had done it in only twenty minutes. Someone else then joked, "That's because he gets paid more."

The real story, when they investigated, was that the production line contained many fumbles, with a great deal of testing, rework, complex flow lines, and delays. The team proceeded to remedy the situation, and although they did not shrink the time to twenty minutes, they did cut it by nearly 75 percent.

Mazda's Fumble Elimination

Fumble elimination is also impressive in auto firms. A Mazda plant in Japan and a U.S. auto plant both had an assembly-line worker place the gas tank on the cars.[1] In both cases the respective employee worked hard and appeared to be doing value-added work. A closer examination, however, exposed something different.

The Mazda worker stood on a platform that moved with the car. His box of tools was directly on the platform, so he never had to reach for it. He did not have to bend around to get the gas tank, either, because a slide-device lifted it up to the car. Interestingly, due to the assembly-line setup, the car was tilted on its side at a forty-five-degree angle, with the two left wheels on the ground and the right wheels high in the air. The worker could stand erect and work on the bottom of the car easily.

What about the U.S. worker? Because the car was not tilted at all, he had to stand in a pit underneath the car and crane his neck. He had to run to get his tools. To get a gas tank, he had to run over to a stack of them, pick one up, then run back to put it on the car. Running back and forth and straining his neck, the U.S. worker was sweating and physically working much harder. Yet it was nonvalue-added work. The Mazda worker, during the time saved, daubed on some tar, attached some rubber spacers, and bolted on some insulating material.

The two assembly lines operated at the same speed, but although the Mazda worker worked considerably less strenuously, he had a much higher percent of value-added work. Mazda's productivity per person was dramatically higher.

Ford's Fumble Elimination

Many U.S. automakers are taking such lessons to heart. A Ford Taurus plant in Atlanta is now one of the most efficient in the world, comparable in productivity to Japanese auto plants. Although many innovative techniques are employed there, one of the most important is the elimination of nonvalue-added work. Workers are thoroughly trained in the concept. In fact, one worker has said, "We want to eliminate no-value work [*sic*]. I put on a part. The value of what I am doing is attaching the part. Walking three steps isn't part of the value. Make every move count."[2]

Eliminate Fumbles First, Invest Capital Later

Making every move count encapsulates the philosophy of LSFI Step 3, Eradicate Fumbles. Furthermore, in all the cases described above, the results were attained by fumble elimination, not by capital investment. When appropriate, capital improvements can be beneficial. But as the previous chapter mentioned in relation to GM, where $50 billion was wasted, if a process has many fumbles in it, the investment may have little value. The new equipment will have a perverse tendency to make the process produce fumbles more quickly.

Eliminating fumbles clears away the underbrush of problems. Then management can more accurately see where to put the capital investment, and that investment can pay off. Once fumbles are reduced, moreover, the efficiency of the system is usually so much improved that less capital is needed. To reiterate, because it can be an expensive mistake: Before making a capital investment, go after the fumbles to avoid wasting much of the investment.

Michael Hammer reinforces this point with an example about Ford.[3] Ford had an accounts payable department of five hundred people, and it hoped that a new computer system would reduce that number to four hundred. Initially, Ford executives were enthusiastic about the proposed computer investment. But then they heard that Mazda had an accounts payable department of five people. Even adjusted for size, the difference in efficiency was incredible; Mazda was 500 percent more efficient.

Computerization was not the answer—that would merely have institutionalized a process that was inferior to begin with. The problem was the fumbles—work that was apparently needed but was not—in which documents were routed to numerous people who made many checks, verifications, and cross-checks. Before it could issue a payment order, for instance, the Ford people had to match fourteen data items between the receipt record, the purchase order, and the invoice. After analyzing the system, Ford reduced that fourteen to three. By eradicating this and other fumbles, Ford achieved an efficiency improvement of 300 to 400 percent. Fortunately, Ford realized that its first step was not to invest in the computer system, but to remove the fumbles.

How Eliminating Fumbles Reduces Costs

Fumbles are often hidden, but by finding and eliminating them, we move farther along our superhighway of no fumbles, significantly reducing time and cost. As the previous chapter showed, the value-added work in many development projects is low—perhaps 5 to 15 percent. By doubling the percent of value-added work, management can reduce the development cost and time roughly by half. Often the improvements are even greater.

Finding Fumbles

To systematically eliminate fumbles, it helps to categorize them (see table 9–1). Two categories of fumbles—market changes and technical delays—are so extensive that two entire LSFI steps are devoted to them. For most firms, the biggest category of fumbles is unexpected changes in the market. When the market shifts, the team must redesign the product in order to sell it. Yet each redesign, and often there are several, is rework and thus a fumble. LSFI Step 4—Place Customers First—is devoted entirely to tackling this very common fumble.

The second and perhaps equally large category of fumbles is delays due to unforeseen technical problems. These delays generally result from a failure to adequately implement LSFI Step 2, Establish Foundations. If new technology has not been fully tested and

TABLE 9–1
Major Sources of Fumbles

- Changes in product design due to unforseen changes in the market
- Delays due to inadequate technological research and foundations
- Delays in dealing with suppliers
- Dealys in support activities and approvals

proven manufacturable by the time actual product development starts, fumbles will almost surely result.

Although these two categories are perhaps the most wrenching—each requiring its own LSFI step—many other onerous categories of fumbles exist. One of the most serious is supplier relations, because for many products, procurement takes up half the development time.

Procurement from Suppliers

Procurement can produce numerous fumbles that go virtually unnoticed. They did not escape the attention of Kim Clark of Harvard, however, when he determined that on a major body die for automobiles, the supplier lead time is thirteen to fourteen months in Japan and almost twenty-five months in the United States.

The prime reason for this difference of close to a factor of two is fumbles. They start right at the beginning, when a U.S. auto firm gives a U.S. supplier an order to start making a die. But the supplier does not start to make the die right away. This is not because the supplier is incompetent, nor is he wasting time. Rather, it is because the supplier knows that the auto firm will soon telephone and say, "Stop working on the die—there's been a change." In fact, he will likely get several of such calls.

The auto firm, because of its own fumbles, decides to make changes. Each one of these changes requires a complex and time-consuming bureaucratic approval process. Moreover, before the supplier can actually implement the changes, it may have to renegotiate its contract with the auto firm. Several rounds of changes and renegotiations often occur. When the supplier finally does start to make the die, another delay ensues. The die has likely lost its place in the supplier's production schedule, so it must await a new turn.

As Clark stresses, the bureaucracy, the changes, and the adversarial relationship all add up to produce delay after delay. Yet most of these delays are accepted as the standard way of doing business. For decades, people have been taught to deal with suppliers adversarially: "Get three bids. Take the lowest. Then beat the lowest down more." The competitive, adversarial approach was the way business was done, and the delays went unremarked. It is difficult for people in that tradition to understand that cooperation and partnership with a supplier are faster, better, and cheaper.

The Japanese supplier lead time was about half that of the Americans because in Japan the supplier is not an adversary but a partner, and both supplier and auto firm will jointly plan, in order to avoid changes and fumbles. Interestingly, to save time a Japanese supplier often starts working on an order without a contract, because the parties trust each other and know they will work out the contract later.

IMPROVING SUPPLIER RELATIONS. Fortunately, U.S. firms are improving their relations with their suppliers. Ford, for one, became frustrated and upset at its many delays in dealing with suppliers. When Ford investigated, however, it discovered that it was frequently the guilty party. If a supplier had an inquiry or question, Ford often took thirty to forty-five days to reply.

In a similar vein, Motorola decided there were too many delays with its suppliers. Chris Galvin, executive vice-president, recalls that management examined the blueprints that were sent to suppliers. They discovered that the blueprints were virtually unreadable, being marked up and covered with changes. Each blueprint also had an average of thirteen documents attached, and each document itself contained many pages of specifications, often scribbled. With blueprints so confusing, it was no wonder there were delays with suppliers. Galvin instituted a rule that limited the number of attachments and required clear, readable prose.

These examples suggest that if a problem with a supplier arises, the fault is not always with the supplier. No mater who causes the fumbles, however, since procurement consumes perhaps half of product development time, management should correct any fumbles in it.

Support Functions and Approval

Innovation requires many support activities, yet because support groups are not administered by the development department their fumbles often escape attention. A fumble is a fumble, however, and must be attacked.

At one large firm that was starting an innovation project, the personnel department required three months to transfer people to the product development team. That was three months of project time wasted. Some readers might be saying to themselves, "Three months is silly—we only take three weeks." But why should it take three weeks? Why not three hours, or even three minutes? Why not call people up and have them drop whatever they are doing and come over to their new assignment?

Paper work and approvals can be completed after the person transfers. Japanese suppliers, as mentioned, start to work before they get a contract or an agreed-upon price. Some changes in corporate culture might be needed to institute this, but to get a project going, transfer the people first and do the paper work later. In product development, time should be the real priority.

Many of the same difficulties exist throughout all the support and approval functions. At Xerox, for example, requests to purchase equipment or materials took two months to process. Xerox cut that to less than a week by eliminating delays and the number of signatures required.[4]

In an extreme example cited by Daniel Whitney of Draper Laboratories, an automotive engineer who was designing one part had to do 350 separate workups.[5] Each of these required an approval signature—a total of 350 signatures for a single part. No wonder, Whitney said, it takes five years for U.S. firms to design a car.

That support and approval processes can strangle product innovation is not always recognized. But once it is recognized, by eliminating fumbles firms can improve those efficiencies.

Techniques to Eliminate Fumbles

Companies employ a variety of approaches to identify and eliminate fumbles, but consider now some special techniques. The first two are organizational in nature, while the latter ones concern data collection.

Organizational Approaches

TIGER TEAMS. Tiger teams are the approach that we saw in the case study of Canon. Here, a team of top people investigates the development process and conceives how to dramatically improve it. The team collects data on where the fumbles are and recommends how to eliminate them. Ideally, the team reports directly to the CEO, so that others will know that they have to cooperate with the team's investigation, and also so that its recommendations can be implemented. To help focus its efforts, the team should be given a clear goal, such as the one at Canon to cut development time in half.

WORKOUTS. General Electric innovated a technique called workout that eliminates specific problems not only in innovation but throughout the firm. Bill Sheeran, vice-president, explains that a workout is a three-day retreat, off-site in a motel or hotel, in which the people involved in a problem attack that problem. The problem might be how to cut nonvalue-added work, how to improve supplier relations, or how to reduce the number of defects in manufacturing. The participants include the people responsible for implementing the recommendations, as well as experts in the process, and worker-level individuals. Depending upon the problem, twenty to one hundred people might attend.

A workout commences with an hourlong overview of the situation. The general manager leads off, then leaves in order to avoid intimidating anyone. To get the participants enthused, they are usually asked: "If all the impediments to your job were eliminated, how much more effective could we be in pursuing our goals?" Usually, the answer is surprisingly high, between 30 and 50 percent. The topic of the workout discussion then becomes how to obtain such improvements. The participants break into teams to examine the problems in detail, and come up with recommendations. During the three days, facilitators help the teams brainstorm, interact, and stay on target.

The pièce de résistance of the workout occurs during its last few hours, when the general manager returns and all the recommendations are presented to him. The recommendations state what should be done, how to do it, its cost, who should do it, and its likely impact. The general manager is given a choice of only three responses: approve, reject for a specific reason, or refer for further study. Moreover, he or she must make that decision on the spot. The number of recommendations usually total well over a hundred, leaving only a minute or two for the general manager to make a decision. It is a grueling period for the general manager, who must make lightning-fast decisions in front of, say, one hundred people. Adding to the pressure on him, the general manager's boss attends this last portion to oversee what happens.

To show GE employees that they count, GE's CEO, Jack Welsh, wants most recommendations approved. If a general manager rejects a suggestion, he is required to have a very good reason. Typically, over 90 percent of the recommendations are approved, only a few percent are rejected, and the rest sent for further study. GE wants the recommendations evaluated and executed immediately, which is the reason for this final portion of the workout.

Three months later it holds a followup to review progress and make adjustments. Any recommendation that was sent for further study is now heard.

Workouts often follow the above format, but they have many variations depending upon the scope of the problem being considered and the individual operating unit. Nevertheless, management at GE from Welsh on down are highly enthusiastic about the workouts. One business unit might hold ten of them a year.

Data Collection Approaches

Once an organizational method to attack fumbles has been established, data should be collected to uncover where the fumbles are. These are some excellent approaches.

WORK SAMPLING. Work sampling means periodically sampling what the staff are doing during the day. Individuals can sample themselves, or another person—often a student—can do it. Every twenty minutes, for example, each person records on a log what activity he or she is doing at that instant, such as getting information on the phone, discussing how to reschedule a project, answering a question from a customer. In an easier but slightly less accurate approach, at the end of the day staff record what they did during the day and the approximate time allotted to each activity.

Richard Schonberger reports a work sample taken by engineers that showed the percent of time they were doing the following activities[6]:

Prepare proposals	32%	Reassignment	6%
Detail	23%	Check	5%
Design	18%	Review Order	5%
Reacquaint	11%		

Note that the engineers spent only 18 percent of their time on design. Also since these data are self-reported, no idle time is reported. The design time itself includes time spent making changes, searching for information, and correcting errors. The time doing actual design—the real value-added work—is thus very small.

These data, however, did give the firm's management insight into which of the engineers' activities to examine. Teams were formed to study the situation and make changes. They discovered that 40 percent of all jobs were designed twice: once for the proposal stage, and then again for the actual job. The teams proceeded to change this as well as other practices, considerably improving engineering efficiency.

Schedule Monitoring

Another data collection approach is to monitor delays in the schedule. Under the direction of Tim Fuller, a consultant and lecturer at the University of Chicago, one product development team held weekly sessions in which they would plan the activities to be done that week. Then they would monitor which activities were finished on schedule. After a few weeks of data collection, they discovered that only 43 percent of all the activities had been completed as scheduled—a fact that flabbergasted management.

Although 43 percent may seem low, this figure is not unusual for firms that have never systematically tried to improve their innovation processes. With a sufficient effort, however, the figure can be changed to nearly 100 percent. At Honda, automobile development projects are consistently finished on time, according to Dave Nelson, vice-president.

In general, the technique Fuller suggests is:

1. Monitor the percent of activities that are now completed on schedule.
2. Analyze the delays that caused the schedule slippages, and isolate their root causes. Usually two or three top culprits stand out, which management can then attack.
3. Continue the monitoring, analysis, and delay elimination until virtually all activities are completed as scheduled.

PROCESS MAPPING. A related technique is to make a map of the process. For each portion of the process under study, the team draws a map of the theoretical sequence of steps involved. Such a map for a manufacturing process appears in figure 9–1.[7] (Similar maps can be drawn to depict information flow.)

Next, the team compares the map that was drawn up with the real process. Nearly everyone who uses this technique discovers that the real process has many more fumbles in it than had previously been realized. Fumbles to look for include:

- rework
- waiting for parts
- waiting for information
- extra steps
- delays or missed schedules
- movement of people or material
- changes in plans
- incomplete information or missing information.

Evaluate every step to see if it is really needed or can be improved. Because the map displays the entire process at once, it often suggests how to make major reformulations and improvements.

Bill Sheeran recommends process maps since they can identify where improvements can be made. Ron Davis, Caterpillar executive, agrees and strongly stresses that they are a prime way to get rid of nonvalue-added work. Executives at Milliken take this one

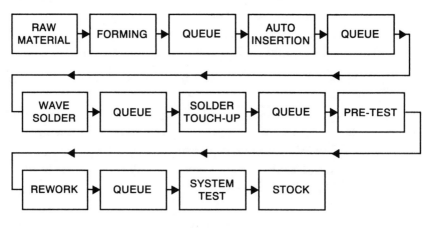

FIGURE 9–1

Manufacturing Process Map

step further. When a problem is posed to them, they often demand to see a map of the relevant process before they will even discuss the problem.

Bottleneck Breaking

In another powerful approach, often used in conjunction with those above, senior executives meet monthly to review progress on the innovation projects. Their role is not to offer advice according to Margaret Dano, executive at GE appliances, but to break bottlenecks. They identify where any delay or queue has occurred, then eliminate the delay. If the model shop is slow delivering a model, senior management will take action not only to get that model made quickly but to prevent such delays in the future. If a supplier is slow with a key part, senior management contacts the supplier CEO and get that part expedited.

Establish Theoretical Limits

Once the basic data are collected, the team can establish the theoretical limits to the efficiency of the process. The theoretical limit is the cost and time of doing the process if every step were done perfectly and there were no extra or unnecessary steps. The theoretical limit becomes the improvement target for which to shoot.

Alcoa pioneered this concept when it considered the energy needed to transform bauxite ore into aluminum. Energy is a major cost factor in aluminum production. First Alcoa found that the industry average was 5.4 kilowatt hours per pound (kwh/lb.) of aluminum smelted, while the best Alcoa plant used 4.5 kwh/lb. Alcoa launched a campaign to improve its operations, and succeeded in getting many plants down to or below the 4.5 kwh/lb. goal. Once that goal was reached, however, the staff stopped their improvement effort, thinking that they had become the best.

Alcoa then conceived of calculating the theoretical limit of its energy use. By considering the basic physics of the process, calculating the energy needed to pull the aluminum atoms away from the ore, they determined that the ideal process would need only 1.2 kwh/lb. That became the new goal, and the staff started improving the smelting process again.

TABLE 9–2
Summary of Techniques to Eliminate Fumbles

Organizational

- Tiger Teams. A small group of top people study the development process to improve it dramatically.
- Workout. In an off-site retreat, the key people involved in a process meet to determine how to improve it. At the end of the retreat, most of their recommendations are approved and immediately implemented.

Data Collection

- Work Sampling. Collect detailed data on the activities of staff to identify fumbles.
- Schedule monitoring. Determine what activities are not completed on schedule. Analyze how to improve the percentage that are finished on time.
- Process Mapping. Flow-chart a process to pinpoint fumbles.
- Bottleneck Breaking. Senior management meets monthly to learn about and eliminate delays.

Theoretical Limits.

Limits on the efficiency of a process that provide goals for improvement.

The underlying concept is simple: Determine the theoretical limit of the process. For processes that are dominated by machines or equipment, engineering analyses can provide this information. For more complex or administrative processes, the theoretical limit is determined by conceiving a process that has no fumbles—a process that is totally value-added work. For example, suppose to approve a purchase order requies ten days. But value-added work occurs only when someone actually reads and signs the purchase order, not when it is sitting in an in-box. Suppose we add up the time it takes for all the people involved to read and sign the purchase order and find that the sum is one hour. One hour is the theoretical limit. One hour then becomes the improvement goal.

Summary

Most firms' product innovation processes are very far from the ideal of a no-fumbles superhighway. Fumbles in the form of delays, re-work, change, and unnecessary work are epidemic. Fumbles occur in all aspects of product development, including marketing, engineering, supplier relations, and support activities. Management needs to identify the fumbles and eliminate them. Techniques that can help them do that including tiger teams, workouts, work sampling, schedule monitoring, process mapping, and bottleneck breaking (see table 9–2).

Place Customers First

The Fickle Customer

Of all the steps in LSFI, none is as important as Step 4, Place Customers First. The worst fumble of all is to create a product that customers do not buy. No sales means no profits means no firm. To innovate products that will sell is paramount. Even a late, over-budget project with flawed planning, weak foundations, and problem-riddled development can be a winner if the product is a hit with the customer.

Yet a major dilemma is to determine what product the customers will actually want. Depending upon the market, between 50 and 90 percent of all new products flop. Eighty percent of new grocery products fail "because shoppers don't want or need them."[1] New industrial products have a success probability of 0.27, while for new consumer goods it is only 0.19.[2] Another study puts the rate at almost two-thirds,[3] but its criterion for success is much looser. Albert Page of the University of Illinois determined that of all new product ideas that started development, only 9.4 percent were ultimately successful, and of all the products that made it to market, only about half were successful.[4] Although the exact percentage varies depending upon the criteria used and the market studied, the studies all concur on one thing: A significant percent of new product introductions fail because customers just do not want them.

Determining What Customers Want

Estimating what new products customers really will buy is very difficult, despite the widespread use of customer-research techniques such as surveys, focus groups, and interviews. (The next two chapters suggest some newer procedures to target the customers' needs.) The overriding obstacle is this: Customers themselves often cannot articulate what new product they really will purchase. How clearly customers express their preferences seems to be proportional to their knowledge of the product or related products. The more they know about a product type, the better they can articulate their reactions.

Focusing on Product Types

Edith Wilson, a Hewlett-Packard executive, uses three categories of new products to explain this concept.

- *Revolutionary.* A revolutionary product is one that is novel or new to the world and has distinctive features unlike those of any existing product. Customers know little about this type of product, and their input about them is not very helpful.
- *Evolutionary.* An evolutionary product is one that is an extension of an existing product line. Since customers already know this type of product fairly well, their input about a new product that is a slight modification can be very beneficial.
- *Special orders.* A special order product is one that is tailor-made to fit a customer's specifications. Customers usually have a good concept of what they want for this type of product.

Revolutionary products are the worst in terms of the value of customer input. Being revolutionary, there are no similar products with which the customer can compare it. Thirty years ago a survey of customers who owned televisions would not have suggested that videocassette recorders would be a success. Wilson recalls that when HP introduced its hand-held calculator, no one had any idea what the future of that product would be.

Steve Hoch of the University of Chicago cites the example of telephone answering machines. When they were first introduced, a market survey might have portrayed a dismal future for the product. In fact, many people did not like them. Answering the phone with a machine, they felt, was rude and discourteous. People had little concept of how useful the product could become.

The leading-edge users, the most advanced people in a field, can sometimes provide guidance on revolutionary products. The leading-edge users—technical "nuts" and computer "jocks"—tinker and experiment in new directions. That often leads to new product ideas. Motorola, for example, is now designing a satellite system for worldwide communication. According to Chris Galvin, senior executive vice-president, the average customer does not understand the implications of this concept. But more informed customers like AT&T can contribute to its development.

Unfortunately, even the top experts have difficulty forecasting some advanced features. Jim Page of Motorola wonders if customers will like pagers with color displays or fax pagers. Don Hoffman of Sun Microsystems notes that his firm is supposed to be a world leader in its field, yet it cannot foretell how advanced areas like network management and multimedia are going to evolve.

The evolutionary product category is somewhat easier. Since customers understand the product, they can state what features or modifications they prefer. Years ago, people did not know about hand-held calculators, Edith Wilson notes, but they are now very knowledgeable, and the market has had to specialize into calculators for almost all uses, including architecture, finance, statistics, and high school math.

Of the three categories, the customers' knowledge of what they want for a special order product is usually clearest. Special orders might include unique equipment that must be designed or adapted to a specific customer's requirements, as well as customized software programs. But even special order products can cause problems. Software is a common malefactor. Dr. Paul Kantor, president of Tantalus, notes that with large software installations, customers rarely know what they want. And once the software is installed, they frequently discover that they want something else. Many customers have a hard time envisioning what a software or hardware product will do.

Further Complications

Even with a product type that they know, customers might not be aware of what improvements can be made in it. Wilson recalls that when Weyerhauser was interested in supplying wood to a furniture maker for tables, the furniture maker declared that it would switch only if the price were at least 10 percent lower. For Weyerhauser to produce the wood for 10 percent less was impossible.

The tabletops being made used two pieces of half-inch wood. However, Weyerhauser figured out a way to replace the two half-inch pieces with a single piece one-inch thick. Some innovative engineering changes were required, but Weyerhauser found it could deliver the one-inch pieces at a substantially reduced price, and it won the contract.

The customer—the furniture maker—had been unaware of the new way Weyerhauser conceived to solve its problem. But that is the point. Customers often are not aware of the possibilities for innovation—after all, they are not technical experts—and asking for their input may not always be helpful.

Even customers who seem to know what they want often respond to questions about their preferences in generalities. When asked about improvements, these customers often reply "More power," "More comfort," or "Easier to use." But in a personal computer, say, it is unclear what "more power" means. Does it mean faster processor speed? Larger size of memory? More additional features?

Furthermore, several different customers may be involved in executing one purchase. With many industrial products, a purchasing agent may buy the product, but a manager will decide which product is needed and a worker will actually use it. General Electric's Bob Hauck is involved in making expensive medical equipment. He notes that purchases sometimes involve a board of directors, in addition to physicians, nurses, and technicians. It is difficult to decide what customers want when the item has many different customers with conflicting needs.

To make things worse, customers' needs today may be different by the time the product actually comes out. Technology advances and economic conditions change. Hugh Barnes, vice-president of Compaq Computer, notes that it is very difficult to know what the market will want with his product eighteen months from now.

What has just been presented is only a brief summary of the issues that people in marketing face daily. In general, the more a customer knows about a product, the more help he or she can provide to new product developers. Nevertheless, many problems and uncertainties remain, and forecasting what the customer will actually buy remains very difficult. Some people suggest that doing such forecasting is like walking through a minefield. It has to be done very carefully, and even then, it is still easy to be blown up.

Case Studies

To make this discussion concrete, three short case studies can show how corporations can misjudge what customers will buy. In all three cases what the customer wanted seemed obvious. Yet in all three cases what was "obviously true" was totally wrong.

John Hauser of MIT recalls a firm that had developed a new dishwashing liquid that had excellent cleaning power. Certainly, the developers believed, customers want very clean dishes. When the firm consumer-tested the product, however, customers reported that it did not clean as well as the competitor's product. The developers were dumbfounded, especially since their own internal tests had proved that their product was clearly superior. When they investigated the situation, they found that the customers had judged cleaning power in an interesting way—they looked at the bubbles. Because the product's bubbles were not the right size or quantity, the customers believed it did not clean well. The product, in effect, failed the customers' "bubble test."

Edith Wilson recalls the time when Hewlett-Packard was developing a gas chromatograph for use in laboratories. It was a significant advancement—able to conduct some fifty different chemical tests, which previously had to be performed by many different instruments. Because it combined so many tests, it was quite expensive. HP feared that the new instrument was too expensive and might not sell. When the designers checked with potential customers—chemists who work in labs—they learned that the real issue was not price but space. Nearly every square inch of space in the labs was jammed with equipment. The size of the instrument was much more important than its cost.

Finally, Jim Pratt of TRW recalls that engineers spent a lot of time and money to design a automobile seat that could be adjusted without noise, since people continually say they want a quiet car. When the product was tested, however, they discovered that people did not like it—they wanted the seat motor to make noise. The

TABLE 10–1

The Difficulties of Predicting Customer Behavior

- Customers often cannot express what they want.
- For advanced or revolutionary projects, customers may not know enough to be helpful
- Customers may not know that their problem is solvable, so they do not express a desire for it.
- Whatever the customer wants today may change by the time the product comes out.
- Many people may be involved in the purchase, each with different desires.

noise gave people instant feedback that the seat was moving more clearly than having felt the seat move.

Again the message rings out: Determining what the customer will like is a risky business (see table 10–1).

Summary

This chapter presented the various difficulties involved in predicting what customers want in a new product. How helpful the customer can be will depend upon his or her knowledge of the product. Nevertheless, even with knowledgeable customers, many uncertainties remain in estimating what customers will buy. The next two chapters, however, consider what might be done about this dilemma.

The Customer-First Questions and Customer Research

The last chapter discussed a basic truth: The customer is very difficult to predict. The situation is far from hopeless, however, and this chapter presents some techniques that can reduce the risk of predicting customer behavior. The chapter begins with the customer-first questions, special questions that help identify what the customer wants. The questions ask, in precise terms, why the customer would buy the new product. Next, the chapter presents several new and powerful customer-research techniques that can also help identify what the customer wants: engineers and managers interacting with customers; quality function deployment; conjoint analysis; cultural anthropology; and kansei analysis. The following chapter will propose a quite different tack, however, that sometimes we should forget about customer research altogether.

The Customer-First Questions (CFQ)

Despite customer unpredictability, certain actions reduce the risk of developing a new product that the customer will not buy. The first and overriding consideration is to understand the goal of LSFI Step 4—that is, to successfully answer the customer-first questions, or CFQ:

1. What major problems that the customer faces does this product solve that no competitor solves?

2. What major benefits does this product provide for the customer that no competitor provides?
3. What is the customer's motivation to purchase this product?

The CFQ were conceived in conversations with Edith Wilson, Hewlett-Packard executive. Wilson notes that most design teams, when asked, cannot provide good answers to the CFQ.

Here is a general methodology for answering the CFQ: First, the firm should identify the needs (and wants) of the customers—the issues and problems that customers would like solved. Some needs, note, are implicit and hidden, as the customer cannot articulate them, yet the customer is still pleased when they are satisfied. Second, for each important need (including price), the firm should evaluate how its product will satisfy that need in comparison with the competition's product. From this information the firm can infer whether the customer will likely prefer its or a competitor's product.

Leading companies follow this approach. For instance, in selling copiers Xerox answers the CFQ by identifying customer needs and wants. According to Peter Garcia, it conducts a detailed analysis of a customer's operation, floor by floor, group by group, and sometimes person by person. It determines what documents must be copied, why, and in what volume. The key documents that are of particular import are singled out. The Xerox shows how its copiers, by cutting cost and turnaround time, can satisfy the customer's document-handling needs best. Xerox even uses computer programs to help it do this analysis. It systematically identifies the specific document reproduction problems the customer has, then solves them.

Similarly, the computer company Next studies how customers use computers. If many people in a target market are using computer-aided design (CAD) programs, Next will try to uncover what problems they are having with CAD. It will then design computers to help solve those problems. As for Microsoft, it tries to find out how customers use software. It looks at features they use frequently, what aspects seem cumbersome, and what problems they have. They determine what in the customer's eyes makes a good word-processing program or good spreadsheet. Using these techniques, these firms strive to develop products that satisfy customer needs and wants better than the competition.

The Kano Model

A new and exciting approach to answering the CFQ is the Kano model, conceived by Noriaki Kano. From the customer's point of view, a product can be considered to have three types of features (see table 11–1). One type are the features that the customer presumes will be there and does not even worry about. A car, for example, will obviously have an engine and heater. The second type are the features by which the customer evaluates the product. Is the car comfortable to drive, and does it have good mileage? The third type are the features that cause customer delight. These are the ones that are totally unexpected by the customer, and that surprise and delight him. Perhaps the car conveys a feeling of elegance, luxury, and great beauty.

The product must provide the features that the customer presumes and expects, and the Kano model takes their inclusion as a given. It is the delight features, those surprising and unexpected ones, that provide the answers to the CFQ. These are the features that distinguish the product from the competition and that provide, Kano feels, the real reasons why customers buy a product.

To use the Kano model, systematically list the features that a new product will have. Then identify the features that customers presume and expect, as well as those designed to delight. Ensure that the product has a sufficient number of the third type of features that it does create delight and consequently sales.

Even with the Kano model, however, answers to the CFQ are difficult to identify with certain products, such as when the customers want style, cool, or pizazz. Indeed, answering the CFQ fully is not always possible. But it is essential for a firm to clarify as

TABLE 11–1
The Kano Model

From a customer's viewpoint, a product has three types of features:

1. Presumed—These are the ones the customer assumes the product will have and pays little attention to.
2. Expected—These are the ones the customer examines in the buying decision.
3. Delight—These are the ones the customer does not expect and that really sell the product.

precisely as it can the reasons the customer will buy its new product and not that of its competitor.

Two Conceptual Approaches to the CFQ

Two basic and seemingly opposite approaches can be used to obtain good answers to the CFQ. The first is customer research. The objective here is to get more accurate customer-preference information, particularly information that the engineering designers can utilize in product development.

The second approach is flexibility. This approach understands that much customer research is unreliable, so it relies upon it less. Instead, the engineers design the product to be modular and flexible. Then, as reliable information about what the customer wants comes in, they revise the product. Indeed, in certain markets customer research is abandoned as too costly and inaccurate. Instead of asking customers what they want, companies "throw" products on the market and see what sells. Actual sales patterns then guide product development.

These two approaches may seem contradictory, since one espouses more customer research, while the other proposes less (see table 11–2). But they are not really contradictory because cost will determine which one to use. If changing a product is costly, the approach will be to use more customer research. Conversely, if the cost of altering a product is small, customer research will not be worth the expense. It will be cheaper to make the product, attempt to sell it, then revise the product based upon actual sales. This latter approach—doing less customer research—is becoming so common

TABLE 11–2

Two "Opposing" Approaches to Answering the CFQ

---

1. Do more customer research.
   • Ensure that the information is useful to the engineers.
2. Create flexibility and do less customer research.
   • Use this if customer research is costly or does not predict customer behavior as well.
   • If the cost of flexibility is low enough, products can be thrown into the market without customer research.

---

and is so important that the next chapter is devoted to it. The first approach is, of course, also very important, and is presented throughout the remainder of this chapter.

Interaction between Engineers and Marketers

In doing customer research, a major problem immediately looms. Lack of cooperation between marketing and engineering design can make it very difficult to conduct the right type of customer research to properly answer the CFQ.

The problem is often arrogance. Each group presumes that it knows what the customer wants and does not want to listen to or work with the other group. Designers frequently feel that they are so expert in the product and its technology that they know what product will sell. Chris Lofgren of Motorola says that many software engineers assume that they are the professionals in software and start coding. In the middle of a project, however, they often discover that the customer wants something different from what they had thought.

Many marketers are no more open-minded. The new product that marketing wants, engineering often cannot be make. Marketing may propose a new product with features like a top-of-the-line Mercedes but want to sell it at a Hyundai price. That would certainly be a hit in the marketplace, but engineering cannot possibly design it. Although this example is exaggerated, marketing nearly always wants a combination of performance, features, and cost that engineering cannot achieve.

The confusion is further exacerbated when marketing passes customer information along to engineering. In the process, the information gets distorted. John Hauser of MIT describes an airline whose marketers conducted a customer survey and reported that the passengers wanted to be "boarded efficiently." What the passengers had really said, however, was that they did not want to be "herded like cattle." The two statements are different and lead to different approaches by the airline. Jim Pratt of TRW likens this problem to the childhood game of telephone, in which kids in a line whisper a secret to their neighbor. By the time the secret gets to the end of the line, the meaning has been totally changed. Similarly, the customer's message gets garbled when it is passed through marketing to the engineers.

Additional friction results from the fact that marketers and engineers have different requirements for information. Marketers need information about market share, product positioning, discount campaigns, and which features will sell. On the other hand, engineers need technical information like where the plug goes, how big the knobs should be, and whether it is all right if the product is a little heavier.

In short, there are many possible points of friction between marketing and engineering, and, as a consequence, what frequently results between marketing and engineering is conflict. Memos fly back and forth, and many meetings are held as the two groups fight for their respective viewpoints.

A Marketing and Engineering Partnership

Since this conflict is harmful and can delay innovation, what is needed is a new partnership between marketing and engineering. Instead of the two being in different departments, marketing and engineering will form a team to jointly develop new products. They will sit together and be trained to interact as a team.

Research confirms the value of good interaction and communications between marketing and engineering. Deborah Dougherty of Wharton studied a number of different new product launches to uncover the factors that lead to success. She investigated the communications between engineers and marketers in areas such as product use, buyers' decision criteria, delivery scheduling, market segments, general marketing, competition, prices, and physical characteristics of the product.

She discovered that successful products are the result of much more communication and discussion between marketing and engineering than are unsuccessful products. In the more successful product launches, she says, the engineers really understood the marketing issues and even the marketing lingo, such as "market share," "customer segment," and "focus group." The marketers and engineers blended together in these firms.

Put Managers and Engineers in Contact with Customers

One excellent approach to getting marketing and engineering to blend is to have managers and engineers visit customers, facilitated by marketing. Simply stated, if a firm wants engineers to believe marketing data, it should involve them in the data collection. In Chapter 1 we saw how James Stryker of Ingersoll-Rand took a joint engineering marketing team around the country to hold focus groups with customers. The team learned that the customers wanted a tool that was durable, easily fixed, hard to stall, and shaped to relieve the hand pain afflicting many operators.[1] Armed with that information, the Stryker team designed a very successful product.

But there is an additional important point. One Ingersoll-Rand executive particularly stressed the value of the team going "belly to belly" with customers. When engineers hear information candidly from customers, it seems to have a much greater effect on them than hearing the same information from their colleagues in marketing. Indeed, what seems essential is the emotional impact of direct contact with customers, as that helps engineers to understand customers' feelings and to create a better product.

There are many ways to get this direct contact. Honda sends its engineers out to car dealers. The engineers speak not just to management at the dealerships but to the repair mechanics in the service bays. Similarly, Motorola managers visit customers, and they speak not just to executives but to the office and factory workers who actually use the Motorola products. Hewlett-Packard has some of its engineers act as salespeople in a store so they can see firsthand what customers like. Microsoft sends its software engineers around the country to speak with groups of users and expert hackers. Participants at these sessions draw up wish lists about what they want in the next version of the software program. Mentor Graphics expects its managers to visit customers twelve times a year. Many firms also have special days when customers are invited to visit the firm and talk about their problems.

To ensure customer contact, Boeing took the novel approach of having eight airline companies assist in the design of its 777 plane.[2] Top people from the airlines attended meeting after meeting with Boeing and contributed their desires on size, range, fuel efficiency, and noise level. The airlines insisted, for example, that the plane's internal configuration be flexible. Despite technical problems with pipes and outlets, Boeing listened and designed galleys, lavatories, and seats that were movable on tracks. The new plan could be re-configured overnight, for instance, from three classes of passengers to two.

Previously airlines had bought planes "off the shelf," whatever the manufacturer made, with only minor modification. Now, according to James Guyette, executive vice-president of operations of United Airlines, "we're back in the laboratory working on the project."

This approach of involving airlines worked impressively for Boeing, because orders for the 777 started flooding in. According to Boeing officials, consulting with the airlines was crucial to maintaining its competitive edge over rival aircraft manufacturers.[3] Phil Condit, vice-president and general manager of the 777 program, stated, "I don't think there's any question that every ounce of airline input is gold."

Speaking directly with customers is popular in many fields and was tried even in as staid an industry as book publishing.[4] Jack Hoeft, president and chief operating officer of Bantam Doubleday Dell, wanted his staff to get "a better understanding of why people buy books, and how we can help our booksellers more." Ever since the advent of computerized ordering, publishers had felt more cut off from the booksellers. Stuart Applebaum, vice-president of the firm, did not want more "ambassadorial" visits, where the publisher visits a few major accounts for a few hours. Rather, he wanted his employees to learn the "nitty-gritty." The publishing people temporarily worked in the bookstores, selling and unpacking books, stocking shelves, and putting up displays. They saw firsthand what type of display posters sell books, and they saw the importance of the cover. They also learned more about why people buy books. For example, the book *Sex after Sixty* was purchased, a customer stressed, as a gift.

Employees as Customers

A firm's own employees can sometimes act as "customers." While Eastman Kodak was developing its disposable Fling 35 camera, according to Al Van de Moere, it encouraged the engineers to use the product as much as possible—for free, of course. One engineer took the camera on a weekend trip to the beach, where he accidentally got it wet. That accident led to the innovation of the Weekend 35 camera, which is totally waterproof and can go almost anywhere.

One American engineer working in Japan had a similar experience. Fujitsu gave him a prototype of a new cellular phone that was under development and told him to use it for his personal calls, free. When he protested that he made a lot of calls to the United States, which were expensive, they said they would still pay for them. They hoped that he might find something out by calling the United States that they would not discover by calling domestically in Japan.

Possible Problems

Getting executives, managers, and engineers in direct contact with customers is extremely beneficial. It can help answer the CFQ and should be required. But the approach is by no means a panacea, and it should be supplemented by other approaches. The problem is that sometimes customers and engineers speak different languages. Bob Hauck, who manages the development of medical equipment at GE, says that the doctors speak cardiology, while the engineers speak bits-and-bytes. Edith Wilson of Hewlett-Packard comments that customers say, "We do integrated circuit testing—we do not want to program the machine," but the engineers ask the customers about data rates. John Hauser of MIT suggests that while customers talk about soap being soft, engineers talk about the soap's chemistry and pH, a measure of the soap's acidity.

The simplest way to overcome this miscommunication, Hauck suggests, is to have an engineer with a good sense of marketing or a marketing person who understands engineering. But, Hauck laments, such two-hat people are rare. Clearly, we must do more, given the crucial importance of placing the customer first. The best approach is to install step-by-step procedures that guide both marketers and engineers to better understand the customer and answer the CFQ. Consider now several techniques, each powerful and novel, that do just that.

Quality Function Deployment (QFD)

Quality function deployment is an organized methodology to translate customer needs and wants directly into engineering issues. It is most applicable to complex products and is widely employed in automobile design, but QFD is valuable for almost any product. It starts not from marketing or engineering but directly from the most important person in product development—the customer. And it is not an interpretation of the customer as made by marketing, but the articulation of the customer's needs and wants in the actual "voice of the customer." QFD hears that voice by collecting customers' unedited phrases, such as, "I like power," or "I want my daughter to be comfortable in the back seat," or, "It is never convenient to change the radio station."

These voice-of-the-customer phrases are transmitted, unfiltered, directly to the marketing-engineering team, who use them to help design products that customers, in their own words, say they want. Employing the customer's original words minimizes distortions and garbling. One garbling situation was previously mentioned about boarding airline passengers. Another revealing example is a customer's words, "I want to be able to wipe up my baby's juice easily if it spills." To the typical marketer, this means exactly what it says—make spills easy to clean. In many organizations, marketing would feed this interpretation—make spills easy to clean—to engineering. But to engineers the original statement means something quite different. To them it suggests a corrosion problem that can be eliminated by using materials that withstand the acids in juices.

As the example shows, for engineers to make detailed technical decisions, they need information that is often lost when it is interpreted by marketing. Jim Pratt stresses the importance of avoiding "baked and shredded" information. By no means does this imply that the customer's words must be slavishly followed, but the original statements are essential and provide undistorted information.

In practice, QFD requires two hundred to three hundred voice-of-the-customer statements. This may seem like a lot, but Abbie Griffin of the University of Chicago notes that pasta—plain old pasta—generated 129 different customer statements. "Who would have believed that?" Griffin comments. Indeed, so many phrases are typically generated that it is generally necessary to sort them into categories. Often five or six major categories are used, each with several subcategories of key phrases.

Griffin also suggests using scenarios to generate phrases from customers. Have customers imagine themselves in a particular situation—on a family picnic, at work, or in an airplane. Then the customers elaborate about using the product in that particular situation. They will use a product quite differently on a picnic from the way they do at home. Presenting specific scenarios sharpens customers' recall and presents a powerful means to obtain the customer phrases.

After the voice-of-the-customer phrases have been obtained and categorized, the marketing-engineering team determines their influence on all the major systems of the product being designed, such as engine, transmission, chassis, and steering. Specifically, a phrase is evaluated to see what product parts it affects. For example, the phrase "good gas mileage" would strongly impact the engine, the transmission, and the car weight, as well as other parts of the car. A matrix array (such as the one in table 11–3) quickly identifies, for each phrase, what systems or components of the product it influences.

TABLE 11–3

QFD Matrix

	Automobile System			Comparison with Competitor	
Customer Phrase	Engine	Body	Transmission	Competitor car I	Competitor car II
"Good mileage"	XX		X	W	S
"Style"	X	XX		B	B
"Comfort"		XX		W	W
"Good pickup"	XX		XX	B	B
"Large trunk"		XX		B	B
"Good in cold weather"	XX		X	W	W
"Prestige"	X	XX		S	B

Competitive Comparison

The coup de grace of QFD comes when for each phrase, the team compares the performance of its product with that of the competition. Consider the phrase "durable paint job," for example. The team rates the product and its competitors' on how well each fulfills this customer desire. The goal is to ensure that the team's product beats the competition's on most of the key phrases. To achieve this, the team establishes a performance target for each of the product's major components. To beat the competition on the phrase "good gas mileage," the team would adjust the performance specifications of the relevant parts, engine, weight, and transmission, to beat the competition. If the team wanted to beat the competition on "have a comfortable ride," the steering, suspension, frame, and seat would be upgraded.

Determining the specifications for all the major components generally requires many meetings. Often tradeoffs must be made. Good mileage and fast pickup might be incompatible, for example, and the marketing-engineering team would have to debate the proper choices and develop innovative solutions. Overall, however, because QFD prevents marketers and engineers from working independently, it forces them to cooperatively and creatively integrate what customers want with engineering needs.

In the QFD matrix in table 11–3, the customer phrases are along the side and the product's systems are along the top. "X" means that the car system is important to that customer's statement, and "XX" means it is very important. Car I and car II are the competitor's cars. The "B" means that the product under development will be better than the competitor's car in that aspect, "W" means it will be worse, and "S" means it will be similar.

In most QFD matrices the different voice-of-the-customer categories are weighted by their importance, ensuring appropriate prioritization. They are also considerably more detailed than the one shown here. For instance, the customer phrase "door easy to open and close" might be broken down into:

- easy to open and close from the inside
- stays open on a hill
- easy to open and close from outside

- operates smoothly
- slam sounds solid

The designers' objective is, nevertheless, to make the product superior to the competition in as many of the important phrase categories on the left of the matrix as possible.

Additional Matrices

Once the initial matrix is considered, the team will develop other matrices that link the customer all the way to the manufacturing-operations process. The first matrix in figure 11–1 is like the one in table 11–3, relating the customers phrases to the product's engineering specifications. In the second matrix, those engineering specifications are tied to the individual parts. The third matrix relates the parts features to how they will be manufactured, and the final matrix ensures that the production operations meet the highest quality criteria. These four matrices help the team determine each aspect of the product, including production and quality assurance, with the objective of satisfying the customer.

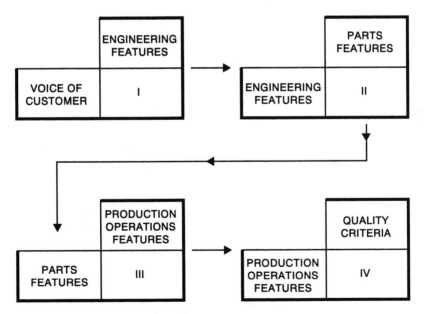

FIGURE 11–1
The Several QFD Matrices

The University of Chicago's Abbie Griffin, who conducted an excellent study of QFD in a number of industries, endorses QFD because it provides a step-by-step process for marketers and engineers to follow. Without it, Griffin notes, marketers and engineers often argue rather abstractly about what the customer does or does not want and about what can or cannot be made. QFD pins down the customers' preferences, forcing the team to methodically examine the facts and determine at exactly what level every component of the product must perform in order to dominate the competition. Agreeing, Dave Miller, vice-president of Clear Communications, declares that before his firm instituted QFD, a team had many disputes because issues were weighed on the basis of personal opinion. Now, under QFD, the facts decide the issues. Further, Miller notes, when disagreements arise now, it is usually because the facts are not known, and the team then tries to obtain more information.

Steps to Implement QFD

1. Assemble a cross-functional team of marketers, engineers, and others. The team should possess not only the expertise to conduct the analysis but, with minimal senior management oversight, the authority to implement its findings.
2. For the pertinent market segments, determine the voice of the customer. Consider all relevant customers, including internal, wholesaler, distributer, and end user. (If verbatim customer comments are not available for all important features of the product, marketing should estimate them.)
3. Organize the customer comments into major categories and subcategories, for ease of analysis.
4. Prioritize the voice-of-the-customer categories in terms of their importance to the customer. This establishes the prime categories to focus on to improve sales. Limit the number of prime categories to about twenty or thirty to make the QFD process manageable.
5. Compare the product's performance against competitors in all the prime categories of the voice-of-the-customer.
6. Identify breakthrough levels of performance, the levels of product performance in the prime voice-of-the-customer

categories that beat the competition by satisfying the customer better.

7. For all systems in the product, determine the performance levels necessary to achieve the breakthrough levels of product performance. To achieve the breakthroughs, the team will probably have to make tradeoffs and be highly creative. Employ a QFD matrix like the one in table 11–3.
8. Specify what performance of the parts is needed to ensure that the systems perform at the breakthrough levels. Similarly, specify the production and quality assurance needed. Matrices like those in figure 11–1 can help.

Where QFD focuses on the customers and relates their voice to the engineering systems and issues, the next technique focuses more on the interface between the customer and the product—that is, on the product's features.

Conjoint Analysis

Conjoint analysis is a powerful marketing technique employed by many firms. A customer is assumed to buy not simply a product but a set of attributes that she finds useful. The product is, in effect, a package of attributes. When a customer buys a television set, for example, she buys its attributes: a sharp picture, nice colors, good reception, an attractive piece of furniture, convenient size (see figure 11–2).

Conjoint analysis assumes that an attribute contributes a certain amount of value (utility) to the customer. Different attributes contribute different amounts of value to the customer. To the customer, the value of the entire product is the sum of the values contributed by each attribute. In other words, adding up the value of all the attributes yields the value of the product to the customer.

For instance, suppose a small radio has three important attributes, quality of sound, size (compactness), and price. Each attribute can be rated on a scale of 1 to 10. When the quality of sound gets a rating of 3 on the 1-to-10 scale, the value of this to the customer is represented as VALSOUND(3). Similarly, let VALSIZE(7) be

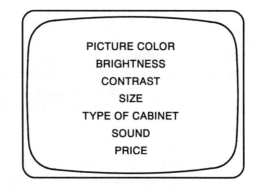

FIGURE 11-2

*Conjoint Analysis: A Product is Considered
to Be a Package of Features*

the value to the customer of the size attribute when the compactness is evaluated at 7. Also, let VALPRICE(5) be the value to the customer if the price level is 5 (where 1 is the lowest price in the product category, 10 the highest, and 5 designates an average price). The radio's value to the customer is the sum of the values of the attributes. Thus, for these ratings, the value of the radio to the customer is represented as follows:

$$\text{Radio value} = \text{VALSOUND}(3) + \text{VALSIZE}(7) + \text{VALPRICE}(5)$$

To implement a conjoint analysis for a product, the first step is to identify the attributes. Next, calculate the value to the customers of the different attribute levels (on the 1-to-10 scale). This is often done by asking customers to compare different products whose attributes are at different levels. Finally, summing up the attribute values gives the value of the product.

In actual practice, computer programs do the detailed calculations. What is important here is the overall concept—namely, that a product can be considered as a collection of its key attributes, each of which contributes value to the customer. All other things being equal, the product with the highest total value should attain the highest market share.

Application to Innovation

Conjoint analysis directly assists with new product development. For a proposed new product, the design team would estimate the performance levels expected for each attribute. From those performance levels, conjoint analysis would calculate the value to customers of the proposed new product. The value to customers of the proposed product can then be compared with that of competitive products.

Conjoint analysis also assists product development by facilitating tradeoff analyses. The value of better sound quality might be compared with the value of more size compactness. Or perhaps the sound quality can be improved, but only at the cost of a higher price. Conjoint analysis helps designers make these tradeoffs and enhance the value of the new product to potential customers.

Westinghouse's Implementation

Conjoint analysis is implemented in several ways. Westinghouse has adapted it to its own use, renaming the technique "value edge." According to Jeff Jury, resident expert there, Westinghouse typically holds a two- or three-day joint session between marketing and engineering. Most interestingly, they also invite a few important customers to the sessions. Westinghouse initially was reluctant to involve customers and expose the details of their products to them, fearing that they might find a competitor's product superior on certain attributes. But Westinghouse has overcome its fear and has found the customers' input helpful and often quite insightful.

During a "value edge" session the participants first determine the attributes customers consider in making purchase decisions. Then they come up with the attribute values, rate the competitive products, and so on. Westinghouse has computerized the process and inputs a considerable amount of marketing data, but the essence remains as described.

Jury notes many instances where the technique has helped Westinghouse. For a component that Westinghouse made for a nuclear plant, conjoint analysis revealed that the customer wanted some improvements in an extrusion process. The engineers felt they had the most advanced process of that type and that nothing about it could be improved. But on the basis of the conjoint analysis information, they went back to the labs. In short order they had several new ideas that generated three new patents, a much better process, and increased sales.

For a Westinghouse transformer, the designers believed that the customer wanted more technical improvements. But the conjoint analysis showed that faster delivery was more important to customers. Such situations are common, Jury says. The information generated by conjoint analysis frequently corrects misjudgements about what customers want.

Concerning price, Jury makes an insightful point. While many people assume that price is the dominant factor in sales, other factors are often more important to the customer. For some products, conjoint analysis uncovered that the Westinghouse product was clearly superior to its competition, and the firm could charge a premium price.

Similarly, Jury notes, companies often overestimate the importance of reputation and image to customers. People tend to think that customers buy from their firm because the firm is good, customers like the firm, and the firm has a good reputation. Conjoint analysis reveals, however, that intangibles tend to be of much less importance than tangibles like price and features.

Motorola's Implementation

Motorola, says Jim Page, uses conjoint analysis extensively. It conducts detailed surveys of customers to determine the value to them of product attributes. Suppose it must reduce the size of a pager. Smaller batteries would enable it to do this, but that would shorten battery life. To evaluate this tradeoff, surveys are conducted to determine how important to customers small size is as opposed to longer battery life. Similarly, surveys might determine how important a large display is in relation to the small size of the overall product, or low price versus additional features.

Before conjoint analysis, Page says, tradeoffs like size-versus-battery-life were evaluated by "gut feel". The marketers would estimate which of the two the customer preferred. But the engineers often did not believe the marketers' opinion, and arguments were common. Since conjoint analysis is based upon data and not opinion, Page states, it eliminated the disputes and helps the engineer design the right product for the customer.

One key to successfully using this approach, Page feels, is to segment the market. Lawyers have preferences different from doctors and salespeople; Japanese, Americans, and Europeans all have different tastes. Motorola has adapted its conjoint analysis models to a large number of market segments.

Limitations

Some critics question conjoint analysis because it assumes that a product can be subdivided into its attributes. Usually this issue is not serious, however, since many products can be reasonably depicted as a sum of attributes. The biggest difficulty with conjoint analysis, at least practically, is the large amount of data collection it requires. Also when the customers are asked to make precise tradeoffs, say how much more important to them size is than brightness, they sometimes find it difficult to make such a comparison in any detail.

Nevertheless, for most products the approach has substantial merit. It forces engineers and marketers to think carefully about what package of attributes and features customers will buy. Moreover, it helps engineers decide how much improvement the product requires to beat the competition. For many products, in short, conjoint analysis can help designers answer the CFQ and innovate a product that will sell.

A Quick Approach to Conjoint Analysis

Since a full-blown conjoint analysis is complex, here is a quick and easy approach (technically not conjoint analysis but possessing some of its key features) taught by William Golomski of the University of Chicago and an international consultant. The process has three steps, as shown in table 11–4:

1. Determine the various product attributes. These are listed as the rows on the table.

TABLE 11–4
Simplified Conjoint Analysis

Product Attribute	Importance of Attribute to Customer	Customer Rating of Our Product	Customer Rating of Competitor A	Customer Rating of Competitor B
Reliable Operation	9.7	8.1	9.3	9.1
Efficient Operation	9.6	9.3	9.4	9.0
Durability Life	9.3	8.4	9.5	8.9
Ease of maintenance	8.7	8.1	9.0	8.6
Ease of installation	8.8	8.3	9.2	8.8
Product Service	8.8	8.3	8.9	9.2

2. Speak to the customers and get their ratings of how important each attribute is to them. A scale of 1-to-10 is helpful.
3. Get the customers to rate those attributes in your product and also in the competition's.

The product in table 11–4 has six main attributes. The second column lists how customers rated the importance of each of those attributes on a 1-to-10 scale. The remaining columns indicate how customers rated the attributes on various products.

What this simple table reveals is often impressive, Golomski stresses. Most companies have little feel for how customers really evaluate their products. In fact, table 11–4 is based upon a actual example Golomski conducted that helped executives to redesign their product to much better satisfy the customer.

Snake Chart

A graphic portrayal of the data is also often helpful (see figure 11–3). For each attribute, the graph shows the customer ratings on a 1-to-10 scale for a firm's truck and for its major competitor's truck. The numbers on the right display the customers' rating of the importance of the attribute.

The success of this approach crucially depends upon listing all the attributes that the customer deems important. Robert Cooper of

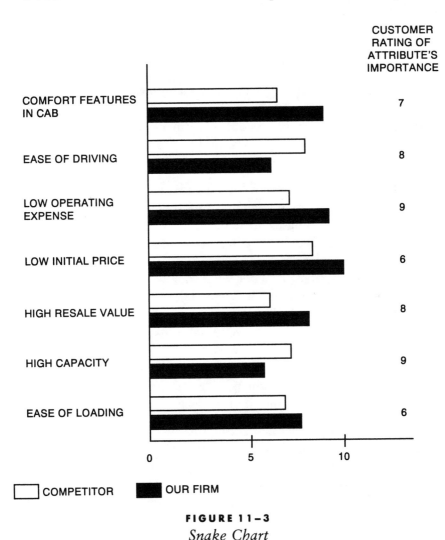

FIGURE 11–3
Snake Chart

McMaster University relates that a firm developed an outstanding computer printer that was one-quarter the price of the competition's and much faster.[5] With such clear advantages, the firm felt sure the printer would be a winner, and it invested millions in development and marketing. But the product was never a success. The firm neglected to consider that the printer needed a special paper that cost a fair amount more than the paper used by other printers. Overlooking that one attribute caused the printer's demise. Indeed, in conducting an analysis, no attribute that the customer might judge important should be missed.

Cultural Anthropology

Most customer-research techniques, including those discussed so far, require verbal input from the customer. Through surveys, focus groups, questions, or discussions, customers express their thoughts about a product or what they would like in a future product.

Three problems, however, arise:

- Customers often do not know features in sufficient detail to assist with the minute engineering tradeoffs required in design. According to Steve Barnett, head of product strategy for Nissan, "People are often not aware of what they are doing and why."[6]
- Customers often state not what they believe but what they think is appropriate. They will claim to an interviewer that they love health foods, but soon after the interview is over, they will gobble down several handfuls of high-caloric junk food. They will claim they want a car with safety features, then purchase one with power, speed, and varoom.
- For revolutionary products, customers lack the experience to provide much helpful input.

A new technique that can surmount some of these difficulties is cultural anthropology. Cultural anthropology borrows an idea from traditional anthropology and considers customers as a tribe, species, or group to be studied. The objective is to observe customer behavior, notice what problems customers have, and then to design new products that solve those problems.

"Just asking people questions isn't going to reveal everything about them," says Robert Calder of Northwestern University. "The best way to get an in-depth understanding of customer values is to watch people buying and using products."[7] Most Americans claim they want good nutrition in a breakfast food, but by watching them, observers learned that enjoyment is a leading factor and that those products are purchased largely on the basis of taste.

By observing customers, Toyota learned that certain automobile drivers consider their cars to be art objects that are on display as they drive. Keeping that in mind, Toyota made advertisements for its Lexus models more like works of art.

An especially powerful way to conduct cultural anthropology studies is videotaping. Microsoft invites its customers into a special office where they are videotaped while using software programs. Microsoft monitors the number of mouse clicks and cursor moves they make, how often they use different features of the program, and when they seem annoyed. Microsoft uses this information to improve the user-friendliness of its software. Nissan also uses videotaping, and according to Steve Barnett, this helped the company change the seat design, storage space, and many other parts of the car.[8] Videotaping even helped with improving the steering wheel. On a videotapes, "you can tell if someone is touching it like a caress or with revulsion," Barnett says.

Privacy

One caveat must be raised with regard to observing people: privacy. This can become a legal question. In order to understand how American families live and their use of transportation, Takishi Morimoto, an employee of Nissan, became a boarder in the home of Maritza and Stephen French in Costa Mesa, California. Morimoto told the French family that he worked for Nissan, and he appeared to be a Nissan executive. Moreover, he got along wonderfully, participated in many of their family activities, took trips with them, and was treated as part of the family.[9]

During this time, however, he was watching every move they made and recording it, taking numerous photographs and filling pages of notebooks. The Frenches did not learn about this until after he had moved out and read an article about him in the *Los Angeles Times*. They were quite upset, feeling they had been spied upon, and they sued Nissan for invasion of privacy, fraud, trespassing, breach of contract, and unfair business practices.

To conform to privacy legalities, many companies now inform people and even pay them to be observed. Many states prohibit taking photographs for commercial purposes without permission.

Use of Cultural Anthropology for Revolutionary Products

With revolutionary products, about which customers have little information, cultural anthropology is one of the few customer-analysis techniques that can help. By observing potential customers, a company can determine whether a particular revolutionary product could save that customer time, money, or effort. If so, the product has a much better chance of success. Black and Decker has a special kitchen where teams watch people do the things people do in kitchens in order to get ideas for new products.

Similarly, Xerox sponsors a study called "A Day in the Life of a Document."[10] Although seemingly unusual, this study is actually very valuable. According to anthropologist Heidi Larson, "I follow a document as it passes through the hands of various employees and departments in the office." She learns how the document accumulates Post-its along the way, gets copied, rewritten, put on a disk, reproduced, stapled. On the basis of such information, Xerox learns precisely what people do with documents and can conceive new products to help them process documents more quickly and easily.

When Square-D wanted to develop an innovative load center (electrical connection box) for houses, it first asked electrical contractors what innovations they would recommend in a load center. The contractors did not know. Square-D videotaped the contractors at work and discovered that they had great difficulty attaching cables to the load center. Interestingly, the contractors were so used to attaching cables that way that they did not even realize it was a problem until the videotape analysis uncovered it. Square-D conceived a novel, quick-attach connection mechanism that delighted the contractors and resurrected the sales of a nearly dead product.

Cultural anthropology provides an effective means to obtain information about customers of which even the customers may not be aware. It, thus, not only sharpens the accuracy of customer research, but can be of use even for revolutionary products.

Kansei Analysis

People tell customer researchers they will buy a certain product, yet they often actually purchase something else. Although cultural anthropology is one means to overcome this problem, kansei analysis takes a different approach. Kansei analysis probes deeper, going beyond customers' statements about a product, to identify their true feelings.

Kansei in Japanese means "sensitivity," and the technique studies the customers' emotional feelings, or sensitivities. According to Xerox executive Richard Greene, kansei analysis has two main branches. The first branch evaluates the more abstract feelings about a product, such as beauty, elegance, and thrill. Suppose a manufacturer of fine china wants to determine what makes a coffee cup elegant. Customers would be shown a variety of coffee cups of different shapes, sizes, colors, and handles. Customers would compare combinations of features and state which of them are more elegant. Through statistical analysis of the responses, the firm can capture the components of elegance and create a coffee cup that conveys it.

Elegance cannot be described in words, yet kansei analysis helps the firm understand it. Similarly, kansei analysis can estimate what makes a suit masculine, what makes a sports car trendy, and other perceptions that are important to sales, yet that people cannot articulate.

As for the other branch of kansei, Greene states it originated through psychological research in the United States. Researchers determined that facial muscles accurately reflect emotions. By putting sensors on the face, researchers identified and classified some fifty different emotions. Most important, research discovered that facial muscle data are more accurate than participants' verbal reports.

Focus Groups Often Wrong

Realizing that compared with facial muscle data, the information customers state is frequently in error, Honda and Mazda examined the record of focus groups. They discovered that about one-third of the conclusions learned from focus groups are wrong. Companies are now putting sensors on the faces of customers and letting them test out prototypes of new products, thereby not only collecting more accurate data but getting in closer contact with the person's emotional responses. As a practical example, if Mazda wants to test a new way for drivers to shift gears, it might put sensors on the face of a volunteer customer and ask him to drive a car and evaluate the shifter. From experience, Mazda knows that customers often state that they like the shifter. But the volunteer's facial data, might reveal that it was causing him difficulty and felt cumbersome.

Reduction of Engineering Changes

The customer-research techniques described here not only determine what the customer wants, they cut the number of engineering and design changes that will be made during product development. During an innovation project, engineers often get ideas for improvements that require changes to the design. Implementing such changes, however, likely means revisions in materials handing, parts descriptions, drawings, and supplier interaction—all of which are costly and time-consuming.

The customer-research techniques presented help minimize the number of changes by making the engineering designers more fully cognizant of what the customer really wants. That helps them target their efforts more carefully, thereby reducing the need to make changes later.

The techniques also provide guidelines to evaluate the possible benefit of a suggested change. If the proposed change will not yield clearly enhanced sales or demonstrably cut costs, there seems little reason to make it. Previously, gut feel determined such decisions, but the various techniques provide more objective criteria for evaluating a proposed change. In fact, when most suggested changes are evaluated in this way, they are found to add little value for the customer.

Louis Sullivan, chairman of the American Supplier Institute, determined that Japanese auto firms have far fewer engineering changes than their U.S. counterparts, and he traces the cause to the Japanese use of QFD.[11] Aisin Warner, a supplier of transmissions to Toyota, says that QFD cut engineering changes by over half and its development time by about half. Toyota states that its development cycle was cut by almost one-third—in significant part because QFD cut the number of engineering changes.

With semiconductors, NEC had similar results, reports Koyoshi Uchimaru, president of NEC's microchip facility.[12] In designing its sixteen-bit chip, the team got four hundred specifications wrong, all of which had to be changed. For the thirty-two bit chip, however, Uchimaru's team did a very sophisticated QFD analysis, with six matrices interconnecting the relationships between customer demands, the basic specifications, and the hardware particulars. Virtually every detail of the design and manufacture was included. As a result, the team did not miss a single specification.

These successes occurred because QFD structured the entire design process. The details of the design, including its manufacture and quality control, were continually checked to ensure that they would deliver what the customer wanted. That minimized the need for later changes and sliced the development time.

The same message holds for all the customer-research techniques presented in this chapter. Indeed, the CFQ will not achieve their purpose if they are viewed as merely marketing inputs to the design process. The specifics of design, manufacturing, and quality control should be continually checked against the answers to the CFQ to ensure that the final product delivers what the customers want.

Requirements Document

One way to ensure that the design satisfies the CFQ and delivers what the customers want is to use a requirements document. This document explicitly records the answers to the CFQ and shows how the product will not only fulfill what the customers want but beat the competition. This document guides the product development process and typically enumerates:

1. *What the customers want.* List this for all customer segments and for all reasonable uses of the product. For

novel or revolutionary products, doing this might be difficult, but a best effort should be made.

2. *How the features of the product satisfy the customers better than the competition.* This should be done feature by feature, and for all customer wants and needs.

3. *How the product will be designed and manufactured to ensure it satisfies the customer.* Validate that when all design manufacturing and quality control issues are implemented, the final product will satisfy the customer's needs and wants better than the competition.

For Revolutionary Products, Beware of Customer Opinion

For revolutionary products that are a significant departure from existing items, consider a clear warning: Be careful about listening to customers, because they are often wrong. For his doctoral dissertation at Harvard, Clayton Christensen studied the computer disk storage industry. He discovered that many firms miss the next generation of their product precisely *because* they listen to their customers.

Although Seagate was a leader in the 5¼-inch disk market, it developed a prototype of the next generation, a 3½-inch disk. But when Seagate's customers were shown these new prototypes, they did not like them. The new generation was not as efficient in storing data as the 5¼, and the customers preferred efficiency to smaller size. Seagate, believing it should listen to its customers, did not develop the 3½-inch disk.

Nevertheless, a large market developed for the 3½-inch. The customers of the 3½, however, were different from Seagate's 5¼-inch-disk customers. Seagate, by listening to its customers, had listened to the wrong customers. The Seagate example, according to Christensen, is typical.

Similarly, Ford's highly successful Taurus and Sable car failed its initial market tests. When customers saw the prototypes, they did not like them. But Ford knew that by the time the car hit the market three or four years later, the customers' opinions would have changed. Automobile firms know not to trust focus groups or customer response. According to Maryann N. Keller, an analyst with the brokerage firm Furman Selz, "If everybody says it's beautiful, it's going to look old by the time it gets to market."[13]

Since innovative products are a departure from the experience of most people, people's comments about the value of such products are often erroneous. Still, listening to advanced or leading-edge users is sometimes beneficial as, being on the cutting edge, they often understand what will be useful in the future. In addition, since they have advanced needs, they often make their own extensions of the product, extensions that have provided many ideas for new products. Microsoft has formed groups of computer hacks, which it frequently consults to get ideas. Hewlett-Packard visits laboratories to see what new applications the researchers are using HP's products on and what difficulties are occurring. That also has led to ideas for many new products.

Another approach to evaluating novel products, as mentioned, is cultural anthropology. If a product provides the customer with a clear benefit—say, in convenience or cost—it has a greater chance of success. Overall, however, with revolutionary or novel products customer research is often misleading. That is one reason the next chapter adopts a totally different approach to answering the CFQ.

Summary

To answer the CFQ, the first approach stresses customer research, particularly information that the engineers can actually use in innovating the new product (see table 11–5). It is very important for the design engineers to understand well what customers want. This can be accomplished by creating a partnership between marketing and engineering, in which executives and engineers assist with customer research and are in direct contact with customers.

More formal customer research methods also help. Quality function deployment (QFD) is used to obtain voice-of-the-customer statements and, by use of a matrix, helps translate them into engineering language. Conjoint analysis highlights the product's attributes and can help engineers innovate new products. Cultural anthropology observes the customer in his natural habitat and provides important information of which even the customer may

TABLE 11–5

Summary of Using Customer-First Questions

Answers to the CFQ isolate the reasons customers will buy the firm's product and not that of a competitor. Part of the answer is to provide the customer with "delight."

Two Major Approaches to Answering the CFQ:

1. Conduct customer research, with engineering designers directly involved in the process.
2. Do less customer research, but build flexibility into the design.

Customer-research should include these newer techniques.

1. QFD, to ensure the product design matches the voice of the customer.
2. Conjoint analysis, to get detailed information of what features customers want in a product.
3. Cultural anthropology, to identify by observing customers' behavior issues customers cannot easily articulate.
4. Kansei analysis, to get past statements customers make about products and identify their true feelings.

For novel products:

- Discount opinions of existing typical customers.
- Check with leading-edge customers.
- Use cultural anthropology.

By answering the CFQ, these techniques:

- guide the innovation process
- target the customer better
- reduce conflicts and the number of decisions based upon personal opinion instead of fact
- cut the number of engineering changes.

A requirements document should be created that specifies how the product will meet what the customer wants and answer the CFQ.

be unaware. Kansei analysis strives to get in touch with a customer's inner feelings about a product. These techniques not only target the customer better but cut the number of later engineering changes, thereby reducing the time of product development.

Above all else, the customer comes first. The techniques in this chapter obtain customer information that will help answer the CFQ and make the innovative product a success. Still, the problem of forecasting what customers will purchase remains elusive. Customer research can help, but it cannot solve the problem entirely.

Flexibility Produces Sales

The customer-research techniques described in the previous chapter are powerful and highly beneficial, but can only go so far. Despite the most valiant attempts to understand customers' needs and wants, foretelling what they will actually buy in the future remains murky and error-prone. The high failure rate of so many new products, even after the most careful customer research, attests to this. The second basic approach to answering the CFQ is intended to surmount this uncertainty. It proposes creating designs that are flexible, thereby making the product easily revised and updated as more information from the customer comes in.

Limitations of Customer Research

Curiously, many firms tend to forget the evidence that product development is highly risky and seem forever optimistic about the next product innovation. If an executive is asked, "In the past, what percent of your new product introductions were successful?" he might reply, "Forty percent." But if he is then asked what he expects the chances of success for the new product he is about to launch, he will likely answer, "About 80 to 90 percent." Past failures are neglected, forgotten, or denied. Hope springs eternal, as the prospects for the success of the latest product are continually and considerably overestimated.

One reason people do this is because customer research is inexact and inaccurate, so wishful thinking tends to fill the vacuum. Clearly we need to do better. Certainly, some guidelines for the use of customer research exist, as mentioned in Chapter 10. Thus, for special order products, customer input is very helpful. For evolutionary products, customer research is often beneficial, while for revolutionary products, customer research is undependable.

But the problem is considerably more complicated. Even in markets where customer opinion ought to be fairly valid, the information learned about the customer may vary depending upon the research method used. Bewilderingly, different analysis methods produce different conclusions about customers' desires and wants.

Abbie Griffin of the University of Chicago was interested in determining what features customers wanted in a potential new product. To obtain that information, she used three standard research methods. One was focus groups; the second asked potential customers about "good things" and "bad things" in a product area; and the third considered differences among brands. All three research methods were carefully conducted by trained and knowledgeable people. All three methods were designed to achieve the same goal— to determine what attributes customers wanted in the new product. The amazing result was that each of the three methods came to different conclusions. There was only an 18 percent overlap among the conclusions generated by the three methods. Depending upon the method used, the conclusions about what customers wanted in the new product were totally different.

It would be as if you took your body temperature with three different thermometers and got three totally different readings. One says you are well, another that you are slightly ill, and the third that you should be in the hospital. Customer-research results may well depend upon which research technique is used. Change the measuring instrument or analysis process, and the results too may change.

The predicament is clear. Understanding the customer is absolutely essential, yet customer research is error-prone and far from perfect. This truth forces us to take a different approach to answering the CFQ.

Flexibility and Modularity: Designing for the Unknown

The crucial step is to admit that customer behavior is very difficult to predict. Once management accepts its own inability to see the future with total clarity, it can proceed to create a design process that takes advantage of this. The second approach to answering the CFQ embodies this notion.

To implement the second approach, the team builds flexibility and modularity into the design process itself. Then it gets feedback from customers on prototypes or on the actual product. Based upon this feedback, it revises and improves the product, which is easy because the system is flexible (see table 12–1).

Cast Study: Software Systems Associates

Roger Covey, CEO of Software Systems Associates, and Jim Franch, his head of software development, utilized these ideas in developing their very successful business applications software program, AS/SET. Throughout the development process, Covey kept certain key principles in mind:

- It is impossible to know what customers want until they make the actual purchase.
- Get a basic product to the market rapidly to see what customers will like.
- Make the design highly modular and flexible to facilitate changes and updates as better customer information comes in.
- Get customer input all along the product development cycle, not just in the beginning. As the product gets more developed, the customer will better see what the product does, and this input will become increasingly valuable.

TABLE 12–1
Principles of Flexibility

Use these principles when the customer, market, or technology is hard to predict or rapid changes are going on.

- Create a flexibile design that permits easy changes.
- Do not permit minor changes or improvements in the midst of development, unless there is clear evidence that sales will improve.
- Build many partial prototypes and mockups during development, and get customer input on them.
- Get the product into the market quickly to get feedback from actual sales.
- Update the product based upon actual sales

To implement these principles, Covey and Franch first provided an overall mission statement: Develop the program by a certain date. Initially, market research explored the market, the competitors, and the desires of the potential customers. Then over a six-month period, two software designers conceived the program architecture.

Frequently during this period co-workers often wanted to add new features the program because "the customers will like it." Covey would always reply, "Does that feature help achieve the mission of the program?" He knew that it is foolish to think you know what the customer wants when you do not. Unless clear evidence existed that a proposed feature was absolutely needed, it was dropped. Only the crucial and necessary features were included in order to get something to the market quickly and get customer reactions from actual sales.

Throughout the period in which the program architecture was being conceived, the software engineers wanted to start coding. But that was not permitted either. First they had to create the basic architecture or framework with as much foresight as they could. The program had to be flexible and modular to allow for the addition of customer-desired features that were still unknown. Coding was secondary and would likely be revised over time anyway. Their paramount task was to create the overall framework that would permit later changes easily and quickly.

Shortly after the coding started, when the AS/SET program was still only 10 to 15 percent complete, Software Systems Associates brought customers in to look at a very early prototype. The prototype was merely a shell—only a few of the major screens had been developed and the data were artificial—but it was enough to give customers a feel for the product and get helpful feedback from them.

When the program was 85 percent finished, the team sent prototypes to potential customers for what is called beta site testing. Beta testing is usually performed at customer sites where people have plenty of time to test a program. Covey, however, selected sites where people were on a rush schedule and desperately needed the AS/SET program. He perceived that those customers would use the program immediately and would discover its problems fast.

The beta site testing revealed the need for two important features that the program did not have. Covey and Franch launched a crash program to add one of those features. The other would have taken too long to implement and was less crucial, so it was held off for the next version of the program.

The AS/SET program came out on time. It was "plain vanilla," with neither advanced features nor an optimized code, but it did an excellent job in the crucial areas that concerned most customers. Based upon information from the initial launch, Covey and Franch quickly developed an improved version. They now added the second feature that the beta site testing had showed customers wanted. Since the code design was modular and flexible, they implemented this and other improvements easily.

Covey stresses the importance of recognizing that you do not know what the customer wants, then taking advantage of that in the program development. In a nutshell, he used a flexible and modular design, had many prototypes along the way to gain customer input, and did not permit changes or additions that might delay development. By getting a good product out fast, he saw what really sold, then introduced improved versions quickly.

Platforms

The AS/SET example displays the relevance of flexibility and modularity to the software industry. For hardware and other products the approach is similar, with the important caveat that the manufacturing plant must also be flexible. The salient concept is to create a core platform that contains the essential technology. Design the platform to allow a wide range of different models or features to be easily built on it. Depending upon what the customer wants, the models or features will be changed, but the platform will remain the same. Periodically, as technological advancements occur, update the basic platform. The platform always permits a full range of models to be easily manufactured on it, however, and whichever models sell, more of them are made.

Case Study: Sony Walkman

The most widely known example of a platform is the Sony Walkman, whose development has been thoroughly studied by Susan

Walsh Sanderson and Vic Uzumeri of Rensselaer Polytechnic Institute.[1] Sony launched the product on July 1, 1979, using its first platform, which weighed almost a pound, including headphones. The platform allowed for easy manufacture of a very large number of models over the entire price spectrum and for just about any application—swimming, at the beach, in the shower, on a belt, on an arm, in any color.

Note that Sony did not rely upon market research to tell it what models to make. Which ever models sold, Sony made more of them, and the platform approach made doing that easy. If pink was a hot-selling color, Sony made more in pink. If a beach model sold well, it made more of them and introduced even more beach models.

The platform concept recognizes that admitting ignorance is a first step toward gaining knowledge. Since many customer desires cannot be known, admitting that ignorance leads to building platforms that easily add almost any features the customer might want (see figure 12–1).

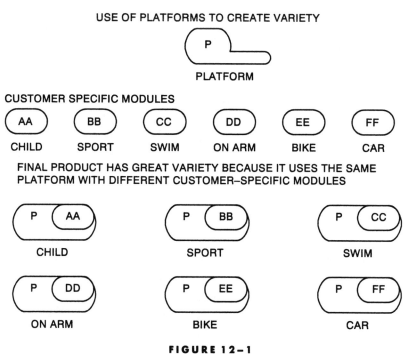

FIGURE 12–1

Use of Platforms to Create Variety

To keep ahead of the competition, over the course of a decade, Sony updated the basic platform, making technical improvements and reductions in weight four times. The newer platforms incorporated a number of advances, including lighter and improved stereo headphones, miniature superflat motors, disk-drive mechanisms, and chewing-gum-shaped rechargeable Ni-Cd batteries. To develop the successor platforms, Sony assigned special tiger teams of top engineers. All told, over the decade that Sanderson and Uzumeri studied, Sony made about 160 different models.

Implementation of Platforms

The platform idea has been used in the automobile industry for years. The average customer thinks that the Ford Probe, the Mazda 626, and the Mazda MX-6 are totally different cars—and they do look different. But they are basically the same car, with the same platform. That is, they have essentially the same chassis, engine, drive train, and transmission. They are even made one after another on the same assembly line at the Flatrock, Michigan, Mazda plant. Only the features the customer easily sees—body panels, passenger compartments, and trim—are different.

Ron Sanchez of MIT studies one of the most remarkable automobile platforms, that of the Porsche 911. After it hit the market in 1964, that basic model survived and continued to flourish. Porsche, a small firm with limited resources, wanted to design a model that was flexible and could be easily updated without large additional expense. The design was brilliant. Not even Porsche foresaw that the model would withstand a quarter-century of advancements like new engines, transmissions, suspensions, pollution controls, different materials, and disk brakes.

A more mundane example of a platform is notebooks for schoolchildren. Kids like to have a picture of their latest craze on the front cover, be it a Disney character, Ninja Turtles, or their latest movie hero. For notebook manufacturers, this posed a problem. The picture they printed was often out of style by the time the notebooks were in the stores, so many notebooks were left unsold. To combat this problem, Mead Paper innovated a clear plastic cover into which the kids could insert a picture of anything they liked.

The ability to be flexible and update easily depends upon the initial design. In a striking example mentioned by Sanchez, Ford created an engine that, by reboring, could easily be increased from two- to three-liter capacity. GM also designed an engine, but to increase its output it had to develop a whole new engine. GM has changed its approach since then.

Product Families

In applying these flexibility concepts, think not of a single product but of a product family. Families have certain parts and designs in common. With the Walkman, for example, Sony made not one product but a family of products, all related by a common platform. Conceiving a family of products enables revisions and improvements to be made without totally redesigning the product every time. "You want to avoid too many clean sheet designs," as Grant Saviers, vice-president of Digital Equipment Corporation, puts it. A major advantage of object-oriented approaches to software is precisely this reuse of modules. Dr. Debashish Sarkar, whom AT&T Bell Laboratories' has designated as a distinguished senior researcher, suggests that because customer behavior and technology are so difficult to predict, the dominant forces in product development in the years ahead will be flexibility and modularity.

Should We Forget Customer Research Altogether?

As the cost and time of product development decline, the feasibility of doing without customer research emerges. Customer research is costly, takes time, and it makes errors. If the cost of new model development is cheap enough, why do the customer research at all? Why not just make a new model and see if people buy it?

This suggestion sounds like heresy, but Sony takes exactly this approach. According to the *New York Times Magazine,* Sony "eschews market research."[2] The article quotes Sony executive Kozo Ohsone; "When you introduce products that have never been invented before, what good is market research?" The Walkman, which was launched without customer research, is typical for Sony.

Sanyo also disparages the value of customer research and suggests that demand for a new product often must be created. R. Jaikumar of Harvard notes that Seiko does not do customer research for its watches. Seiko has a fast, inexpensive design process that is computer assisted, and its flexible, automated factory can make virtually any design. Every season it "throws" three hundred new models onto the market. Those that sell, they make more of; those that do not, they drop. Citizen follows a similar policy.

Merlyn Rutzky, vice-president of Action Advertising, often attends gift and premium shows and has observed that the Japanese seem to offer a lot of variations on a product. They offer a watch with a bottle opener, a watch with a pen, a watch with a light, a watch with a good-luck charm. They do not know beforehand what will sell, she said—"they try everything."

This flexible approach applies to complex products, not just to simple gift items. Ralph Gomory, president of the Alfred P. Sloan Foundation, once asked a Japanese colleague if his firm had done market research on a computer printer. The answer he got was a polite no. The Japanese friend explained that his firm could get an entirely new printer out in only eighteen months. It preferred to adapt to people's actual buying patterns.[3]

Do not misunderstand this approach: The top firms like Sony, Sanyo, Seiko, and Citizen keep very close to their customers and try diligently to discern what they will like. For these firms, however, the cost of throwing products onto the market is cheaper than doing customer research, with its inherent costs and errors. For them, it is less expensive and more accurate to see what people actually buy.

This approach is the ultimate conclusion of LSFI Step 4, Place Customers First, since it sees what the customer buys, then makes adjustments. As the time and cost of developing new products drop, this approach will become more common. One of the prime reasons for this is that it facilitates multiple learning trials from the market, which is discussed next.

Dynamic Flexibility and Multiple Learning Trials

Flexibility permits not only great variety in product models but fast learning from the market. A firm throws a product onto the market. Based upon feedback from actual sales, the firm learns what customers want, then revises the product. Flexibility allows this learning cycle of feedback and revision to be done quickly and many times (see figure 12–2).

A baseball analogy can help here. Old-fashioned design processes afforded a firm just one time at bat. A fast, flexible system, however, affords multiple opportunities. No matter what happens the first time at bat, we will immediately step up and have a second, third, and multiple chances. Moreover, each time we do so, we are getting feedback from the customer about how to hit even better next time.

The length of the learning cycle then becomes very important. How long it takes to develop a product, obtain feedback from the customers, and get the new revised version out becomes crucial because it governs how many attempts there will be to learn from the market. Barry Bebb, consultant and retired vice-president of Xerox, compares the situation to learning how to play the piano. Practicing every day makes progress twice as fast as practicing every other day.

Roger Bohn of the University of California recalls that IBM's lap-

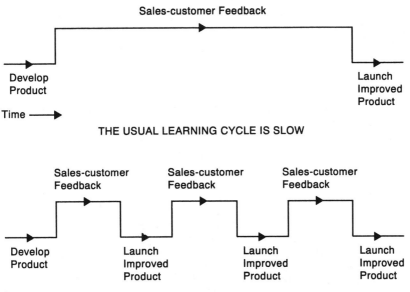

INFLEXIBLE SYSTEM—SLOW LEARNING FROM MARKET

Sales-customer Feedback

Develop Product

Launch Improved Product

Time ——▶

THE USUAL LEARNING CYCLE IS SLOW

Sales-customer Feedback   Sales-customer Feedback   Sales-customer Feedback

Develop Product

Launch Improved Product

Launch Improved Product

Launch Improved Product

Time ——▶

FLEXIBLE INNOVATION PROCESS. RAPID-CYCLE LEARNING FROM MARKET PRODUCES FASTER IMPROVEMENT.

FIGURE 12–2

Rapid-Cycle Learning

top computer, the Convertible, was an excellent first model. But IBM did not follow up with changes and improvements for a few years afterward. Meanwhile, Toshiba started out with a model that was clearly inferior but kept putting out improvements. Toshiba had three cycles of learning to IBM's one. Soon, Bohn recalls, Toshiba was far ahead.

Much of the Japanese success in consumer electronics, and indeed in many product areas, can be traced to this rapid-cycle learning. The rationale for why Sony, Seiko, and others throw products onto the market is now perhaps clearer. It helps them learn about customer wants and improve more quickly (see figure 12–3).

Many experts feel that a flexible, fast process is the key to successful innovation because it permits quick introduction of improvements and enhancements. If the customer likes them, they are retained, while if the customer does not like them, something else can be quickly tried. Customer research is no longer necessary when one can get much more accurate information from the market itself (see table 12–2).

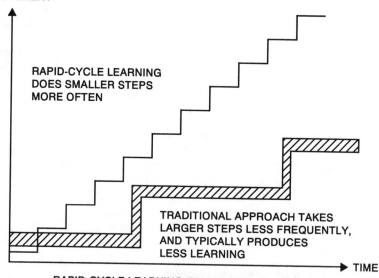

IMPROVEMENT

RAPID-CYCLE LEARNING
DOES SMALLER STEPS
MORE OFTEN

TRADITIONAL APPROACH TAKES
LARGER STEPS LESS FREQUENTLY,
AND TYPICALLY PRODUCES
LESS LEARNING

TIME

RAPID-CYCLE LEARNING, BY TESTING THE MARKET
MORE OFTEN PRODUCES FASTER LEARNING

FIGURE 12–3
Rapid Cycles Learn Faster

TABLE 12–2
Summary of Rapid-Cycle Learning

- requires flexible modular design
- "throws" product onto the market in rapid succession
- learns what sells and makes revisions in each cycle
- permits quick introduction of enhancements
- uses actual sales to learn and quickly improve

Note that it is difficult to make certain large complex systems, such as cars, jet engines, and airframes, highly flexible. For them, customer research will still be necessary. With certain other products, however, customer research will be reduced or eliminated, because flexibility and rapid-cycle learning from the market will be superior. Even though large complex products will still use customer research, they will likely adopt some of the ideas of flexibility, at least in portions of their design. Overall, flexibility is a fundamental and powerful concept, and in the future more and more designs will take advantage of it.

Summary

Determining what the customer wants is the biggest challenge in product development, and the CFQ give direction to this effort. Nevertheless, considerable uncertainty remains about what customers want. With a product design that is flexible and modular, that uncertainty can often be managed. In fact, if the cost of flexibility gets low enough, it might be better to omit customer research altogether and simply see what sells. With fast feedback from the market, this option speeds learning. It will become increasingly common.

Develop a Business Strategy

13

The Business Strategy
of the Product

We are almost ready to start to innovate a new product or product family. We have done the overall planning, put the foundations in place, and gathered information about the customer. The next LSFI step—Develop a Business Strategy—requires evaluating the product's marketing, distribution, and other relevant business aspects. The business strategy is concerned not with specifics but with the overall concept and features. This step must be finished before conducting the detailed design, because the design will change depending upon the business strategy selected.

Dave Siefert of NCR studied some twenty-five different innovation projects to analyze the reasons for their success or failure. The failures, he determined, typically occurred when management lost sight of the business purpose of making a product: ensuring it will be purchased and profitable. Speed and cost are essential in product development, but not at the sacrifice of cutting corners and endangering the business objectives. Siefert's principle, although applicable throughout the development process, is most important at the beginning, when the product is being specified. If the general features and specifications of a new product are improperly cast, expensive revisions will surely follow.

Case Studies

General Electric Business Strategy

Paul Raymont of General Electric confirms this strategy of standing back before starting design, in his works, "to think through the business equation." For his product—industrial lighting panels—volumes are high, costs and quality are important, and the market is very competitive. Under the old approach, marketing determined what features the customer wanted; then, based upon those features and a cost goal, engineering would design the product. But Raymont has changed that. To conceive the business strategy, he sends a cross-functional team of engineers, systems, marketing, and sales people off-site for an intense concentrated session. Raymont feels it is important for all the key players to jointly discuss and understand the broad business view of the financial, marketing, and design issues.

As one of its first tasks, the cross-functional team talked to customers and discovered that a fast lead time from order to delivery of product was essential. The previous products had been delivered in four to six weeks. For the new product, the team decided that every U.S. customer should receive delivery in less than one week.

Providing fast delivery demanded that the team institute many changes. Sales orders had always been processed manually, for instance. To speed that for the new product, they created a data link between the sales engineers and the factory. Also, to make a part previously might have required six to ten steps, including stripping metal to certain widths, making a blank, making a general outline, bending and forming, and tapping. The team sliced the manufacturing time by limiting the number of steps needed to fabricate most parts to three. Allowing only three steps also forced the engineers to be much more direct and simpler in their design, facilitating the one-week delivery.

Most important, since all the products were custom designed, the GE team had to conceive a new manufacturing process. No longer could it use the old time-consuming approach of making and storing batches. Rather, it modularized and standardized the design using common parts. In fact, from only a couple of hundred basic parts, GE is now able to make 250,000 different customized variations.

By studying the overall business concerns, the team examined the marketing issues, determined the goal of one-week delivery, and then conceived several innovations to achieve that goal. The final document the team produced listed the overall features and specifications for the product, and after approval by top management, it guided the actual design process.

Motorola Business Strategy

Motorola adopts a similar approach for its business strategy phase. According to Jim Page, a team of engineering and marketing people evaluates technical feasibility, marketing, and other business factors. Based upon the team's recommendations, top management decides whether to actually develop the product. The team pays special attention to estimating the size of the market, potential sales, costs, and profits. They also carefully forecast the market window of opportunity—the time when this product must hit the market before it would be surpassed by the competition. If team does not believe that the development of the product can be completed within that window, they stop the project.

As part of the market window analysis, the team investigates any major technical risks. For the Bandit pager, three alternative technical approaches were considered: make the new pager capable of automated assembly using surface-mount technology (SMT); adapt an existing receiver that was already close to SMT; or develop something new.[1] By comparing the three methods on paper, the team determined that only by adopting something already close to SMT could they meet the schedule. Without this technical risk analysis, they might have chosen the wrong technology and missed the market window.

How much technical risk is allowable will depend, according to Page, upon a product's strategic purpose. If the product must get to the market fast, little risk is permissible. If the product is to be more innovative or to "reach out," more technical risk might be necessary.

Paul Noakes, vice-president of Motorola, calls this business strategy step the "blitz phase." *Blitz* means "lightning," and Motorola wants these decisions made quickly. At the end of the blitz phase, Noakes notes, the team should delineate a clear conception of the product and its general specifications: What are its expected sales and customers? Are the technical risks reasonable? What resources will be needed? And most essentially, why will this product will be successful in the marketplace?

Interestingly, Motorola found that the final documents that the teams were developing were getting longer and longer. In fact, they were so long that executives were not reading them but were delegating the reading to subordinates. This eroded one of the major purposes of the blitz phase, since top managers were no longer evaluating the product or making decisions to proceed. Noakes expressly suggests that the final document of this phase be no more than twenty-five pages long, not including appendices.

Successful Product Criteria

Wilson's Criteria

Edith Wilson of Hewlett-Packard identifies ten crucial success points that seem to distinguish the successful projects from the unsuccessful. Her conclusions are based upon her Stanford University thesis, when for a year she probed seventeen projects in such diverse areas as microwave and communications, electronic instruments, analytical instruments, medical products, and work stations.[2] The ten success points are:

1. **CUSTOMER AND USER NEEDS.** The entire team must understand the needs and the problems of the potential user or customer and identify how the product will satisfy those needs or resolve those problems.

Difficulties in this area are typically caused by the team:

- not allotting sufficient time or resources to studying customer needs, perhaps because of insufficient funding;
- segmenting the market improperly, or grouping several markets together;
- not calling on the right customers;
- not being properly trained in customer research methods, or using them improperly (this might occur if the team is top-heavy with technical people and lacks adequate representation of marketing); or
- not calling on users of competitive products, so the team does not understand why the competition is successful.

2. STRATEGIC ALIGNMENT. The product must fit into the long-term strategy of the business unit. Otherwise, it may not get the support it needs from senior management, marketing, technical or other groups.

Strategic alignment problems often occur because senior management has not planned a long-range strategy. Or if a corporate strategy has been selected, the goals of the various groups in the organization may not be aligned with it. Indeed, without clear and consistent strategic goals, various groups might be unwilling to commit their resources in any particular direction, fearing that a later shift in strategy will undermine their efforts.

3. COMPETITOR ANALYSIS. The team must understand not just the products that competitors develop but how the competitors are satisfying the needs of the customer and solving the customer's problems. The team's product must do those things better than the competition is expected to do at the time of product release.

Problems might arise here if the team looks primarily at a competitor's product but misses the competitor's distribution channels, marketing strategy, or product support.

4. PRODUCT POSITIONING. The product must be properly positioned in the market relative to other products. In the market segment, the product must provide a higher value to the customer than any competitor's product.

Major problems here are the failure to identify the right market segment and the failure to describe in sufficient detail why the customers in the segment will find that the product has more value than the competitor's product.

5. TECHNICAL RISK LEVEL. The level of technical risk must be appropriate for the strategic purpose of the product. Risk analysis should be done for all facets of the product, including piece parts, processes, and marketing plans. High levels of risk should be addressed early in the development process.

Frequent problems here include:

- poor assessment of the limitations of the technology or the skill base of the team;
- too much risk for the purpose of the product;

- too much risk for the time and budget allotted;
- failure to understand that a key component obtained from a supplier might soon be superseded by the supplier bringing out a new generation of that component.

6. PRIORITY DECISION CRITERIA LIST. The team should establish a list of priority goals and performance standards. A typical list would include:

- manufacturing cost target
- time to market
- the product's key features
- quality, reliability and design for manufacturability goals
- technology strategy
- strategy for flexibility and modularity (platforms).

Without a clear list of priorities, a team lacks direction and tends to drift, change, and revise its decisions. Failure to specify priorities often occurs because the team has an inadequate understanding of what is required to make the product successful. That often results from:

- insufficient understanding of the customer
- insufficient understanding of the competition and why the competitor's product sells
- failure to project what the market or competitor will be doing at the time of product release
- lack of understanding of what can be achieved technically within the time and budget provided.

7. REGULATION AND GOVERNMENT COMPLIANCE. The company should know and comply with government requirements on patent infringements, health and environmental regulations, UL standards, and global standards.

A common concern here is that different countries have different requirements and standards.

8. PRODUCT CHANNEL ISSUES. The right distribution channel must be selected or developed. The team must also develop the channel issues sufficiently ahead of time, so they are ready at the time of product release.

9. ENDORSEMENT BY UPPER MANAGEMENT. Senior management must approve the project and support it with staffing and financing and when difficulties arise in its development. Problems here might occur if senior management does not understand how the project helps the firm reach its strategic goals.

10. PROJECT PLANNING. The team should develop detailed staffing and funding requirements based upon accurate schedules and financial projections.

Problems here might include:

- erroneous budgeting
- the shifting of staff or budget to complete another late project.

Failure to Implement Points

A failure to consider or implement these points might cause the failure of a product. Wilson mentions a large telecommunications system that was originally developed for one customer. Based upon its success, the design team decided to market the system to other customers as well. The team neglected to study the market, however, and learn that each customer was unique and needed a specialized version of the product. The team also failed to study why the competition was successful. In particular, the competition had understood the requirement for specialized versions and had tailored its product design to easily adapt to different customers.

The team also did not examine the marketing channel issue. Its product cost more than 2 million dollars, so that general managers and vice-presidents had to be involved in the sales negotiations. Moreover, because the product had to be customized, the customer's factory-level people had to be involved, too. Not realizing that so many people were involved, the team was unaware that the sales negotiations would be very time-consuming. In addition, the team neglected to examine the global regulatory issues and thus could not sell its product in several countries.

Many other examples of failure are connected with omitting points on Wilson's list. For instance, with its instant camera, Kodak discovered the importance of patents and intellectual property when it ended up paying Polaroid nearly a billion dollars in infringement damages.

Also, when implementing Wilson's point 8, about marketing channels, do not overlook the sales force. Frito-Lay, a powerhouse in snacks, tried to innovate by marketing some health food. The product was excellent, but the sales people were not prepared to sell it, and the new nutritional product failed. The salespeople did not normally call on customers for this type of product, and they were not properly trained in selling this food type.

Bob Lusko, a Ford zone sales manager, recalls a similar experience in auto leasing.[3] A competitor launched a major leasing program that faltered because the salespeople did not understand leasing and did not get any incentive for it. The salespeople even steered customers away from it, saying, "Well, leasing's not really for you." Lusko declares that "then everything fell on the floor."

Also relative to Wilson's marketing point, recollect that distribution, too, can cause disasters. When Campbell's innovated a line of refrigerated goods called Fresh Chef, the product had excellent taste and seemed destined for success. Campbell's had many trucks—but nearly all were designed to deliver frozen goods. Few existed to deliver refrigerated products. An otherwise excellent product floundered because it could not be shipped to the stores.

Distribution can disrupt even technically driven markets. Bruce Walter, president of Grid Systems, says that the market for laptop computers "is already so crowded that the issue is not the product but the distribution of the product."[4] There are too many different manufacturers and models for all of them to be distributed and displayed to customers.

Perspective on Wilson's List

Wilson's list highlights the fact that meeting criteria for marketing and technical success is by no means enough. Many other issues impact the success of a product. Sometimes, in their exuberance to develop an exciting product, companies overlook crucial factors. Wilson's list serves as a check on that oversight. To conceive the proper business strategy, a team should thoroughly evaluate all ten of her success points.

NewProd Criteria

Robert Cooper of McMaster University has developed a set of criteria similar to Wilson's which he has incorporated into the software program NewProd.[5] NewProd has been validated on actual new product introductions and can often predict if a product is likely to be successful with 70 to 80 percent accuracy. In a typical application, a cross-functional team of experts evaluates the potential of a new product concept. First, each team member independently answers thirty questions about the product. Then they get together to discuss any different answers and share insights. Finally, they jointly answer the thirty questions as a team. The software evaluates their answers and provides a final score on the product's likely success in the market.

Cooper has divided the thirty questions into major categories as follows:

1. *Resources required and alignment with company.* Does the company have the right talent and sufficient resources to develop this product, including R&D, engineering, marketing, financial, production, distribution, and sales?
2. *Newness to company.* The less experience a firm has with a product, the harder it is to develop and sell it. Is the product new to the company? Will the customers, technology, or competitors be new to the company?
3. *Product superiority and economic advantage to the user.* Will the product offer customers unique features and be superior to the expected competition? Will the product be priced properly relative to the competition? Will the product satisfy customer needs that no competitive product does? Do customers have a clear need for this product?
4. *Clarity of opportunity and of the project.* Is the product revolutionary? Are the technological and marketing challenges clear? Are the market, customer needs, and competitors well understood?
5. *Market size and growth, and competitive situation.* What is the estimated size and growth potential of the market? Is the market highly competitive? Are customers highly satisfied with competitor's products? Is the market or the technology rapidly changing?

Not only does NewProd forecast the product's potential of being a hit, but by pinpointing weaknesses, it can help the team develop a product that is more likely to be successful.

Delta Analysis

Many companies will like the approach Northern Telecom uses to evaluate the success potential of its new products. According to Jerry Dehner, director of manufacturing strategy, the technique is called delta analysis. Particularly for the marketing and technological aspects of the business phase, the team considers the following five success criteria:

1. *Customer needs.* Will the product satisfy the customer's specific requirements?
2. *Product quality.* Will the product be defect-free and reliable?
3. *Development cost.* What will it cost to develop the product?
4. *Manufacturing cost.* What will it cost per unit to manufacture the product?
5. *Development time.* How long will it take to get the product to market?

For each of these factors, the team determines where Northern Telecom is now and where the competitors are expected to be by the time the new product is developed. The difference between those two—where Northern Telecom is now and where the competitor will be—is called the delta (or gap). The delta represents the progress Northern Telecom must make in order to best its competition.

If the team beats the competition on all five criteria, the new product will better satisfy the customer and have better product quality, lower development cost, lower manufacturing cost, and faster time to market. A product that can do all these things will almost surely be a winner. Achieving all that is no easy feat against the competitors that Northern Telecom faces. But most of its big successes, Dehner notes, occurred when the team exceeded the deltas.

In doing a delta analysis, Dehner feels that the most important issue is the composition of the team. Having a full range of experts on the team is crucial so that all bases will be covered. There is a tendency to have too few people on teams because of cost or other pressures. That is shortsighted, Dehner observes, and leads to costly mistakes. For example, because customers and suppliers play major roles, they should be on the team.

Do not merely take whoever is available, Dehner urges. Pull people in from other jobs if necessary, but get the best people on the team. Their knowledge, insight, and creativity are essential to conceiving the right product.

Product Strategy

So far for this step of LSFI, we have been discussing the concepts. Now we must examine its implementation. The first issue in implementation is to determine the product's strategic purpose.

Panasonic introduced a bicycle that was custom-designed for its owner.[6] Having a bike custom-fitted to one's own body dimensions is a vital advantage, particularly for professionals or amateur racers. A bike shop has a special mockup of a bike on which the customer sits, and the exact dimensions of the custom bike are then determined. Those dimensions are faxed to the factory, where a computer translates them into the bike design in three minutes. A highly automated and fully flexible production line makes the bike in three hours.

With such fast production, Panasonic has the capability of getting that bike back to its customer the next day. But it chooses not to do that. It prefers to wait two weeks to deliver the bike. The two-week wait, Panasonic feels, builds anticipation and excitement in the customer.

A tailor-made bike is a brilliant idea, but the crucial aspect here is the way the business strategy meshes with the product design. The customization is possible because the design is totally modular and highly flexible, allowing eleven million variations. Indeed, the capability of the design to be customized is what allows pursuit of the business strategy.

Another example, albeit less successful, involves a firm that installed a totally automated production line that could make products without any human assistance. The line required a sizable capital investment, and the firm considered its installation a major step forward. Unfortunately, the line that was installed was intended to make several different products. To change the new line to make a different product took over a day. This was due partly to the design of the products and partly to the automated production line itself. Since the firm's products were low-volume, it had to do the time-consuming changeovers frequently. The cost of this soon forced them to scrap the automated line. Because the firm had not considered its business strategy—low-volume production of many products—it made the wrong decisions about how to design the products and the production line.

Blockbuster versus Small Improvements

A product's business strategy should thus drive its development process. To probe this, consider two very important business strategies. One is to produce a blockbuster product, and the other is to make frequent, small improvements. The blockbuster or "home-run" approach strives to introduce a "wow" product so impressive and exciting that people cannot help but buy it. Polaroid, for instance, built itself on this strategy. Every several years, it introduced a totally new series of instant cameras. Each new series was so dramatically improved over the previous one that, Polaroid hoped, people would rush out to buy the new models. That strategy was successful for decades. But eventually the competition caught up, and the advent of one-hour processing for 35-millimeter film dampened the need for instant cameras.

Opposing the blockbuster approach is the strategy of frequently making small improvements. Japanese firms follow this strategy in video cameras and recorders, faxes, consumer telephone equipment, 35-millimeter cameras, stereos, Walkmen, computer printers, and computer peripherals. In this strategy a firm makes small improvements on the product frequently—sometimes every few months. Over time, the many improvements add up, and the product as a whole becomes strikingly different and superior. (This strategy is so important and has been so successful that the entire next chapter is devoted to it.)

Which strategy a firm adopts will depend upon its product, the market, and the technology. For a very complex piece of equipment, such as a large mainframe computer, an automobile, a jet engine, or an airframe, the blockbuster strategy is almost required. Small improvements are not easily implemented because the product is an entire and very complex system. To make an improvement in a jetliner, supply parts might have to be changed, pilots retrained, maintenance people retrained, new software written, and new manufacturing procedures introduced. For very complex integrated systems, then, the blockbuster approach is almost a necessity.

These two different strategies require different design processes. Since the blockbuster approach introduces a new and significantly improved product every several years, it encourages major and dramatic innovations. The frequent small improvement strategy, however, requires a modular design that easily allows small upgrades and encourages small innovations. (Frequent small improvements, however, can work with certain components of a blockbuster product.) The point remains, therefore, that the choice of business strategy determines the product's design.

Fast to Market versus Low Price

Since the business strategy step of LSFI is so crucially important, consider two other very important strategies: the fast-to-market-strategy and the low-price strategy. Compaq Computer used a fast-to-market strategy for many years. As long as it had an excellent machine and was first, it could charge a premium price. Every strategy, however, has at least one counter. A counter to the fast-to-market strategy is the low-price strategy. The low-price strategy usually enters a product into the market later, but if the product performs well, it can steal business from the pioneering entry.

Both strategies can be viable depending upon their execution, but each requires quite different product design activities. The low-price strategy usually requires low-cost, efficient production. That could entail very lean and well-conceived designs and the manufacture of certain parts by very inexpensive suppliers overseas. But careful designs and distant suppliers usually require extra time.

The fast-to-market strategy, in contrast, cannot take this extra time, so it omits certain steps from its design process. Sony's designs, according to MIT's Karl Ulrich, often have extra screws and wires or other complexities that an excellent low-cost design would not have. But Sony wants to be first, not least expensive.

Fast-to-market entries can grab the market for themselves and, until competitors enter, enjoy the advantages of a monopoly. When Compaq introduced its 386 model, it hit the jackpot. It had the market to itself for a year and reaped the profits. But to be successful, the first-to-market strategy requires that a firm have a comfortable head start on the competitors. After its 386 success, Compaq's lead was slashed, and thereafter its competitors sometimes beat Compaq to the market with new products. This caused severe profit problems for Compaq and forced it to change its strategy and lower its prices.

Striving to be first is also sometimes hazardous because no one knows if the customers will really like the innovation and purchase it. RCA lost millions when it introduced a video disc format that few wanted, even though it was first. Sony launched the VCR first with the Betamax. But the VHS format, introduced later by Matsushita, provided longer recording time and finally came to dominate the market. Sony eventually had to admit defeat.

Nor are low-price entries by any means risk-free. A low price usually means lower margins and less profits per unit sold. Also, because the low-price entry is usually a later entry into the market, it may be too late and miss much of the market. Each strategy thus possesses its own advantages and risks. Nevertheless, the choice of which strategy to follow should be made in the business phase, because each requires a different design approach.

Sometimes a firm can have the best of both worlds. Motorola apparently did so with its personal cellular phone. It was the smallest cellular phone made, and could fit into a pocket. To get that phone out quickly, the team had to develop it quickly, so its initial design was complex to manufacture. After the first model hit the market, however, it had time to do a low-cost design, which was incorporated in later models.

Overall, as these examples have illustrated, a product's business strategy defines and determines much of the innovation process and how the product is designed.

Risk Strategy

As part of the business strategy step of LSFI, before design gets under way, the team should enumerate the potential risks. Will the customer buy this product? Are the technical issues solvable on time and on budget? Risk is inherent in innovation, and as we have seen, good risk management is inherent to good innovation.

The business strategy of a new product determines how much

risk should be taken. Northern Telecom's Jerry Dehner recalls that at the time digital technology was being introduced, the older analog technology was cheaper and more easily manufactured. Digital was then riskier because the engineers were not fully acquainted with it, yet digital yielded higher performance. The choice of which technology to use depended upon the strategic purpose of a product. If performance was paramount, digital would be selected, despite the greater cost and risk.

The risk of introducing too much new technology is real. A leading manufacturer of major medical equipment tried to introduce five significant changes in one new model, including changing software language, computer platform, and other aspects, as well as changing major suppliers. Each single change introduced some risk, but introducing all five at once was too much, and it delayed the project over two years.

Toshiba takes an interesting approach to risk, according to Steven Eppinger of MIT. In designing the next model for consumer products, Toshiba wants improvements in 20 percent of the design. Less than that, it feels, is not worth the expense of introducing a new model. More than that, the risk is too great.

In Xerox's approach to risk is also novel, as the company wants "no surprises." In other words, it wants to be prepared. Management knows the future is impossible to predict, but they want to carefully consider the likely possibilities and be sure they have adequately prepared for any reasonable eventuality.

Research Foundations

This decision of risk spotlights the importance of LSFI Step 2, Establish Foundations. A firm with a solid research base has a pool of technologies "on the shelf," tested and ready for use. Utilizing unproven technologies significantly elevates the risk and danger. Indeed, if the research has not been completed before the business strategy step, costs may skyrocket.

GE's appliance division fully understands this, according to Bill Sheeran, vice-president. It no longer allows any invention during the process of product design. GE ensures that the technology used in a new product is fully proven and manufacturable in advance.

This requires extra expenditures on research, but the reduction in risk is worth it, Sheeran declares, since a delay in getting a new product to market would be much more costly.

Evaluating Risk

There are various approaches to handling risk. Ford, according to Phil Barkan of Stanford, has several useful criteria for introducing a new technology. Ford will introduce it only if the technology:

- adds true value to the product or process;
- is essential to world-class product status;
- is not an end in itself—not intended solely to satisfy the ego of its designers or inventors; and
- is simple enough to be used by designers, manufacturers, and customers.

Xerox, Barkan continues, also has excellent criteria for the use of new technology in new products. The company requires that a new technology:

- be thoroughly proven over the full range of design constraints in the required environment;
- meet all performance objectives;
- meet cost projections;
- meet life-cycle requirements—maintenance and service; and
- be manufacturable with a process with which manufacturing engineers are comfortable.

Clearly, these criteria help the team evaluate the risks in a project.

Risk Document

The risk analysis table 13–1 can help a team evaluate the risks and implement the "no surprises" concept. Under each area, such as technical or marketing, the team enumerates the specific risks, and for each risk it determines the countermeasures to be taken. Suppose a new technology would significantly boost performance, but its development is risky and may not be successful. The team would list not only that risk but also its countermeasure—perhaps to si-

TABLE 13–1
Risk Analysis

Area	Risks	Countermeasures
Technical		
Software		
Marketing		
Intellectual Property		
Competitors		

multaneously develop a backup technology. Or a competitor may come out with a special feature, but this is not known for certain. That risk, too, would be listed. The countermeasure might be to make the design modular, so that if the competitor does bring out the special feature, the firm could easily introduce it into its product.

Marketing Strategy

Although the business strategy step of LSFI examines many issues, marketing often devours the most time, and considerable effort is spent answering the customer-first questions. The CFQ (presented in Chapter 10) require that the customer's reasons for buying the product be clearly understood. Answering the CFQ demands an analysis not just of how the firm's product will meet the customer's needs but of competitive products as well. Indeed, if the new product being innovated cannot answer the CFQ well, then the risk of failure in the market escalates enormously.

Dave Siefert of NCR goes even further, suggesting that specific customer checkpoints be built into the product development process itself. Such checks would verify that the product under development will still satisfy the customer's needs well. Markets, customers, and technology change so fast, Siefert notes, that a product that was initially right on target can, just a few months later, be totally off. These checkpoints should be entered into the business strategy step and should be conducted after major phases of the project are completed.

Siefert thinks that these periodic reviews, involving actual customers, should be formal. The customer should be shown prototypes, even if they are very rough. These sessions should also produce a written document of what the customer seems to want.

Cost Strategy

Ultimately, the financial numbers—the costs and profits—mold and shape business strategy. At the end of the business strategy step, senior management evaluates the innovation project to decide whether to proceed. To make that decision, the business strategy step should generate expectations of the product's development costs, manufacturing cost per unit, and other relevant costs such as distribution and selling.

The reader might object, "I do not know those numbers. How do you expect me to know those numbers if the product hasn't even been developed yet?" Edith Wilson of Hewlett-Packard points out that architects build tall skyscrapers, yet are able to estimate the cost to within one percent. Auto mechanics know the cost of an overhaul or tune-up. The secret that lets them do that, she suggests, is an excellent database.

With the exception of truly revolutionary products, the larger part of most new products has been designed before—only a small portion of the design effort is actually new. This is true even if many portions of the design seem to be changed. Examined carefully, often only a few items within those portions are really novel. The problem, according to Wilson, is the lack of a database or model that can estimate costs more precisely. Her message to firms is to build up this database.

Such databases are now becoming more widespread. For instance, Sunder Kekre of Carnegie Mellon University and his colleagues have developed a model for General Motors that estimates the cost of lights and lamps.[7] In addition to headlights, a typical car contains fifteen to twenty lamps, including brake lights, side markers, license plate lights, and interior lights. Some may be several feet long and wrap around the car. These lights and lamps are very important to the style of a car. According to designers, especially for certain types of cars, such as vans, "the lamps sell the car."

The model can tell the designer how much a lamp design will cost before it is made. Factors the model considers include the complexity of the mold, the material costs, labor, overhead, and quality. Using the model, the designer can make such style decisions as whether one continuous six-foot lamp is worth the cost, or whether using two three-foot lamps would be preferable.

Similar models exist for a variety of electronic, plastic, and metal items, according to Mike Duffey of University of Massachusetts. The same holds true even for software, where costs are notoriously hard to estimate and often run 100 to 200 percent over budget. But depending upon the project and the calibration, software cost-estimation models can often forecast costs with 80 to 90 percent accuracy, according to MIT's Chris Kemerer.[8]

Strategic Cost Forecasts

Databases and cost models help a team make not only financial projections but also two strategically important financial forecasts—the cost to break even and the cost of being late to market.

COST TO BREAK EVEN. Hewlett-Packard, as seen in Chapter 7, has found the time-to-break-even projection very valuable. Suppose development of an innovation takes one year and will cost $100,000. Suppose profits from the sale of the product are forecast at $50,000 per year. This means that the time to break even is three years: one year for development, and two additional years until the profits cover the development costs.

The time-to-break-even number is useful because operationally, it forces a team to ponder not just the development aspects but what happens after the product hits the market, including marketing and distribution. Financially, Hewlett-Packard believes, time-to-break-even provides the big picture in a snapshot.[9] It focuses the team on the one overriding concern: returning the R&D investment as quickly as possible.

COST OF BEING LATE TO THE MARKET. The cost of being late to the market is another very important strategic financial measure. Suppose a firm is expected to have a new product out in six months. If it is late and takes longer than six months, it loses sales to competitors. In terms of sales (or profits), the amount per week that the firm loses from its lateness, is its cost of being late to market. Karl

Ulrich of MIT estimates that for every week a new camera is late to market, Polaroid loses about a million dollars in sales.

The cost of being late itself has two components: the cost of lost profits, and the cost of the development activity, since people will still be working on the project. For example:

Lost profit (per week of being late)	$100,000
Additional investment (salaries, overhead, and other project costs per week)	<u>$200,000</u>
Cost of being late to market (per week)	$300,000

The cost-of-being-late figure can help ensure that adequate resources are allocated to a project. Unexpected delays often occur in the middle of a project, and additional resources are needed. By using the cost-of-being-late figure, which is usually sizable, the project manager can more easily argue the importance of freeing up additional resources to avoid any delay.

In Chapter 7 we saw that one department did not have the $200,000 in its budget it needed to hire two engineers. Because the $200,000 was not spent, the firm lost millions of dollars in being late to market. Had management known the cost-of-delay figure, it might have been able to free up the additional funds for those two engineers. Indeed, the cost-of-being-late figure is frequently sobering, and its magnitude often forces the entire development team to think of ways to speed up the development process.

Implementation of the Business Strategy

As an example of this LSFI step, Motorola, according to Paul Noakes, wants its blitz (business strategy) phase to last no more than a month and to be performed by a small team consisting of senior people from marketing, engineering, and manufacturing. The team's purpose during this phase is to consider, on a general level, the pertinent business factors and to decide if actual development of the product or system is warranted. The final document, which is to be presented to top management for approval, should have the following information, Motorola suggests:

1. Marketing Strategy
   - Customer requirements
   - Results of market research

- Windows of opportunity
- Market risk and obstacle identification
- Strategic objectives, market-by-market
- Distribution strategy / delivery requirements
- Sales forecast:

  market-by-market
  sales history
  pricing by market
  service strategy
  competition and other external factors

2. Production Description Outline

- Key features / attributes / estimated production cost
- Technology required and availability
- Manufacturing process assessment
- Technology risk identification and assessment

3. Program Investment Estimate

- Proposed Schedule
- Estimated resource requirements, by discipline
- Estimated total program costs

4. Financial projections

- Investment required, net present value calculations, and internal rate of return
- Profit projections

5. Summary and Conclusions

- Estimated schedule for the next phase of development
- Estimated resources for the next phase of development
- Recommended actions

Senior management should review this document and hear the team's presentation on it. Based upon that, management would determine if the expected return is worth the investment. If so, it should determine whether the financial and human resources in the relevant disciplines are available. Depending upon their evaluation, management has several options, including:

- continue to the next phase
- investigate this phase further
- put the project on hold pending further developments
- kill the project.

The scope of the project determines the level of management that is involved in reviewing and approving the document. If important

Summary of Business Strategy Considerations

An experienced cross-functional team examines a product concept to see if it makes business sense and if detailed development should be undertaken.

- Get excellent people involved; do not skimp.
- Include customers and suppliers.
- Do it quickly.
- Submit the report to top management for approval and funding of subsequent phases.

The team should consider:

1. The customer-first questions, and why customers would buy this product and not the competition's
   - Get formal customer input throughout development
2. Marketing issues, including segmentation and positioning
   - Estimate market window of opportunity.
   - Examine distribution channels and sales.
3. Competitor strategy and issues
   - Interview customers of competitors.
4. Risks, technical and market
   - Risk should be appropriate for product's mission.
   - Have minimal technical risk, if fast to market.
   - Do a risk analysis and ensure "no surprises."
5. Costs, resources required, and financial projections
   - Estimate the cost to break even and the cost of being late to market.
   - Develop databases for cost estimation.
6. Major targets and conceptual issues
   - Develop technology strategy.
   - Develop manufacturing strategy and targets for manufacturing costs and quality.
   - Develop marketing strategy.
   - Estimate time to market and cost of development.
7. Strategic goals of firm, and level of support from top management and other groups
8. Governmental issues such as intellectual property and regulations
   - Evaluate for international sales.

efforts from several divisions are required, the general managers of those divisions should be included.

How lengthy and formal should the business strategy step of LSFI be? The governing factor is the firm's experience with the product. If the product is a significant departure from the firm's previous experience—if the product is quite innovative or is a new generation, or if the market or technology has changed substantially—the business strategy step must be executed carefully and thoroughly. On the other hand, if the new product is an update or minor revision of an existing product, considerably less effort might be necessary.

For other firms, Motorola's suggested practice should be adapted and revised as necessary. It even varies among Motorola divisions themselves. The calculation of the time to break even and the cost of being late might also be included, for example.

Summary

LSFI Step 5 evaluates whether a project has a reasonable chance of being a business hit. This is not the time for technical details but for the larger picture. Most important, it is the time for creative approaches for conceptualizing the product and for conceiving how to make it a profitable success (see table 13–2).

Usually a cross-functional team of engineers, marketers, and other relevant experts—often including suppliers and customers—conducts the analysis. The team examines marketing issues, determines the product's strategy, and does a careful risk analysis. It estimates the key costs, as well as the cost of breaking even and the cost of being late to the market. Generally, this step should take about a month. Based upon the conclusions of this team, top management can make the decision on whether to proceed with the product's design.

Platforms, Reuse, and Modularity

The strategy of platforms, reuse, and modularity (PRM) is effective over a wide range of products. It is one of the most powerful product strategies to be developed in recent years, and for many products PRM should be the conceptual basis for the business strategy step of LSFI. PRM creates some important strategic advantages:

- greater tailoring of the product to the individual customer
- easier upgrading, allowing the product to be continually improved and enhanced
- lower cost of both product development and manufacture
- faster introduction of new models
- faster introduction of new technologies.

Some aspects of PRM have already been introduced in this book. Chapters 11 and 12 presented it relative to platform products like the Sony Walkman, and Chapter 12 presented the idea of making frequent small improvements. This chapter examines the PRM strategy in general: its major considerations and value, its implementation, and some detailed examples.

Modularity

PRM represents the creative confluence of two powerful concepts. The first concept is to consider developing a product family. Ordinarily when one thinks about developing a product, one thinks about developing the product itself. PRM suggests thinking instead about developing a family of products—and not just one generation of the family but several generations. As Susan Walsh Sanderson of Rensselaer Polytechnic Institute states, managers should envision not one cycle but multicycles, to exploit synergies across the family of models and across generations of families.

The second concept is modularity. This allows the parts of the product to be easily switched or changed, permitting flexibility, adaptability, and variety. Suppose someone launches a new automobile firm and decides to design three car models. One way to do that is to do exactly that: design the three models. But a different way is to design modules that fit together. For simplicity, suppose that a car consists of four modules: the exterior body, the engine and drive train, the chassis, and the passenger compartment. The firm makes three different styles or types for each of the modules— that is, three body styles, three engine styles, and so on. One body style might be sporty, a second may have two doors, and the third may have four doors. The three engines might differ in power or fuel economy, and the three chassis styles might provide different rides and feelings of the road. To produce a car, the firm takes one style from each of the four module sets and puts them together. By considering all the different permutations, the second approach yields eighty-one different car models, rather than only three.

The first approach considered the car as a product to be designed. The second approach designed a family of cars. This second approach is the PRM approach, and it has many advantages. Clearly more models are generated, but that is only the beginning. Suppose, for example, that the customers do not like the sporty body style, and sales drop. A new sporty body style can then be designed to remedy the situation. Because of modularity, moreover, only the body needs to be redesigned—not the entire car. This gets the new body style introduced much more quickly, with the hope of boosting sales much more quickly. Or suppose that some emergency antipollution laws are enacted. To comply with them, the engine module needs to be altered. Again, this can be accomplished quickly because the entire car need not be redesigned.

This technique capitalizes on the rapid-cycle learning presented in Chapter 12. The car can be continually improved on a short cycle by updating and improving the modules. Whatever modules the customers do not like are replaced, and technical improvements in a module can be quickly introduced—because the modules can be easily and quickly replaced and updated.

The example of an automobile is, of course, ahead of its time. Cars, because of their complexity, are not likely to be made totally modular for a number of years. But the concept is already being applied to automobile components. Daniel Whitney of Draper Labs notes that Nippondenso builds car generators, alternators, voltage regulators, and radiators in this manner.[1] In making a radiator, for instance, a team of marketing and engineering people decides how to modularize the design and the number of variations there will be in different parts. The variations are designed to be interchangeable and to fit together physically and functionally. If the radiator has six parts, each of which has three variations, for instance, then 729 models are possible. Indeed, the fact that this technique uses parts in many different models leads us to the next aspect of PRM.

Reuse

Reuse (often called multiple use) is an essential feature of the PRM strategy. In the traditional practice of making a product instead of a family, each model is designed independently, and most of the parts in the models are different. Under PRM, due to the family concept and modularity, certain parts (actually, part numbers) are used in many models.

Reuse is important because, for one thing, it permits a wide variety of models to be easily made. Chapter 12 already introduced the most widespread use of this idea—platforms. A base platform is built that contains the key equipment or technology. The platform serves as a foundation on which, by use of modules, different features are added to make the different models. The platform, in other words, is reused. The platform concept allows great flexibility and variety and is the notion behind the Sony Walkman and much of the Japanese consumer electronics industry. Sony was so efficient at changing customer feature modules, as we saw in Chapter 12, that it did no market research when it introduced the Walkman, but simply saw what sold and made more of that.

Cost

Reuse can dramatically lower costs. An executive at a leading electronics firm wanted to buy a particular type of tailor-made semiconductor. He discovered that he could purchase one from a Japanese manufacturer at one-third the cost of a U.S. supplier. Especially considering that wage rates in Japan are higher than in the United States, the price disparity was surprising. The reason, it was determined, was that the U.S. firm had designed the semiconductor from scratch. The Japanese exploited reuse and conceived the chip by piecing it together from previously designed portions— a considerably cheaper technique.

Karl Ulrich of MIT explains how such cost savings are possible. A firm manufactures a nozzle for industrial use, and the nozzle has four major features. Customers want each of the four features in four different styles. So to cover all combinations of styles, the firm has to make 256 different models of the nozzle. One way to manufacture all 256 is to fashion 256 molds, one for each model. Applying reuse, however, the firm needs four molds for each of the four features—a total of 16 molds. The parts made by the molds would be modular, and putting the parts together would still produce all 256 models. The reuse approach therefore requires one-sixteenth the number of molds, with comparable savings in inventory and overhead.

Speed in Product Development

Reuse, moreover, allows new models to be developed relatively easily. In the motorcycle war between Honda and Yamaha described in chapter 1, Honda came out with a new model virtually every week. It was able to do that because the new models were not totally new. Don Clausing of MIT suggests that 75 percent of the parts in each new model came from other models—that is, they were multiply used. A new model would have only 25 percent of its parts changed—but that was more than enough for the model to look very different to customers.

The reasons for Honda's speed are now clear. When only 25 percent of the parts are new and the design is modularized, the different models could be developed quickly. Manufacturing benefitted, too, because the same parts were employed in many different models. This reduced the total number of part numbers needed, which in turn cut the expense of storing, scheduling, and supplying the parts. Honda had mastered the reuse and modularity notions, and Yamaha—at that time—had not. Similarly, in the early 1980s Xerox's Japanese competitors, by exploiting reuse, were coming out with models twice as fast with half of the engineering effort. Xerox has since adopted the reuse concept.

Frequent Improvements

The identical idea is also the secret behind the frequent-improvement strategy of many Japanese firms, mentioned in the previous chapter. Most of the modules in a product stay the same, and only a few modules are updated. Apple's Macintosh followed this approach—its basic computer is little more than a frame into which modules are placed. It modularized its 3 ½-inch floppy-disk drive and continually upgraded as the technology advanced from 200 kilobytes to 400K, 800K, and 1.44 megabytes. Apple also modularized its memory module with standardized connections for quick change.

Now leading PC makers have redesigned their machines so that even the novice user can install an upgraded module. When a new microprocessor comes out, a secretary can snap it into the computer in minutes. If a new graphics card is needed, that is snapped in too.

Periodically—say, every few years—a firm using PRM will introduce a major improvement, a new generation of the product. But between those times, it makes many small improvements, a module at a time. Moreover, the many small improvements add up to a large improvement after a short while.

Sales Increased

Most important, the small improvements produce sales. Ron Davis, Caterpillar executive, states that in the past, Caterpillar had followed the blockbuster approach, redesigning the entire product— the engine, transmission, torque convertor, frame, and body. This was a lengthy and costly undertaking. But it learned that PRM produces profits faster, because even small enhancements can create sales. Increasing ease of use and convenience for the customer is particularly helpful, Davis says. Adding some comfort features in the cab, for example, generated a nice boost in sales. A major competitor enhanced its own sales just by changing color scheme and decals, since that gave the equipment a fresh new look.

Reuse Applicable to Any Aspect of a Product

So far, the reuse discussion has focused on parts, but the concept can be applied to any product aspect. Designs, manufacturing processes, and even marketing brochures and distribution channels can be used again and again. Susan Walsh Sanderson of Rensselaer Polytechnic Institute reports that Ford developed CAM V8 engines by emphasizing their reuse and commonalities. These engines had common combustion chambers, common valve trains, and a common basic structure. Using the PRM approach, Ford could introduce new engines for $60 million, rather than the $500 million it had cost when each new engine was designed separately. In electronic design, certain parts like gate arrays and silicon compilers can be reprogrammed, which is a type of reuse. Compared with the old approach of using parts, gate arrays cut the cost of a TV tuner in half.

In related instance, the University of Chicago's Abbie Griffin visited a U.S. firm that had installed a computer-aided design (CAD) program. Previously, the engineers had designed by hand, but now the computer had eliminated their drafting work. Still, CAD did not speed up the design process as much as it had been expected to. Griffin wondered what was going on. Then she recalled another firm that made a similar product, but that had significantly speeded up its design with CAD. That firm had stored previous designs of the product in the computer's memory. When a new product had to be developed, the team would take out the old designs and make modifications. The reuse of the old designs made the design process much faster.

Software

Because it prevents bugs, one the hottest fields for reuse is software. Most programmers like to create new routines. But places like Mentor Graphics sternly resist that. All new routines contain bugs and must be tested and validated—an extremely costly and time-consuming process. Unless it has compelling reasons to reprogram,

Mentor Graphics requires the reuse of old routines, since they are already proven and validated. (Reuse of software is so important that a detailed example is presented later in this chapter.)

Managing PRM

For a management perspective of PRM, consider the experience of General Electric as related by Bill Sheeran, vice-president of the division that makes large home appliances like refrigerators, washing machines, and dishwashers. Several years ago, GE managers noticed that because the company wanted to satisfy customer demand, it held a big inventory of finished goods—nearly a billion dollars' worth. To hold that inventory was costing them, when all the associated costs were considered, close to $200 million annually.

GE wanted to be sure that whatever a customer wanted would be in stock, so it had an excellent warehouse system to store all that inventory. In fact, its records indicate that it was out of stock in a item—unable to satisfy a customer's request—only a small percent of the time. It was doing a fine job. Or so it thought. When GE decided to have a multifunctional team examine the situation, it found that the real out-of-stock situation was much different from what the figures indicated. The figures counted only orders received that could not be filled. If a customer informally called up for refrigerator model X and that model was not in stock, it was not counted as an out-of-stock because no order had actually been received. The percent of times that GE did not have what the customer wanted, the team discovered, was much higher than the numbers said.

The team also learned that GE's forecasts for future product demand were almost always in error. Since manufacturing had to plan for about three months ahead, product demand had to be forecast at least that far ahead. The aggregated-demand forecast for a product like refrigerators was usually fairly good. For any particular model, however, the forecasts were usually poor, often off by as much as 50 percent. Some managers suggested better forecasting as a means to improve the inventory situation. But that approach would be hopeless, the team knew, because customers and the competition are too unpredictable several months in the future. As Sheeran puts it, "Forget forecasts."

The situation was that despite a very large and expensive

finished-goods inventory, GE was still out of stock frequently and not satisfying customer demand well. What was GE to do? First the team probed for the underlying cause of these problems. After a careful study, they fingered the real villain: a lengthy production cycle. To make a product took close to three months. With an item being made only once every three months, at least three months' worth of stock (plus some safety stock) had to be held in inventory.

The team conceived a solution: Change the three months to three days, and make to order. In other words, three days after an order would come in, the product would be made and shipped. No longer would it be necessary to make the forecasts. No longer would it be necessary to hold all the finished-goods inventory. No longer would a customer be disappointed because a specific washing machine model was not in stock.

Although reducing three months to three days sounds extreme, the team knew it could be done. First, they improved the order handling and the manufacturing process, cutting the production lead time from ten or twelve weeks to two or four weeks. That was a great help, but it was still not three days. To get to three days, they had to change the design of the product using PRM concepts. They modularized, and they did so in an insightful way. GE developed a common chassis on which the unique features of the model are added very late in the production process. Sheeran calls this "late-point product identification."

A product—say, a heavy clothes dryer—is kept very general for almost the entire length of its production run. Only when it is very close to completion are the customer-selected features added: special fabric handling, temperatures, and drying cycles. No matter which model a customer wants, the product can be made to those specifications very rapidly. The three-day goal was achieved. Inventories evaporated, costs dropped, and the customers are much happier.

But the GE team did not stop there. They also introduced the capability of changing and improving the product every year. Previously, the product had been redesigned every five years. But the heat of competition and the rate of technical advancement made that too long. By modularizing the design, it became possible for GE to make annual technical improvements in the product. Annual change may not be as rapid as the couple of months possible in some electronic goods, but it is excellent for a refrigerator or dishwasher.

Planning for Reuse and Flexibility

PRM can be very valuable for many products. But because it alters the way a design is made, it must be considered up front in the business strategy step of LSFI. Gary Reiner notes that companies like Panasonic "conceive of planning as two separate activities."[2] First, they plan a product class based on an underlying platform. This platform will generally be modularized and permits not only customization for the buyer but easy inclusion of technological advances. Second, they consider the development of the individual models.

To implement PRM, a company should first consider its product's position in the graph in figure 14–1, which was conceived by Susan Walsh Sanderson and Vic Uzumeri.[3] This will provide insight into the type of modularity and flexibility needed. In particular, it should be decided whether the design will easily allow:

- model variety,
- rapid improvements,
- a combination of both, or
- neither.

Fast-changing products like memory chips must permit frequent rapid improvements, which requires modularity and reuse in both the product and its designs. Products that require many models will require a flexible production capability that allows a variety of models to be manufactured easily. Products of a more dynamic nature will need a combination of both model variety and rapid improvements.

Once the overall strategy for modularity and reuse is clear, table 14–1 can help identify the specific modules used in each model of the product. Note that the reuse concept is applied here not just to parts but to design processes, marketing, manufacturing, and other areas. The last line of the table shows the customer features that depend upon the model. Those features differentiate the models and create the variety.

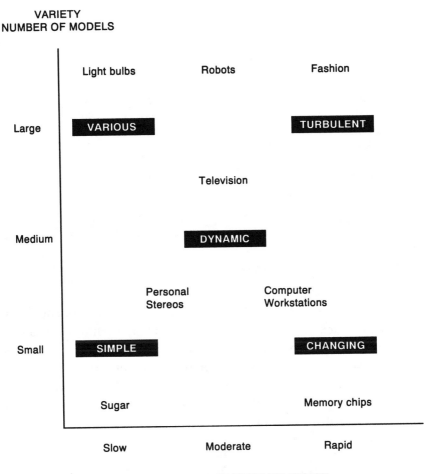

VARIETY
NUMBER OF MODELS

RATE OF CHANGE OF PRODUCT DESIGN

FIGURE 14-1
Strategy of PRM

An "X" indicates that this particular module (design, system, subsystem) will be used in the model. Observe that software A will be used in all models, so it serves as a platform. "U1" through "U5" indicate features unique to that particular model. To allow these unique features to be easily installed in each model, modularity must be built into the basic design and manufacturing process.

TABLE 14–1

Reuse and Variety in Models

	Model 1	Model 2	Model 3	Model 4	Model 5
Designer Module	X	X	X		
Low-Cost Module		X	X	X	X
Software A	X	X	X	X	X
Software B	X		X		
Motor A	X	X	X	X	
Motor B	X	X	X		
Mail Order			X	X	
Retail	X		X	X	
Plant Line A	X		X	X	X
Customer Features	U1	U2	U3	U4	U5

Introducing Improvements

For a family sedan, table 14–2 shows which improvements will be installed in which models and when. Such a table forces engineers to create a flexible design now that will easily permit insertion of new technologies into the product in the future. It also indicates when specific technologies must be developed and ready for insertion into the product. For example, the fifty-miles-per-gallon technology will be introduced into the model upgrade that is scheduled to come out in October 1995.

TABLE 14–2

Introducing New Technologies: Family Sedan Improvement Schedule

	Jan 95	Mar 95	Oct 95	Jan 96	Mar 96	Oct 96
Low-Cost	X	X				
50 MPG			X	X	X	X
New Exhaust		X	X			
Low-Cost Phone				X	X	X
Back Seat VCR					X	X
Voice Control Steering						X

The Importance of Balance

As with any good idea, an overreliance on PRM concepts can lead to trouble. In the early 1980s General Motors strove for reuse of many parts across many models. Although this was seemingly a great idea, it failed. Because so many of the parts were used in common, the cars all looked alike, and sales suffered. Pontiac customers did not like their car to look like a Chevrolet. GM learned to be careful about features and parts that customers can easily see. Those parts should be different so that each model looks distinctive. The parts that are multiply used should be hidden.

The issue here is one of balance. With too many parts in common, model variety is destroyed. With too many unique parts, the virtues of commonality and reuse are lost. In particular, U.S. autos had numerous options that customers could select, thereby providing great variety. They could choose seat style and fabric, steering wheel tilt, trim, transmission, engine, wheel style, body style, and headlight style. The customer choice was enormous, but coordinating all the different options and features on the factory floor was very cumbersome, impairing quality and driving up cost.

The Japanese auto firms took a different approach. In order to exploit reuse, they limited the number of customer options to only a key few. That restricted variety, but it made the car much easier and less costly to produce. Still, which options the Japanese did offer had been carefully determined through detailed market research. That way, they ensured that the options they did offer satisfied the most customers. Customers found a reasonable set of options and, in addition, better quality and lower price, which the reuse helped provide. At present, many U.S. auto firms have adopted these concepts and have become quite competitive.

PRM Case Studies

Let us consider two case studies of implementation of the PRM concept: software and consumer telephone equipment.

Software

Software quality is very costly and very difficult to achieve because bugs are rampant. Even the best programmers make bugs that necessitate prolonged, expensive, and frustrating removal. Reuse is of great benefit here, as we have noted, because reusing a previously coded and debugged module, routine, or design can dramatically reduce the number of bugs. Reuse also cuts programming time.

Against this background, consider that in certain areas of software, Japanese firms have two to ten times fewer bugs, yet they often produce a code in half of the time. This situation began to come to light a few years ago through the careful research of such experts as Michael Cusumano of MIT, and more recently, through probing by practitioners such as Bob Yacobellis at Motorola and Gordon Bell, an independent entrepreneur.[4]

The Japanese firms develop software that fast and with excellent quality because they create libraries of old routines, modules, and designs that are repeatedly used. To illustrate, if Hitachi is asked by an electric power firm to develop software to help it schedule its generators, a Hitachi team would first examine the situation at the power utility. They would say to the power company, "We can give you a program that will do the following for you, and it will cost Y yen. That program will reuse many of our old routines. But if you want additional features, they must be specially programmed, and the price will go up to Z."

In other words, by reemploying many old routines, Hitachi can develop a program quickly and cheaply that does most of what the customer wants. To do everything the customer wants, however, requires programming new routines, which takes more time and money. The customer decides which approach is preferable. Over the years, Hitachi has built up an extensive library of programs, so that in most cases it can do almost all of what a customer wants without much additional programming.

Once the project is agreed upon, a team of Hitachi software experts examines it in detail. They target areas where old routines can be reused and where new routines must be programmed. When they do program new routines, they are programmed not only to be used this time but to be reused in the future. Making the routine reusable costs a bit more, but when the company reuses that routine in the future, the savings are enormous.

In addition, individual programmers are given goals for the amount of reuse. Their work stations are also programmed to bring up old routines and to permit easy adaptation of those routines. It takes programmers a while to get use to this approach, but the pay-off is clear.

For many business and process-control applications, the software programs produced have 70 to 80 percent repeat use. Compared with starting from scratch, this provides a considerable savings in time and money, and it produces many fewer bugs. Although the Hitachi example is typical of the top Japanese firms, leading U.S. firms like Mentor Graphics, EDS, Arthur Andersen, Motorola, Borland, and Microsoft vigorously pursue the same approach. Also, as these firms are discovering, new programming methodologies like object-oriented software design can make reuse much easier.

Consumer Telephone Products

AT&T Consumer Products makes telephones, cordless phones, answering machines, and related products. Several years ago, according to Con Brosnan, general manager, it was losing sales and market share to Japanese manufactures like Panasonic and Sony. The Japanese were introducing new models three and four times faster, "stealing" the customers. But AT&T installed a new product development process that has let it fight back, become competitive, and boost market share. Based upon PRM concepts, it is best illustrated by the time line in figure 14–2.

The entire cycle to develop a product, including getting the production ramped up and the product into distribution, takes twelve months. Observe, however, that the development of the new, improved model starts in just five months, overlapping the last model under development. That greatly enhances the team's ability to get an improved product into the market quickly and to quickly adjust it to the market. Notice, in particular, that this implements the rapid-cycle learning concept discussed in Chapter 12.

To conceive the general specifications for the product, AT&T utilizes a cross-functional team of marketing people, design engineers, and process engineers. All the team members co-locate in New Jersey to foster good interaction. Although the manufacturing

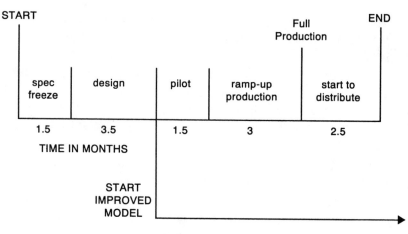

FIGURE 14–2

Modularity and Model Introduction Timeline

is not carried out in New Jersey, the process engineers go there for the first phase to hammer out the specifications.

The team is given only one and a half months to finish the specifications. After that, the specifications are frozen, locked in, and the team is not allowed to make any additional changes or improvements. Anything they missed or want to add or improve (unless it is of overwhelming importance) will be inserted in the next model, which starts development only a few months later.

Detailed design then takes three and a half more months, followed by pilot testing and the start of manufacturing. At the end of the detailed design, however, the new, improved model starts development. Anything anyone wants to improve can now be fed into the new model.

Speed drives this approach. The time line shows how, by freezing specifications and overlapping product development, AT&T introduces new improved models in rapid succession. Modularity, moreover, is crucial to this process. It allows quick improvements to be made in portions of the product, without having to redesign the entire product.

Con Brosnan thinks of telephones as a collection of modules. If a cordless phone has one channel, the team obtains a two-channel phone by using two such modules. Paging, memory, redial, and indeed almost all the features are also modular. Putting together a new model means interconnecting and packaging different feature modules.

Research Base

Each feature, moreover, has its own separate research team working on and improving it. This is done off line, independent of the design of any particular product or model. When a research team develops a better module—say, a pager—it then becomes available for use in products. Whenever a development team starts a new model, they put the product together by selecting from among the most current modules.

Notice that the product development teams themselves do not invent new concepts. That is done off line by the research teams, and only proven technology is employed in the modules used by the design team. This follows the philosophy of LSFI Step 2, to establish a solid research foundation, thereby avoiding the risk of trying to invent or use unproven technology in product development.

Customer Research

The role of customer research here is particularly interesting, since some of AT&T's arch-competitors like Sony and Panasonic do not utilize it. Con Brosnan feels that customer research does help target the markets better. He estimates that it costs $200,000 to put out a new model, including the costs of printing brochures, designing service manuals, and distribution. Customer research helps the company cut back on the number of models that customers do not want and that are therefore wasted. Although AT&T differs from Sony and Panasonic in its use of customer research, all three use feedback from actual sales in the same way, constantly supplying it to the development teams.

If the cost of developing and marketing a model is low and if the period between model introductions is short, customer research is not needed. Information on what actually sells is fed into the next model under development, which will come out quickly. On the other hand, if the cost of a model is high or if the time between model introductions is long, customer research can often help target the customer somewhat better.

Overall, the AT&T approach provides a structured and carefully considered way to implement many PRM concepts. In fact, Brosnan believes, without its new approach, AT&T Consumer Products would be out of business.

PRM Strategy

PRM is a powerful strategy to use in the face of uncertainty. A firm that employs modularity and reuse can easily produce a wide variety of models and introduce new improvements rapidly and cheaply. But despite its virtues, the PRM approach is not for every product. Kempton Smith, general manager at General Electric Lighting Products, notes that for 60-watt bulbs, GE uses a different approach, with no modularity and no reuse. Because it makes millions of them, GE employs a dedicated production line to produce the bulbs in high volume and at very low cost.

On the other hand, GE Lighting Products does take advantage of modularity and reuse for specialty products. Smith notes that for certain products it has achieved 95 percent commonality in use of parts—despite the fact that those products employ quite different technologies, some incandescent and others metal halide (like the high-intensity lamps used in stadiums).

The deciding factor in choosing between these two different approaches is the degree of uncertainty—of the market, customer, and technology. With a stable and relatively certain market, a dedicated production system can be more efficient. For 60-watt light bulbs, the best strategy is to forget flexibility and churn out the bulbs as fast and cheaply as possible. But when there is uncertainty, when

TABLE 14–3

Summary of PRM Concepts

Permits rapid-cycle learning

Facilitates rapid introduction of new models

Permits model variety

Allows model specifications to be frozen and changes to be quickly introduced in new models

Improves quality and cuts cost by resue of designs, systems, parts, modules

Is effective for software and hardware

Is employed by many Japanese and U.S. firms

Facilitates concept of "throwing" products into the market without customer research

Avoid reuse of parts where customers can see them.

the customers are unpredictable and the technology is evolving rapidly, PRM comes into its own.

Summary

PRM was born by marrying the concept of product families with the concept of modularity (see table 14–3). Much of a product family can multiply use parts, which makes it much cheaper to introduce a variety of models and to frequently improve the products. In most markets customers are demanding more and more models, and technology is proceeding rapidly. Especially for those markets, platforms, reuse, and modularity helps companies stay ahead.

Design the Product

15

Concurrent Engineering: The Concept

At this point, all of our previous work comes together because this LSFI step actually designs the new product. Accomplishing that, however, is a subtle and complex process. First, the development team determines the product's overall technical concept. Then the detailed engineering-design work on the product's systems, subsystems, and piece parts begins. Prototypes are built, and pilot models are tested. Last, manufacturing starts debugging its operations and ramping up for full production.

A powerful technique for orchestrating all those tasks is known as concurrent engineering (also called simultaneous engineering). Concurrent engineering strives to do the right job right the first time. It results from synthesizing two fundamental observations. The first is that changes become more and more costly, the later in a project they are done. The second is that doing the different steps of a project in parallel—simultaneously—gets the project done more quickly then doing the steps sequentially, one after the other.

After presenting these two fundamental observations, this chapter will articulate the technique of concurrent engineering. The next three chapters will delve into concurrent engineering's operational details. Concurrent engineering has been quite successful and has often cut development time and cost by over half.

The Cost of Change

Catching mistakes early in new product development is very important because for most products, the later a change or revision is made, the more expensive it is to make. As Jan Benson of General

Motors notes, automobile design is a typical example. During the initial phases, design is done mostly on a computer with perhaps some clay models. The designer can make changes easily, often with little more than a computer keystroke. But later in the process, when the tooling needed for production has been made, changes become enormously expensive.

Suppose a car hood, Benson suggests, has five main parts. To make each of those parts might take five dies, so making a hood requires twenty-five dies. Some of the major dies—the ones used to stamp out parts on the thousand-ton presses—can be very expensive, costing a quarter of a million dollars. Just to make a hood, auto firms invest millions in dies and the associated tooling. Now suppose that after the dies are made, someone discovers a mistake in the hood, and the dies must be redone. The cost of making that change would be outrageously high.

Although perhaps less apparent, the same principle holds even before any tooling is made. The design process generally consists of at least two phases—a high-level design phase that decides the overall concept, and a detailed design phase that designs the individual systems and parts.

Making a correction or revision in the high-level design phase is generally easy. But after that, alterations become increasingly difficult and costly. In fact, when the detailed design phase is well under way, the different aspects of the process are so interconnected that a small change is almost a fiction. Making even the most minute change requires making new engineering drawings. Schedules, machinery, and specifications probably have to be revised. Changing one part may necessitate changes in the parts to which it connects. Purchasing might have to notify or even change a supplier. Bills of material, parts lists, and documentation may have to be revised. Any one correction or alteration is very costly because it sets off an avalanche of other changes (see figure 15–1).

Factor-of-Ten Cost Increase

Confirming these observations, *Business Week* has reported the costs of change for a major electrical product in each phase of its development.[1] The table that shows these costs is called a factor-of-ten table because each subsequent phase multiplies the cost of change by a factor of ten.

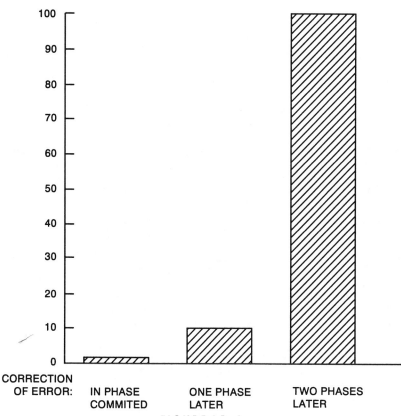

FIGURE 15–1

Increasing Cost of Correcting an Error, If Corrected in Phase Committed or in Later Phases

During design	$1,000
During design testing	$10,000
During process planning	$100,000
During test production	$1,000,000
During final production	$10,000,000

The $10,000,000 figure may seem high, yet if a sizable number of products have already been made and have to be altered, the cost could easily equal that. In the GE refrigerator debacle (discussed in Chapter 4) changing the failing compressors cost GE over $400 million.

For its midrange AS/400 computer, IBM determined that a change in the testing phase cost thirteen times more than a change in the early design phase, and that a change after installation at a customer site cost ninety-two times more.[2] These are data for a very well-designed, highly modular product, so for many other products the numbers might be even higher.

Software

Software seems as if it ought to be easier to modify, since it is all in the computer. But that is not the case, either, because for software the issue is almost as bad as it is for hardware. Barry Boehm of the U.S. Department of Defense lists the phases of a typical software project as being requirements, design, code, development test, acceptance test, and operations.[3] Boehm determined that from one phase to the next, the cost of change or correction increases by a factor of two to three. This is cumulative. Suppose, for instance, an omission is not caught until two phases after it appears. Fixing it then would cost four to nine times more than if it had been done caught right away. Considered over all phases, the cost of correction, change, or revision rises by a factor of about one hundred.

Costs Are Also Locked In

The point here is that many crucial decisions about products are made early, like the basic shape, the performance, the overall logic, the types of materials. Once these basic features are set, that limits and locks in much of what occurs later. Indeed, not only do changes become harder to make, but costs also get locked in as well. Robert Winner of the Institute for Defense Analysis notes that the concept development phase spends only one percent of the total cost of the project, but determines 70 percent of the life-cycle cost of the product.[4] When the advanced development phase is completed, 7 percent of the development cost has been spent, but 85 percent of the life-cycle costs are determined.

General Motors discovered that the design phase determines 70 percent of the cost of truck transmissions. For two thousand parts studied at Rolls-Royce, the design phase settles about 80 percent of the final manufacturing cost.[5] More generally, about 60 percent of a product's life-cycle costs are set in the concept formulation phase, and 75 percent before full-scale development starts.[6]

Changes Are Common

Despite the expense, many engineers want to revise, make improvements, and create the "perfect" product, even late in the project.

"Creeping elegance" is what Dave Kinser, vice-president of Claris, calls these changes. Kinser recalls a firm in which certain vice-presidents constantly wanted "improvements," even late in the project. Fortunately, one project manager was very hard-headed and, despite the vice-president's requests, would not permit such changes. That particular project was the only one completed on schedule.

Do the Early Part Right

Getting the job done right the first time is essential. Do the up-front work thoroughly, even at the price of lengthening that phase, because correcting an error or omission in a later phase can be so expensive.

Many accounting people and budget-cutters will likely scream at an approach that calls for thorough initial planning. They might say that the best time to save money is early in a project because that leaves a lot of time to revise things later. That is incorrect, however. It is much more cost-efficient to spend the money up-front to do the job right. As Paul Noakes, vice-president of Motorola, says, it is better to add five extra engineers at the beginning than to add fifty, often with overtime, near the end.

Steve Cook, a former student, mentions a firm that tried to speed up late projects by taking people off projects that were just starting up and switching them to a late project. The firm felt that since these other projects were just starting, taking staff away from them would cause no problem. That firm did not realize that initial conceptualization is crucial, and that many of the problems that caused their frequent furious last-minute rushes were the result of skimping on the up-front work.

Parallel Processing

If the first observation that later changes are costly is empirical, the second observation is based on straightforward logic. To cut the time it takes to get a new product to market, one can perform many portions of the development process concurrently—that is, in parallel. Much of product development must be done sequentially—the overall software architecture must be finished before the detailed coding can begin. But astute management can often do numerous steps concurrently, saving time. Fuji-Xerox calls this the *sashimi* system, after the slices of raw fish arranged on a plate, one slice overlapping the next.

Conceptually, management can accomplish concurrent engineering in three basic ways: overlap generations of products, overlap phases of a project, and overlap steps of a phase.

OVERLAP GENERATIONS OF PRODUCT. Product generations frequently overlap with semiconductors, cars, and many other products. Before design work on one generation is finished, design work has already been started on the next. According to Bill George of Motorola, creating a new generation of semiconductors requires five to six years. By overlapping generations by a couple of years, George observes, the Japanese get new generations to the market in about three years. The AT&T consumer products case history in Chapter 14 overlapped also. The team started developing the new model just a few months into the development of the previous model.

OVERLAP PHASES OF THE PRODUCT DESIGN. Traditionally, product design was conducted sequentially in distinct phases: market analysis, overall design, detailed design, testing, and manufacturing startup. These phases can be overlapped to a considerable degree, saving time.

OVERLAP STEPS OF A PHASE. Within any one phase, many of the detailed steps can be done concurrently. For example, many of the parts constituting a product can be designed in parallel, or software modules can be coded simultaneously.

IBM overlapped phases for its AS/400 computer project and thereby reduced the development time 40 percent, compared with the previous system. With its sashimi system, Fuji-Xerox does parallel activities not only among project members but with suppliers. It feels that for one advanced copier, the system helped shorten the development time from thirty-eight months for an earlier model to twenty-nine months. Dan Dimancescu reports that Boeing Commercial feels the sequential process caused it up to 30 percent of its design rework.[7] To eliminate that waste for its 777 plane, it made the development process parallel from the very first day.

These two fundamental concepts—do the up-front work carefully to avoid later changes, and use parallel processing wherever possible—are united in the technique called concurrent engineering.

Concurrent Engineering

The key to concurrent engineering is that the entire development process is managed by a cross-functional team of experts from all relevant departments, including marketing, design, and manufacturing. The central notion is that the team is responsible for conceptualizing the product correctly up-front. Each expert ensures that the problems that could later occur in his department are, to the greatest extent possible, avoided, thereby dramatically reducing later changes. But what about the parallel processing of the different phases such as marketing, design, and manufacturing? The cross-functional team already consists of experts from those areas, so it sets up and manages the parallel processing, too.

With all the important areas represented right at the start, the cross-functional team conceives the product correctly, manages parallel processing, and cuts delays and waste. By contrast, the traditional approach kept the marketing, engineering design, and manufacturing phases separate and performed them sequentially. When one group was finished, they "threw their work over the wall" to the next group. The different groups communicated little and had numerous misunderstandings, so costly delays and changes ensued. Concurrent engineering is clearly a superior alternative.

Compare the old sequential approach shown in figure 15–2 with the concurrent engineering approach shown in figure 15–3, to see how concurrent engineering eliminates potential fumbles up front.[8]

Successes Achieved

Concurrent engineering has cut product development time by 20 to 70 percent, boosted white-collar productivity 20 to 100 percent, and increased sales five to fifty times.[9] Without calling it concurrent engineering, many Japanese firms follow its principles and achieve excellent results. For example, Motoo Suzuki, director of passenger car development and engineering at Mitsubishi, has said that his three thousand engineers produce three times as many new car designs as their eight thousand counterparts at Chrysler. "There is no secret to it," he says. "We bring in our suppliers and marketing

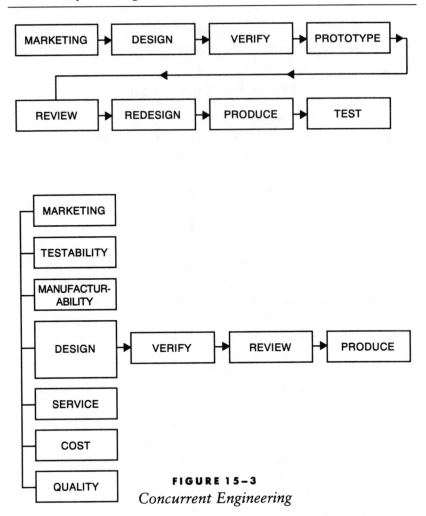

FIGURE 15–3
Concurrent Engineering

people from the start, and do it together. They bring in the budget cutters."[10]

Selecting a few from the many possible examples, Robert Winner of the Institute for Defense Analysis put together the chart in table 15–1, which shows how concurrent engineering has produced savings in cost, schedule, and time.

The Cross-Functional Team

Place the best and brightest on the cross-functional team—this is a necessity on which all the top firms agree, because they know the

TABLE 15–1

Savings Due to Concurrent Engineering

Case Study	Cost	Schedule	Quality
McDonnell Douglas	60% savings on bid for reactor and missile projects	Significant savings (reduction from 45 weeks to 8 hours) in one phase of high-speed vehicle preliminary design	Scrap reduced by 58%; rework cost reduced by 29%, nonconformances reduced by 38%; weld defects per unit decreased by 70%; 68% fewer changes on reactor
Boeing Ballistic Systems Division	Reduced labor rates by $28/hour; cost savings by 30% to 40%	Part and materials lead time reduced by 30%; one part of design analysis reduced by over 90%	Floor inspection ratio decreased by over 66%; material shortages reduced from 12% to 0; 99% defect-free operation
AT&T	Cost of repair for new circuit pack production cut by at least 40%	Total process time reduced to 46% of baseline for 5ESS	Defects reduced by 30% to 87%
Deere & Company	30% actual savings in development cost for construction equipment	60% savings in development time	Number of inspectors reduced by 66%
Hewlett-Packard Instrument Division	Manufacturing costs reduced by 42%	Reduced development cycle time by 35%	Product field failure rate reduced by 60%; scrap and rework reduced by 75%
IBM	Product direct assembly labor hours reduced by 45%	Significant reduction in length of design cycle; 40% reduction in electronic design cycle	Fewer engineering changes; guaranteed producibility and testability
Northrop	30% savings on bid on a major product	Part and assembly schedule reduced by 50% on two major subassemblies; span time reduced by 60%	Number of engineering changes reduced by 45%; defects reduced by 35%

importance of this team and that it must conceive the product correctly. Reap the benefit of those highly paid creative people discussed in chapter 3. For certain high-priority projects, these people could be "stolen" from lesser activities. The highly successful Bandit project at Motorola is reputed to have done this, which is partly how it earned its Bandit name.[11] Jerry Dehner of Northern Telecom notes a tendency to skimp to save money, but that is faulty and shortsighted. Dehner suggests, "Get top people even if they must be grabbed from other tasks."

The concurrent engineering team usually consists of a core four to six people representing all key areas such as marketing, engineering, and manufacturing. People from less crucial areas participate as they are needed. If suppliers play an important role in product development, supplier representatives should be on this team as well. For most products, as Dehner stresses, a customer should be on the team.

Typically, line workers are also part of the team. Spartan Motors designed and built its Metrostar fire truck in a lightning-fast two and a half months by having engineers and assemblers work alongside each other.[12] About 20 percent of the engineering, it estimates, was done by assemblers.

For very small projects, the team itself does the entire development. For moderate-size projects, the team manages others, and for large design projects like a computer mainframe, automobile, or airframe, the team might manage hundreds or even thousands of people. General Motors' Flint Automotive division has a core team that directs the development of a car. Reporting to that core team are teams for each of the six major systems—chassis and power train, trim, electrical, heating and cooling, body structure, and bumpers, and glass. In treelike fashion, each of these teams is broken down into still smaller teams. All these teams are cross-functional, containing not only technical staff from materials purchasing, marketing, manufacturing, and assembly line but also suppliers and even financial and accounting representatives.[13]

Project Director

The most crucial position on the team is that of the project director. Top management should select that person very carefully, as he or she will direct the cross-functional team and the entire development effort. In the word of Harvard's Kim Clark, the project leader should be a "heavyweight." Many projects get delayed by power struggles between departments. The project director should be of sufficient stature with colleagues and top management to ensure that this does not occur.

To run the project efficiently, the project director should have budgetary and personnel authority for the project. The team members should report directly to him, and the project director will typically evaluate the team members for pay and promotion while they are on the team. Granting such authority to the product director seems necessary because if it is not granted and people are assigned to the team only temporarily, they will still report to their old bosses. Those bosses will often pull the team members away for work on other projects. Or they will meddle and give team members directives on the innovation project itself, causing confusion and delay. The U.S. auto industry is only recently overcoming difficulties of this kind.[14] Detroit firms have now adopted an approach in which senior management gives a team its initial overall directions, then the team is left alone to get the project done.

Implementing Parallel Processing

To implement the parallel processing component of concurrent engineering, the cross-functional team can utilize a time/concurrence plot delineating the tasks to be done in parallel. Dan Dimancescu, president of TSG of Cambridge, Massachusetts, suggests this procedure.

Consider the simplified example in table 15–2. For weeks 1 and 2 of the project, both the marketing and the engineering staff will visit with customers. In weeks 3 and 4 all participants will be involved in quality function deployment (QFD). During week 5, all participants conduct a careful review of the design and progress made. In week 6, while marketing and engineering are doing the system design, manufacturing and suppliers are working on the tooling.

In actual practice, the time/concurrence plot will be considerably more detailed, and the tasks listed on it would include the specifics of exactly what should be accomplished. Overall, however, this table depicts when coordination will be required between what groups, and how different tasks will be done in parallel.

Coordination

Parallel processing, as the time/concurrence plot suggests, requires careful coordination and communication. For one complex avionics

A Time/Concurrence Plot

Week	Marketing	Design Engineering	Manufacturing	Supplier
		Department		
1–2	Visit customer	Visit customer		
3–4	QFD	QFD	QFD	QFD
5	Review concept	Review concept	Review concept	Review concept
6–9	System design	System design	Tooling concepts	Tooling concepts
10–12	Verify with customer	Parts design	Parts design	Tooling development
13–14	Verify with customer	Pilot tests	Pilot tests	Tooling development
15–16		Production prep	Production prep	
17			Start production	

system, many design steps were done in parallel but without coordination. The team that designed the radar met their goals and completely finished their unit on time, on specs, and on budget. Other parts of the system came inconsiderably overweight, however, and the radar designers were required to go back, redesign, and cut forty pounds. The radar team was thus forced to design their unit twice. With better coordination, however, much of that double work might have been avoided. As soon as the other parts began to get overweight—and it was noticed early in the design process—the radar designers should have been immediately informed. Then they could have made weight adjustments during their first design.

By contrast, good communications produces good results. Kim Clark of Harvard discusses the design of an automobile body panel and the dies that will be used to stamp out the panel. To parallel-process and save time, the die-maker starts constructing the dies before the engineer finishes the design. Since the design is not complete, the die-maker must provide leeway for changes and make some guesses. Mistakes are made, and revisions occur. The two parties need a high level of mutual trust for the process to be successful, and their communication, in Clark's word, must be "dense."

The die-maker could wait and not start his work until the body panel is completely designed. But that would be a waste of time. Furthermore, it would prevent the die-maker from providing his expert feedback to the designer and helping the designer design a better body panel. Overlapping activities thus produces a better product in addition to saving time.

Parallel processing, like any other scheduling technique, requires good management. If the staff is not used to coordinate and communicate across group boundaries, formal training and management support are helpful. In coordinating with its suppliers, Fuji-Xerox has each side visit the other's plants and keeps information channels open at all times. Any change or potential problem is immediately discussed.

Innovation Through Co-location, Dedication, Isolation, and Concentration

Since the cross-functional team is responsible for the product's conceptualization, it must be highly innovative. Scientists suggest that life on earth might have been created by lightning striking certain organic material. We want the lightning of excellent ideas to strike our team, and certain techniques can help with this, including co-location, dedication, isolation, and concentration.

Co-location

Co-location means that the team members all sit together in one room. Paul Noakes, Motorola vice-president, observes that the old system impaired communication. Team member A phoned B, who was not in her office. When B phoned back, A was not there, and the missed phone calls bounced back and forth, especially because these people were busy.

Pat Robertson, Pratt and Whitney manager, has worked under the old sequential system, where groups were separated, as well as under the newer co-location approach. He strongly prefers co-location. Suppose he gets an idea. Under the old approach he would have to wait a week for a meeting. Then at the meeting, according to Robertson, "someone would shoot it down," or "someone would say that it was the responsibility of some other department and that I shouldn't bother about it." Under co-location, where key people are in one room, "ideas are developed together with much less hassle and conflict." Robertson can tap someone's elbow and talk about the idea. Someone else might chime in, and soon a really creative idea is developed.

Fuji-Xerox agrees. According to a *Harvard Business Review* article by Hirotak Takeuchi and Ikujiro Nonaka, "When all the team members are located in one large room, other people's information becomes your own with little effort. You then start thinking in terms of what's best or second best for the group at large. . . . Initiative and compromise emerge as a result."[15]

Although the team should be together in one room, in many firms office space is a problem. Delays may result while the team leader tries to obtain a location for the team. Do not waste that precious time. Use whatever space is available. Roger Covey, president of Software Systems Associates, sometimes sends a team of programmers off to a motel to live and to work. As long as they bring their computers along, they have all the support they need (besides pizza and beer). As for the Motorola Bandit program, according to its team leader, Russ Strobel, "We had a dinky lab back in the bowels of the factory, next to the sprinkler system and fire alarms."[16] The initial Nissan team that developed the top-of-the-line Infiniti consisted of twenty people in temporary quarters.

Needless to say, I am not arguing that concurrent engineering can be done only in dilapidated surroundings. Some firms like NCR have very nice facilities that are especially designed so that when a project starts, the key people involved can quickly move together.[17] But avoid wasting time looking for space. What counts is the team's creative interaction, not the beauty of the physical facilities.

Dedication

Dedication, the next concept for an innovative team, means the team must be dedicated to the project full time. If one team member is away on another assignment, it destroys the entire purpose of the co-location. (That happened in Dave Sartorius's story—see chapter 8.) Allow nothing to distract the people on the team from their project. It might even be useful, as Paul Noakes of Motorola mentions, to screen out nonproject-related mail.

Isolation

Isolation, in which the team and all others working on the project are put into a separate facility, or "skunk works," is often beneficial. This idea was brilliantly implemented by Kelly Johnson at Lockheed, which developed a slew of innovative aircraft including the XP-80 Shooting Star, the F-104 Starfighter, the U-2, and the SR-71 Blackbird.[18] Roger Covey did this with the AS/SET project (see chapter 12). The highly successful Apple Macintosh was also conceived this way.

At IBM, Abe Peled got fed up with the firm's slow-moving bureaucracy and convinced top executives to let him set up a secret lab outside the normal channels. In less than two years—a breakneck pace—his "skunk works" team was able to develop a powerful graphics supercomputer.[19] IBM is now convinced that the skunk works approach speeds products to market.

The skunk works has the advantage of getting a top-notch group away from interference and distractions. But do not cut the designers off from key resources. The Bandit project, for instance, was located right next to the manufacturing line, so the team could continually validate their ideas in test production.

Sometimes isolating the team members for the entire length of a development project is impossible. The team members, being top people, are often in demand for other activities, or they may live in geographically distant places and have to go home. In such cases, isolate the team at least for the initial conceptualization phase, so that the major up-front decisions can get the intense focus and concentration they need. AT&T, as we have seen in Chapter 14, flies the key people to New Jersey for that phase. Similarly, GE and Motorola send cross-functional teams away for that phase to a motel or resort for an "eagle" session.

Concentration

The benefit of co-location, dedication, and isolation is that they promote concentration. Innovation occurs when a team wrestles with a problem so profoundly that they know every part of it and it obsesses them. The really good ideas come from really deep analysis. The problems, issues, and complexities must play over again and again in one's mind for the breakthroughs to come. But interruptions thwart deep analysis, which is why the team needs concentration, which, in turn, is attained through co-location, dedication, and isolation.

The team might talk and discuss for hours and hours, because creativity and innovation are great fun. As William Spencer, president of Sematech, writes, "When they get out of the bed in the morning, there is nothing they want to do more than to go to work." For the team to attain that, however, concentration is vital.[20] Indeed, the entire purpose of co-location, dedication, isolation, and concentration is to forge a crucible in which the lightning of innovation can strike.

The Role of Senior Management

Despite the efforts of cross-functional teams, some of the most sizable fumbles related to concurrent engineering occur in the executive suite. Senior management must understand that their role is to "clear the tracks" so that the team can function effectively. Phil Barkan of Stanford investigated the highly successful GE lighting panel development, which reduced the number of plants from six to one, cut salaried personnel by 75 percent and hourly personnel by 55 percent, and produced a dramatic increase in market share. Many factors contributed to this success, but one of the keys, in Barkan's words, was the "excellent support of top management."

Unfortunately, such support is not always forthcoming. Top management, for example, may not allot the team sufficient time to do the up-front planning. They often want to see something real, like chips or code, quickly, and somehow they feel that any problems can be easily tidied up later. These beliefs are unwise, of course, and if top management skimps on the up-front work, they could pay double or triple later.

Further, top management is responsible for the quality and speed of the various support activities, as these can be a major source of fumbles (see chapter 8). If the team needs information from purchasing, it should not have to wait long for that information. If a model or prototype must be made, it should not take long. More pointedly, if the team needs a decision from senior management, that decision should be made promptly. Top management is the only group that can ensure that all support activities—including themselves—are lightning quick.

To speed progress, top management may need to correct the physical separation of the activities. Several years ago, AT&T Consumer Products' development activities were so spread out that communications were almost impossible.[21] Physical design and electrical design were on different floors of the building, and the test lab was on still another floor. Drafting was in a different building, and style design was in a different state. To make matters worse, model construction was in the Far East. By contrast, a major Taiwanese competitor had all its major activities close to each other on the same floor.

People who are spread out cannot communicate and coordinate well. Realizing that led senior management at AT&T to relocate their operations to the same spot, making coordination fast and effective.

Godfathers

To facilitate top management in helping the team, many firms like IBM, Quantum, Mentor Graphics, and Accuvue use "godfathers." A godfather is an executive, often a senior vice-president, who oversees a program and shepherds it through problems. The godfather stays in direct contact with the team and ensures that any delays or problems are handled expeditiously. If marketing is slow in providing information to the team, a call from a senior vice-president can get action. If top management is meddling with the team's decisions, the godfather speaks to them. The godfather uses the authority of the executive suite to clear away problems and obstacles.

Even though the godfather can help most projects, some projects are so important that the project director should report directly to the CEO without any intermediaries. This arrangement should be reserved for only the most crucial innovation projects. It ensures that the top person in the firm is directly involved in the project and will personally ensure action (see table 15–3).

A Case Study

If a firm is used to the old approach in which the functional areas operate independently, consider what happens should it shift to concurrent engineering. GM's Flint automotive division (which is responsible for the Buick, Oldsmobile, Cadillac, and Pontiac) underwent this shift, as mentioned, so that a core team would man-

TABLE 15-3

Responsibilities of Senior Management in Supporting the Cross-Functional Team

- Provide funding and resources
- Allocate time to do up-front planning
- Ensure that support activities actually support the team and do not delay it
- Organize the firm physically to promote innovation
- Appoint a "godfather" to oversee the project
- Select an excellent project director

age the overall project, with supporting teams for each system and part.[22] With representatives from such diverse areas as the functional groups, finance, and suppliers on the team, the participants had to learn to listen to one another and cooperate. Because everyone talked, people became frustrated at the delays, and one program manager said, "There were times I had to bite my tongue not to say 'Just do it my way.'" Personality differences arose, and it took time for team members to get used to one another. A fifty-year-old purchasing agent with thirty years of experience had to master the task of listening to a green twenty-two-year-old engineer who was fresh out of school. As Randy Wrightman, assistant chief engineer, says, "A lot of people thought we were slowing the process down and not accomplishing anything."

But GM's concurrent engineering effort paid off, because as the individuals argued back and forth, their differences were worked out and problems eliminated. People expert in their own areas realized they were ignorant of the other areas and learned that the collective wisdom on the team far exceeded that of any individual. By working together, the team could make the tradeoffs necessary for the entire part or system to work properly. Moreover, under the old approach the staff had had to wait for approvals, since decisions went up and down the hierarchy. Now each team had cost and performance goals for its own portion of the project and was empowered to make decisions themselves—a task greatly aided by having a team member from finance.

The GM teams eliminated innumerable problems in the early stages that would have been exposed much later in the development process. One team cut the number of parts in a bumper system by half. Moreover, assembly workers sitting on the teams made many

TABLE 15–4
Summary of Concurrent Engineering

A cross-functional team of experts is responsible for the design and management of the product development project. They should:

1. Do the up-front work carefully to avoid costly later changes, and
2. Implement parallel processing.

The team should include top people from all the key areas that will be needed in the development. Including customers and suppliers is often helpful.

Creativity can be enhanced, and time and cost reduced through co-location, dedication, isolation, and concentration.

suggestions about how to simplify assembly. In one case they complained about the twenty-seven parts needed to make the front and rear door frames. The engineers then redesigned the part to consist of one piece. Despite the growing pains of learning how to use it, under concurrent engineering the H car platform—the Buick Le Sabre, the Pontiac Bonneville, and the Oldsmobile 88—was brought to market in thirty-four months (compared with fifty-five previously), with 40 percent fewer parts and 20 percent shorter assembly time.

Summary

Many expensive delays can be avoided by understanding parallel processing and the idea that later a change is implemented, the more it likely will cost. Concurrent engineering implements these two concepts (see table 15–4). A cross-functional team of top people from the key areas envisions and oversees the design of the product. It is important to have the best people on this team because they are responsible for doing the up-front conceptualization properly and for managing the project. Moreover, good team management through co-location, dedication, isolation, and concentration can enhance innovation. Top management plays a major role and should ensure that the rest of the organization, including themselves, does not get in the way of the innovation process but vigorously supports the team.

16

Concurrent Engineering and the Contract Book

The previous chapter presented the overall concepts that drive concurrent engineering. This chapter delves into concurrent engineering's operational aspects—in particular, the contract book. The contract book is a document that structures and guides the entire development project by providing the basic plan for its execution.

The Contract Book

The cross-functional team's initial objective is to plan the project properly. As the previous chapter stressed, that plan should ensure that potential difficulties in the project are virtually eliminated. The team's first task, therefore, is to ferret out problems. That is usually done by seeking input of customers and by testing the product's technical features and manufacturing. Once those aspects are accomplished, the team will delineate its plan to execute the project in a special document called the contract book. The contract book should evaluate all important issues in the product's development, manufacture, and marketing and furnish the tactical blueprint to conduct the innovation project. Motorola, says Paul Noakes, suggests that the contract book present the teams's methodology to attack the issues listed in table 16–1.

Freezing Specifications

The contract book does far more than analyze and plan the issues listed in table 16–1, however. It is a document, as Noakes emphasizes,

TABLE 16–1

Issues Included in the Contract Book

Market Issues

- Market strategy and prioritization
- Market timing (windows of opportunity)
- Delivery requirements
- Market price experience curve
- Demand forecast
- Expected revenue

Project Control Criteria

- Project schedule (including major milestones and product support introduction)
- Total project cost, including all aspects of implementation
- Critical technology, feasibility, and alternatives
- Fatal events defined
- Specific criteria for ship acceptance
- Specific criteria for program completion

Product/System

- Specification and definition
- Product structure plan
- User feature state event diagram
- Finalized ergonomics
- Safety plan
- Styling model

Development Plan

- Resource plan, by function
- Development plan and schedule including major milestones
- Manufacturing cost; goal time

Manufacturing Plan

- Order flow plan
- Manufacturing plan and schedule, including major milestones
- Quality plan
- Product verification and validation plan
- Sourcing plan
- Supplier plan

Sales and Service Plan

- Distribution plan
- Service and installation plan
- Replacement parts plan
- Training

Announcement Plan

- Literature
- Announcement budget

that is actually an agreed-upon contract, which all members of the cross-functional team sign. After the issues are examined, all the team members—from marketing, engineering, manufacturing, and quality—stipulate in writing precisely what product they will deliver. Because it is a binding signed contract, it is very important.

Moreover—and this is crucial—once the book is signed, the specifications are frozen. This means that essentially no additional changes will be allowed in the product. Freezing the specifications may sound quite outrageous, but it has a purpose. It forces people to think very carefully in advance about the product development activity.

Imagine for a moment being on a team and having to sign the contract book. You are surrounded by team members from different backgrounds and from departments that have different needs. Soon you find yourself in a discussion with experts from, say, marketing or quality, trying to agree and jointly develop the best possible product. You would work out the differences, perhaps run some tests and experiments, and in doing so, realize many creative insights. But because your signature will be on the line and you must deliver on your promise, you exhaustively assess what might happen to the product in the future.

The freezing of specifications is clearly designed to eliminate the problem of making later changes. These, as we have seen, can be extremely expensive. Although this approach may not entirely eliminate changes, it certainly slices their number enormously. As Scott Schumway, vice-president of Motorola, emphasizes, the philosophy is that you can not bluff or "wing it." You sign the document, you are committed, and after this, everything becomes frozen. Only if an extraordinary, unexpected event occurs will later changes be allowed, and then only after careful approval. Caterpillar executive Ron Davis agrees and stresses the importance of not continually changing and adding to a product but defining and sticking to that definition. GE executive Margaret Dano and others concur and declare that freezing is essential for fast, effective product development.

Handling the Unpredictable

Still, things do happen that no one can predict, like changes in customer wants or technological advances. But beware of this argument: Some people use it to excuse changes they should have foreseen. They might blame the need for a change on some market shift instead of the real cause—their own failure to think through the issues in the first place. That is precisely what the freeze strives to stop.

Moreover, by implementing the previous LSFI steps, there should be little need for change. Under LSFI Step 2, the difficult technical challenges would be already solved. Under LSFI Step 4, how to handle what the customer wants should be fairly clear.

Nevertheless, uncertainty pervades innovation, and the unexpected will occur. The contract book handles that by enumerating risks and providing appropriate contingency plans. For example, computer logic chips are notoriously hard to test, because they contain literally billions upon billions of logical paths. Indeed, the number of paths is so large that only a small fraction of them can ever be tested, and manufacturers hope the untested paths will not cause any problems to users. Testing is clearly a risk area which the development team for such chips has to discuss in the contract book and institute special action.

Other products have different risk areas that the team should list in the contract book. Suppose, despite applying LSFI Step 2, that the development of an important technology is uncertain. To manage the risk, the team could commence work on the problem immediately, put extra people on it, and plan backup approaches. Kodak knew that the tooling for its disposable Fling camera (later renamed FunSaver) was going to be very difficult to make. Therefore, it sought the best tool-makers, involved them early, and made sure they would have time to work on the problems.

Modularity and Platforms to Manage Risk

Chapter 14 outlined another powerful way to manage risk, through flexibility and modularity. If the team selects this approach, they design the product to be easily changed and updated. Under this approach, the specifications are frozen at the end of the contract book phase. Any later changes or improvements will be incorporated into the next model, which will come out in short order.

When GE adopted this approach, Bill Sheeran, vice-president of General Electric Appliances, noticed a curious phenomenon. Under the old system, delays had occurred in the design process because the next new design would not come out for five years, so engineers had to cram as many improvements as possible into the product, even if its completion was seriously delayed. Now, with modularity, new models come out annually, so the engineers simply save their improvements for the next model. The delays, Sheeran notes, have disappeared.

The flexibility and modularity concept is especially useful because it prevents changes from disrupting one model, yet allows them to be incorporated into the next, which will come out only a short time later. The team thus freezes and risk-manages simultaneously.

In sum, during the contract book phase, any product aspect whose future is moderately certain should be frozen—and freezing is the strongly preferred approach, since later changes are so costly. Any aspects of the product for which the future is highly uncertain should be risk-managed. In particular, the contract book should list all likely problems, as well as backup approaches for each problem. At Honda, management checks on this and ensures that the team enumerates both potential problems and backups.

No Surprises

An approach used at NEC takes this theme further and should be part of the contract book.[1] The NEC team not only lists the possible risks ahead, it monitors what problems actually do occur. Often problems that are forecast do not occur, while problems that had not been forecast pop up. NEC studies the actual problems that occur and feeds the analysis back, both to improve the development process and to help the people forecast problems more accurately next time. This approach not only risk-manages, it systematically increases expertise (see figure 16–1).

Avoiding Later Problems

The objective of the contract book is to eliminate potential problems and fumbles before they occur. A general approach for eliminating potential difficulties is known as robustness. A robust product is one that will withstand the uncertainties and fluctuations that

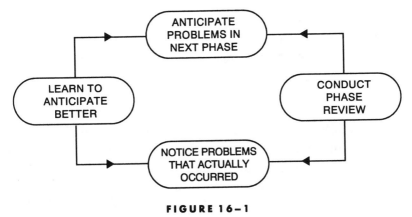

FIGURE 16-1

Anticipation Paradigm

will occur during manufacture, normal use, and occasional customer abuse.

Robustness

Years ago I was director of a project in educational technology for the government. Salespeople would troop into my office with their firm's latest, most sophisticated computerized machine for helping students learn in the classroom. After they pulled the device out and showed it to me, I would ask them, "Can I drop this on the floor?" Most salespeople would gasp, "Of course not! You'll break it!" But the battering that students in a classroom would give their device would be far greater than that from my drop test. Still, few firms had prepared their machines for that reality.

The robustness of a product should include a large array of conditions. Users will press the wrong buttons, spill coffee on it, and use it in the tropics and in the Arctic. Suppose an automobile door is open, and a 250-pound person leans on it. The weight may bend the door very slightly, causing the door to leak in a heavy rain. A robust design, however, would prevent that leak.

Robustness applies not only to customer use but to the product's own manufacture. The phrase "Quality Is Job One" is more than just an advertising slogan at Ford. Job one at Ford is the first preproduction run of about twenty cars off of the assembly line. Traditionally, that run caused a slew of engineering changes because parts were not right and did not fit. Internally at Ford, "Quality Is Job One" means to plan ahead and design the parts right, thereby avoiding the engineering changes.

Many Variables

In creating robustness a large number of variables usually interact. Consider a manufacturing process that depends on five major variables: heat, pressure, chemical mixture, humidity, and time. Each variable is supposed to be at a standard value. But in actual manufacturing, these variables are not easily controllable. Each of the five variables, in fact, could be at any of three possible values—low, correct, and high—creating a total of 243 possible settings for the key variables of the manufacturing process.

Testing all of those 243 settings might be very expensive. Yet missing any one might force a delay to redesign the product if that setting later causes a problem. To avoid such problems, Genichi Taguchi pioneered a statistical technique (discussed in Chapter 18) that quickly tests a large number of circumstances that might later necessitate a redesign or other change. Fuji-Xerox utilized Taguchi's method for its best-selling 3500 copier, and eliminated so many potential problems that it cut the development time from an anticipated five years to two.[2]

Despite the importance of these formal techniques, there is no substitute for firsthand knowledge. Most top firms require their design engineers to learn about production processes. Taking that one step farther, General Motors sends its design engineers to the assembly line, where they spend days installing a part, such as a steering wheel or bumper, just to learn the problems and to eliminate any possible bugs.[3]

Design Reviews

Explicit design reviews can also eradicate many potential problems. At key stages of the team's work, a group of technical experts check on the design of the systems and the major components. In software, where such reviews are often called "walkthroughs," the code might be analyzed line by line. NEC strongly advocates design reviews, having discovered that reviews significantly cut the need for later design changes.[4] Phil Walker, Motorola executive, agrees, declaring that design reviews are "critical." During the rush to get projects finished, teams have a tendency to skip the reviews, but Motorola insists they be done.

Dan Dimancescu, president of TSG in Cambridge, Massachusetts, suggests very detailed major design reviews, with the team and reviewers locked in a room together for a couple of days. He also recommends that a "designer's scorecard" be used to judge progress. The scorecard might evaluate parts that are difficult to test, cost targets, quality targets, and manufacturability targets. Use of a scorecard ensures that the review thoroughly examines the crucial aspects of the product's development.

The reviews are typically performed by experts not only in engineering design but in marketing, manufacturing, and quality. At Hewlett-Packard experts from manufacturing check to ensure that the design can be easily manufactured. Cadillac has had excellent results in letting workers review design plans. A team of assemblers found three hundred problem areas in the 1992 Seville. They identified the electrical system as particularly difficult to install. Engineers then redesigned it, eliminating seven pounds of wire.[5] (For a number of other powerful techniques that prevent future problems, see chapters 17 and 18.)

Setting Goals

Although much of this phase is devoted to eliminating potential problems, the contract book should also clearly specify the goals for the product's performance. Precise goals will help focus the cross-functional team on what is really important to make a product a success. Otherwise, as Edith Wilson of Hewlett-Packard explains, the team has tendency to drift and waste time on less important issues.

These goals should be set sufficiently high to ensure that the product beats out the competition. In developing its personal copier, for example, Canon set these targets:

- copy quality as good as IBM
- $1,500 price, compared with the then-current lowest price of $3,000
- 20 kilograms of weight.

Similarly, for its AE-1 camera, Canon wanted a high-quality, compact, easy-to-use single-lens camera that was 30 percent lower in price than those of the prevailing competition.

Process Goals

Goals should be set not only for the product's performance but for the entire process of ordering, manufacturing, and delivery. General Electric, says executive Gerald Hock, feels that the speed of responsiveness to customers can provide a powerful competitive advantage. To provide that quick response, GE stresses the goal of cutting the interval between orders and deliveries. This goal forces the designers to consider not just the manufacturing time but the order-processing and delivery times.

Indeed, the contract book should establish goals for almost all areas of the product development process. According to executive Frank McFarland, Motorola has goals for

- the schedule for completing the design documents
- the standards for evaluating and certifying new suppliers
- the cost and time of testing
- the schedule of milestones (the major steps in the detailed design, start of manufacturing, and so on)
- the reuse of designs, parts, software
- manufacturing (number of steps in the manufacturing process, inventory, scrap, layout, processes and machines needed, time it takes from when a customer places order until shipping)
- quality (defects per unit, scrap, warranty costs, cost of quality)
- costs (cost of parts purchased from suppliers, direct labor cost, overhead cost, indirect cost, testing cost, energy cost)

Manufacturing Goals

To ensure that the Motorola team meets their manufacturing goals, they plot out, step by step, what will happen during typical production. Then they run tests to validate that the goals will be achieved. In many manufacturing operations, for instance, overhead is a sizable expense. If the expected overhead is above target, the team changes the product or production process to reduce the overhead—perhaps by cutting inventory, the movement of materials, or the scheduling complexities. In this regard, Daniel E. Whitney of Draper Laboratories strongly recommends that the team carefully examine the product's assembly, including running tests and experiments as necessary.[6] Assembly is one of the last steps in a product's manufacture, is inherently integrative, and often exposes problems in previous steps. Setting goals for the efficiency of assembly can help the entire production process to go well.

Goals for manufacturing compel the cross-functional team to consider virtually all features of the manufacturing process in precise detail and to eliminate any potential problems before they occur. As Dan Russell of Motorola declares, "People do not realize that a simple factory is a lot of work."

On this issue, consider the Saturn automobile's slow startup of production. According to automotive consultant James Harbour, "Saturn's manufacturing processes should have been proven before the plant went into production."[7] Saturn wanted the cars produced perfectly and defect-free because that would be essential for customer satisfaction and sales. Nevertheless, Harbour feels, producing those defect-free cars would have been much easier had Saturn pre-planned and avoided the bulkiness of the startup.

Quality Goals

To attain manufacturing excellence, almost in one voice the people in Motorola state that the quality goal is the most crucial, because achieving high quality requires nearly everything to be done right. If there are too many parts, or the design is too complex, or if there are too many steps in the manufacturing process, quality will suffer. Nearly any imperfection in the system can harm quality—including movement of material, rescheduling, storage, poor design, and inadequate suppliers. Motorola sets very high standards for quality because it squeezes out waste and forces a very efficient system.

Material and Information Flow Goals

To think about the various process and quality goals, an easy way is to visualize two flows (as in figures 16–2 and 16–3). Most activi-

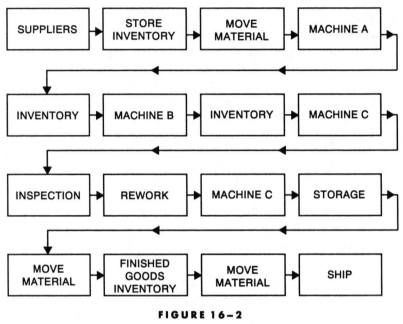

FIGURE 16–2
Simplified Flow of Material

ties in a production operation pertain to one or the other of these flows. The first is the flow of material through the system. Some of the material starts at supplier, is held in storage, undergoes inspection, and passes through machines. The other flow is the flow of information. This flow starts from receipt of the customer order, then goes through administrative processing, scheduling of production, and other steps, until the actual shipment of the material and the billing.

Analysis of these two plans is vital to attaining efficiency. In particular, setting challenging goals for the various aspects of the process forces those two flows to be very efficient. Conversely, eliminating wastes and delays in these two flows helps reach the goals.

As an example, Bumper Works of Danville, Illinois, supplies bumpers to Toyota. Toyota set a goal for Bumper Works to have raw steel coming in the door and get turned into a finished bumper on the same day. Also, Toyota wanted the time it took to change dies speeded up from ninety minutes to twenty-two minutes. The faster die change allowed the production process to be flexible enough to handle twenty types of bumpers.[8] Bumper Works had to

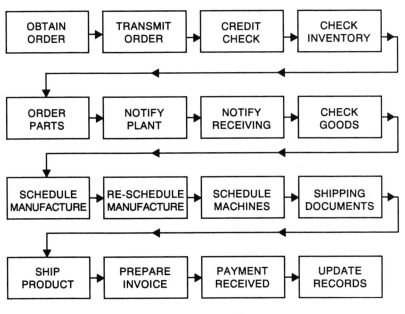

FIGURE 16–3
Simplified Flow of Information

considerably improve its flow of material and flow of information to achieve these goals.

Staffing-level Metrics

Goals force the cross-functional team to plan ahead, to avoid problems, and to be innovative. But the serious question remains of how to anticipate how much time and staff will be needed to achieve the goals. Motorola, according to executive Phil Walker, is developing staffing-level metrics to do this. Based on the complexity of a design, the team can forecast the time and person-hours needed to develop the product with a pager, for instance, they consider the software, manufacturing process, mechanical parts, integrated circuits, and circuit design. Suppose a pager will require fifteen mechanical parts, with ten of those reused and five that must be newly designed. Motorola can estimate fairly accurately, based on historical data, how much staff effort will be needed to design those parts. Similarly, for the software, the team estimates how many lines of code will be reused, how many must be newly programmed, and how many require only minor adaptation from previous code. From that information they calculate the staffing level needed for the software coding. They even have data on how long it takes to procure items from suppliers.

Through analysis of historical data, companies can generate staffing level metrics for how much effort is required to carry out almost any step in the design process. Using these metrics, the team can estimate the time and staff required for different design approaches and to develop the product.

Later Engineering Design Phases

With its several sections, the contract book provides a powerful approach to conceptualizing the specific plan to develop the product. If the contract book passes senior management review, the development team starts on the remaining phases of product development. These typically consist of the following phases, which usually overlap:

- detailed engineering of the systems, subsystems, and piece parts, building and testing prototypes
- designing and building the dies, tools, and equipment needed for manufacture
- pilot manufacturing and ramp-up, in which the factory builds up to volume production.

The contract book should delineate the important issues in these subsequent phases, including risk management and manufacturing. Since the completion of the contract book fairly well locks in most of the product's features and costs, as Jerry Dehner of Northern Telecom states, the remaining phases are almost inconsequential— virtually everything important has been settled. Because of this, the remaining chapters of this book will not provide precise details on the later phases. Instead, they will articulate some universals, some general techniques that can be applied. Before moving on to that, however, consider an example of concurrent engineering at General Electric.

A Case Study

GE, according to executive Brian Gott, successfully used concurrent engineering and a cross-functional team with its air-cooled generator. Firms from Sweden, France, Germany, and Japan had been beating GE out of the market for smaller generators. (*Small* is a relative term here—these generators are sizable machines capable of spewing out 10 to 100 megawatts of power.) The unpleasant option GE faced was either to drop its small generator line or to fight back with an innovative redesign. Dropping the line would have been easy, since GE was still selling larger generators profitably, and most financial analysts suggested this course. GE chose, however, to fight.

Gott formed a cross-functional team to manage the overall project, with people from all aspects of the business: engineering, manufacturing, purchasing, finance, and marketing. Although most of them were not full time on the project, a core team of three people within this larger committee were dedicated full time. First the team conducted a competitor and market analysis and determined performance targets for the new design. These targets provided the goals for the development process and were divided into two sets:

- external goals driven by the market, such as price, performance, and delivery-cycle time
- internal goals for direct, indirect, and overhead costs, as well as for reduction in the number of parts, reduction in the number of designs, standardization, and reuse of parts.

For each major design area, the team formed a subgroup to analyze the issues. Interestingly, each subgroup launched its work with a brainstorming, idea-generating session. Literally hundreds of ideas were suggested, and the team screened them on the basis of their cost, practicality, time required, and risk. They generated so many good ideas, in fact, that not all of them could be implemented in the first model, and some had to be saved for later.

Value Analysis

To reach the goals, the team employed a powerful technique called value analysis (see Chapter 18 for more on this). Value analysis scrutinizes the functional use that a product must satisfy and the most effective means to accomplish it. Before, Gott noted, GE had looked at the old generators, seen the parts it contained, and made a new generator with basically the same parts. Using value analysis, however, the team examined function, not parts. What functions had to be performed? Could a function be performed with fewer parts, or could a part do more functions?

Generators have a big heavy frame, called the stator, that holds steady a part, the armature, which rapidly rotates. Value analysis revealed that the stator, however, had not one but two functions. One was to hold the rotating part, and the other was to guide the air cooling with a series of baffles. The value analysis concluded that instead of one giant part for both functions, there should be two parts, one for each function.

Having two parts produced a significant simplification. Previously, the baffles for the air flow had been portions of the heavy stator frame and so were subject to great forces and had to be very strong. They had to be made from one-inch steel, which is expensive and difficult to fabricate. Now, because it was a separate and distinct part, GE could make the baffles from cheap and easy-to-fabricate sheet metal.

The separation into two parts also permitted parallel manufacture. Before, the wire had to be wound on the stator, and only after that could the pipes for the air circulation be installed. Now they did the wiring on one piece and simultaneously installed the piping on the other piece. The parallel manufacture of these parts significantly cut the time it took to make the generator. Along with other improvements, the team cut the time it took from order to delivery from twelve or fourteen months to four or five months.

By gathering market information, specifying performance goals for the product, and then creatively conceiving a new product, this cross-functional team created a new design that reestablished the company as a major force in the market.

Summary

This chapter presented some operational specifics about concurrent engineering and the cross-functional team. By constructing a contract book, the team plans the project with the objective of eliminating potential problems and fumbles (see table 16–2). The contract book specifies all pertinent aspects of the product: production, marketing, quality, costs, and supplier relations. Most important, these specifications are frozen. The contract book phase is the time

TABLE 16–2

Summary of the Contract Book Phase

The team tests and validates concepts to minimize later delays and changes. It plans out the remainder of the project.

1. Freeze specifications to minimize later changes.
   * Emmumerate possible problems and backup approaches.
   * Anticipate future problems—no surprises.
   * Use platforms and modularity, if appropriate.
2. Establish goals:
   * for product's performance
   * for the design process
   * for the manufacturing process
   * for quality
   * for costs
   * for order, delivery, and the time from receipt of orders to delivery
3. Ensure robustness.
   * Implement design reviews.
   * Use Taguchi methods.
   * Involve hourly workers in the design.
   * Ensure engineers gain experience on the factory floor.
4. Use staffing level metrics to estimate resources and staffing needed to complete the project on time.

for innovative concepts, and providing goals for important aspects of the development can often enhance that innovation. After the contract book is completed and approved, the subsequent phases of the development get under way, but most of the important issues in them should have already been determined in the contract book.

Scheduling

Actual development projects in most organizations are driven by the schedule—what is supposed to be done and when. The schedule is management's prime tool to organize and direct the activities of the design and development staff. In fact, most of management's daily life is devoted to keeping a project on schedule. This chapter presents techniques to determine and keep a project on schedule. Under good management, this chapter suggests, most projects should be completed on time.

Two Scheduling Levels

Project scheduling generally consists of two levels. The macrolevel divides the work into large blocks or phases, and the microlevel handles the day-to-day activities.

The Macrolevel

The macrolevel comprises the project's overall major phases or stages. A phase often lasts several months, and each phase has specific tasks to be accomplished during it. At the end of each phase, senior management usually conducts a review to check progress and decide if funding for the project should be continued. The phases are often done concurrently, overlapping somewhat, to save time.

The Microlevel

The microlevel comprises the detailed day-to-day or week-to-week work to be conducted within each phase. The schedule for this work provides a key technique for management to keep the project on time. It helps identify slippages, enabling management to take corrective action and meet the project's timetable.

Phase Review (Macrolevel)

The macrolevel scheduling is often called phase review, because it divides the project into phases with specific tasks to be accomplished in each phase. At the end of each phase, senior management typically conducts a review to evaluate progress and decide upon future funding.

Abbie Griffin of the University of Chicago discovered that compared with go-for-it and just-plowing-ahead approaches, almost any phase-review process can cut the time of development, often by a third. This occurs because the phase review arranges the work into a logical sequence and, through the periodic reviews, ensures that what was supposed to be done was actually accomplished. Further, the reviews provide the opportunity to kill ill-conceived projects that might otherwise struggle on until suffering a costly death in the market.

The phase-review process is a means to determine and structure the phases of the project after the contract book phase. The exact number of phases will depend upon the product, often running from four to seven for the entire development process. A typical example appears in figure 17–1, which shows six phases with reviews between them.

With parallel processing, the phases would overlap (see figure 17–2), so that some of the work in phase 2 starts before the review

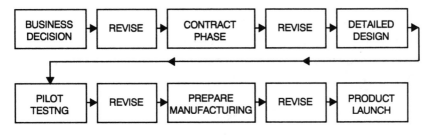

FIGURE 17–1

Six-Step Phase Review

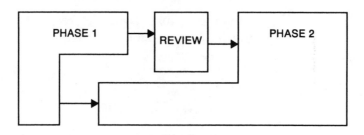

FIGURE 17–2
Parallel Processing of Phases

of phase 1 occurs. The review at the end of phase 1 would typically also review the work already started in phase 2.

Many firms, including General Electric, Kodak, NEC, and 3M, employ the phase-review process. General Motors, according to Gary Dickinson, vice-president, and Al Jordan, head of phase zero development, has a four-phase process (technology and concept development; product/process development and prototype validation; process validation and product confirmation; production and continuous improvement), with major reviews after each phase. Because car development is so complex, however, it holds nearly 180 smaller reviews and checkpoints along the way.

The phase-review approach is sometimes called stage-gate, with the phases of development comprising the stages, while the reviews form "gates" that control the project's progress to the next stage. A generic phase-review process (adapted from Robert G. Cooper and Elko Kleinschmidt of McMaster University) appears in the chapter appendix.[1]

Success Criteria

Ron Davis of Caterpillar calls the specific tasks that are to be performed during each phase success criteria because their accomplishment provides for the success of the project. As examples, here are some tasks for the contract book phase:

Marketing with Support from Engineering
- Meet with customers and obtain their reactions
- Gather information on competitors
- Do analysis of market trends, segment by segment

- Make a demand forecast
- Consider distribution and sales issues
- Estimate market window of opportunity
- Do QFD matrix

Strategic Considerations

- Develop a product family
- Conceive plans for platforms, reuse, and modularity
- Consider how to introduce future improvements
- Do risk management and consider how to respond to market shifts and uncertainty

Marketing and Financial

- Estimate pricing
- Estimate return on investment
- Estimate time to break even, and cost of being late to market

Engineering and Manufacturing

- Determine major features of product
- Develop goals for reuse of designs and parts
- Enumerate and test technological approach
- Enumerate and test manufacturing approach
- Conduct risk analysis
- Provide goals for production cost
- Provide quality goals
- Provide service goals
- Provide goals for time from customer order to delivery

Software

- Develop plan for software
- Decide platform and programming approach
- Analyze integration of software and hardware

Support and Schedule

- Estimate staff required by specialty
- Estimate funds required
- Estimate time required and schedule

Governmental

- Investigate intellectual property, environmental, regulatory and other governmental issues

The tasks of the subsequent phases are heavily dependent upon the product and would be listed similarly. Generally, they will include some of the following:

Design Reviews (see chapter 15)
Review all major designs and components to ensure they meet goals for:
- quality in terms of defects/warranty costs/field service
- elegance of design
- cost of manufacture
- reliability
- ability to satisfy customer needs and wants
- ability to meet product specifications
- integration with other systems and parts
- time and cost of development

Build Prototypes
- Develop prototypes to meet goals for cost, reliability, quality, ease of manufacture, customer satisfaction
- Have potential customers examine the prototypes

Manufacturing
- Involve suppliers
- Design tools and dies
- Ensure ease of manufacturability and assembly
- Build pilot models
- Ensure that overhead costs meet target
- Minimize inventory and movement of material
- Ensure that total manufacturing costs meet target
- Ensure that speed of response to customer orders meets target
- Build test equipment

Software
- Develop plans for reuse of design, modules, and code
- Do high-level design
- Do low-level design
- Do detailed coding
- Conduct software reviews and walkthroughs
- Ensure integration of modules
- Do documentation
- Prepare training
- Build prototypes and get customer feedback on prototypes
- Ensure ease of maintenance and upgradability
- Prevent and get rid of bugs

Companies should decide beforehand the tasks and the review criteria. Northern Telecom spent a million dollars to develop its phase-review process and specify what tasks are to be done when and how to evaluate them.[2] Indeed, as Dan Dimancescu, president of TSG, stresses, a well-conceived delineation of the tasks and review criteria can prevent the team from drifting, ensure that the right tasks are done, and speed progress.

It should be clearly noted, however, that this approach should not become a straitjacket. A not uncommon circumstance, in fact, is that the review criteria become too strict, so that only outstanding projects get passed to the next phase. Quite reasonable but not spectacular projects get sent back to do minor additional tasks, or they get totally blocked and canceled. Phase review is meant to provide guidelines to facilitate innovation, not regimentation to thwart it.

Review Procedures

Robert Cooper has investigated more than two hundred projects to pinpoint what makes phase review a success.[3] He states that the senior experienced people who conduct the reviews should have the authority to approve funding for the next phase. Otherwise, delays will ensue while their approval is sought. Further, the reviewers should be highly knowledgeable, so they can be helpful to the development team. Indeed, nothing is as central to a review's success as the expertise and knowledge of the reviewers.

According to Jerry Dehner, director of manufacturing strategy at Northern Telecom, the work done during a phase should be reviewed by the people who will be using it. Manufacturing, for instance, should review the engineering design. If the design does not adequately consider manufacturing needs, it should be sent back to the engineers for correction. The reviewers must undertake their role seriously, and as Dave Siefert of NCR emphasizes, fully preparing and studying all the pertinent documents and materials might take several days.

Anticipation—No Surprises

The reviewers, being experienced and knowledgeable, should implement the LSFI concept of anticipation and help the team anticipate any problems that might occur in the next phase. A reviewer might alert the team that the product must withstand a special high-stress customer use, or that a specific test may take a lot more time than the team believes. In particular, the team and reviewers should implement the NEC idea mentioned in chapter 16. Specifically, it should anticipate likely problems in the next phase, monitor what problems actually do occur, and then feedback that information to improve.

Problems

Despite the value of reviews, problems can arise. In some firms teams consider the reviews not helpful but a pain to be endured. Just getting ready for a review can devour time, as Paul Noakes, vice-president of Motorola, notes, because the team members must prepare for it, develop presentations, and draw charts. In addition, as Abbie Griffin comments, a month is often required to schedule the senior people to hold a review, during which time the development team does little but wait to see if the project will be approved for the next phase. If five reviews are scheduled into a development project, that means five months wasted. Such holdups in the project, obviously, cannot be allowed.

Meddling

Unfortunately, many firms have a considerably worse quandary: Senior management meddles. They impose ridiculous criteria and require that the team make unnecessary changes and do unnecessary extra work. Perry Gluckman, president of Process Plus, recalls that years ago at Rolm, the review team would put such demands on the development team that product development was delayed for months and months. Frank Lloyd, vice-president of Motorola, agrees that meddling or second-guessing by senior management can severely delay a project. He suggests that they should "stay out of the way."

A contradiction appears: On the one hand, senior manager involvement can help, yet on the other hand, it can hurt. But this contradiction can be resolved because the overriding issue here is the expertise of the senior management. If senior management lacks sufficiently detailed knowledge to be helpful, they tend to become meddlesome and should be excluded. However, when top management is knowledgeable and can truly be helpful, they should actively participate. Bill Gates, chairman of Microsoft, is constantly reviewing projects and making brilliant suggestions. "He has this laserlike ability to home in one the absolute right question to ask," says Brad Silverberg, vice-president of Microsoft's Windows development program.[4] "He'll know some intricate low-level detail about a program, and you wonder, 'How does he know that?'" In cases like that, top management's participation is not just beneficial to the project's success, it is absolutely essential.

Detailed Work Scheduling (Microlevel)

Once the phases and reviews are set at the macrolevel, management must schedule the day-to-day work within each phase—the microlevel. Many experts believe that fairly detailed scheduling, week to week if not day to day, helps promote progress. An individual can easily go down the wrong path or get stuck on an issue if frequent consultation with management does not occur. At Canon, for example, the development team for a copier might consist of twenty people, who would have weekly group meetings to review progress and plan the next week's schedule. Microsoft previously left its programmers alone for weeks. But that allowed bugs to go undiscovered for weeks. Management now requires programmers to test their work daily, and the manager must run checks and tests on the work weekly. The frequent checking also promotes better coordination among the different groups that are working on the program.

TABLE 17-1

Phase Review

- Organizes project into logical steps
- Provides opportunity to kill ill-conceived projects
- Provides checkpoints after each phase
- Establishes beforehand the tasks for each phase
- Establishes beforehand criteria for each review
- Reviews important designs
- Ensures top, well prepared people conduct the reviews
- Anticipates problems of next phase
- Ensures reviews are scheduled expeditiously
- Involves senior management if they can be helpful and not meddlesome.

Project-Management Procedures

For his microlevel scheduling, Motorola executive Ralph Quinsey employs an exceptional project-management system. It helps him not only to schedule but to eliminate potential problems by quickly spotting difficulties so that corrective action can be taken. First he breaks the work down into what he calls assignable tasks. Assignable tasks are work-units—clearly identifiable, specific elements of work for which one person is responsible, like ordering software for the system design, making preliminary layout of the IC semiconductor, or making die estimates. Although the entire project may require thousands of assignable tasks, Quinsey concentrates on the most important few hundred.

For each task, Quinsey specifies two types of information:

1. The task itself—what exactly must be done, how long it will take, what resources are needed and who is responsible.
2. The surrounding tasks—including precedent tasks which must be done before this task can start, and dependent tasks, which depend upon the present task and cannot start until this task is finished.

With this information, the show starts. Quinsey assembles everyone in a room for a couple of days to discuss what is going to happen. The questions fly. Suppose task F depends upon task E, so F cannot start until E is done. Do the people undertaking E know that? Will they really deliver what F needs? And does F really need those inputs?

Many problems arise at the interfaces between tasks. These discussions make sure that a task will deliver exactly what any dependent task needs. Omissions are uncovered, such as the need for a special test. Ways to cut time or cost are suggested, and how to do the tasks in parallel. Most important, Quinsey notes, with everyone in on the discussion, the process not only identifies problems but obtains perhaps its most crucial benefit by enhancing communications and commitment. Indeed, Quinsey declares, these free-for-all discussions significantly cut development time and cost.

Once the work is under way, Quinsey uses a project-scheduling program on his personal computer to keep track of the project.

On a simple chart he can plot what tasks are ahead of or behind schedule.

Enhanced Management Control

A major difficulty in project management occurs when a project starts to run late but management cannot determine exactly where the problem is. Quinsey says that he previously used the approach of plotting milestones, but it was not precise enough to locate the errant task. If the project missed a milestone, the information was not available to isolate what task was causing the problem. By contrast, the new approach tracks specific tasks and lets him pinpoint the task that is causing the trouble so he can provide assistance.

Quinsey recognizes that before the advent of the personal computer, this approach was too difficult to implement. Now, scheduling programs available at every software store make it easy.

Even more sophisticated computer packages are presently being developed for scheduling, according to Steven Eppinger and his colleagues at MIT.[5] Eppinger's program identifies tasks and activities that during product development will be heavily dependent upon each other. General Motors used the program to plan a brake development project. The program discovered certain tasks that would need much interaction, but they were located in different buildings. GM moved the people closer together and, along with other changes, significantly cut the time of development.

The Fear Issue

Scheduling procedures like these can be of great benefit in avoiding delays, but a very serious underlying issue persists: fear. In many firms people hide problems because, as Edith Wilson of Hewlett-Packard points out, "the bearer of bad news is shot." An employee fears that when the manager hears about a schedule delay, the manager will evaluate him as incompetent. Problems then remain hidden, and management cannot take action to quickly solve them.

This problem is critical, and Wilson suggests several approaches to help:

1. Make sure the work-breakdown structure is detailed enough so that it is clear what each person is supposed to be doing at any given time.
2. Have good project reviews periodically, with experienced reviewers who know what they are doing and who cannot be bluffed.
3. Ensure that management is on top of the day-to-day activities and learns immediately of any problems.

Most essential, Wilson notes, is to create a corporate culture without fear, in which people quickly come forward with problems so that help can be provided. In particular, an open culture of trust and mutual support is crucial (see Chapter 4).

No Delays Allowed

But let us take the discussion of schedule delays one step further: Why have delays at all? A powerful approach to avoiding delays is simply to not let them occur. For some firms, this might sound preposterous. Nevertheless, if the work tasks have been well thought out to begin with, this is, in fact, possible.

The Motorola Bandit project finished remarkably quickly, largely because the team did not allow any delays.[6] Says Scott Shamlin, "The schedule was our religion." Suppliers were dropped if they could not operate in that environment. Russ Strobel comments, "We were not going to miss any of those major prototype dates. When those cells were to be on-line, they were on-line."

During the Bandit project several prototypes were built, and management had established clear dates on which the prototypes were to be assembled. If on that date any group had not fully completed its scheduled portion, they had to simulate by hand and submit a document stating what was incomplete and the corrective actions to be taken.[7] The date scheduled for the prototype, however, was not allowed to slip. The powerful pressure of these clear deadlines forced people to plan and execute very well.

Likewise, when Amdahl was building a large mainframe computer, the team never missed a milestone, according to K. C. Vennugopal—much to the surprise of its competitors. It did this, Vennugopal says, by carefully managing the details—that is, by planning the details, scheduling the details, and watching the details. Honda is similar and, according to Dave Nelson, vice-president, consistently gets its car development projects completed on time. The Honda teams do a careful contingency analysis and must have a backup determined for any possible problem. If a problem does arise, they quickly implement its backup procedure. Further, Nelson states, management checks to ensure that good contingency planning is done.

Finish on Schedule

Most delays stem from the following sources:

1. *Failure to implement LSFI Step 2 and build the technological foundations.* The engineers then must invent and conduct research during the product development project, which is a risky endeavor.
2. *Failure to freeze specifications.* Changes, as we have seen, are a notorious cause of delays.
3. *Failure to provide adequate resources.* This includes not being able to call on resources when they are needed during the project.
4. *Failure to properly monitor the project's progress and to quickly correct for any slippages.*
5. *Failure to think through and plan the project up front.* Inadequate planning often results from failure to involve the right expertise, including, where appropriate, suppliers, customers, and factory-floor workers. Also, the up-front effort should include careful contingency planning and provide backup approaches.
6. *Failure to get quick support services and management approvals.* The clock does not distinguish between delays caused by R&D and delays caused by the model shop, by purchasing, or in obtaining management approvals.

Since good management can remedy most of these difficulties, there should be almost no reason for not completing projects on schedule.

Summary

The schedule typically is the prime means for management to control and direct an innovation project (see table 17–2). Most projects need scheduling both for the major phases of the project and for the detailed day-to-day work. The phase-review technique divides innovation into logical phases, with checkpoints between them. It can also structure the phases of the project after the contract book phase. The tasks to be done in each phase, and the review criteria should be delineated ahead of time. The detailed microlevel scheduling of work helps management to monitor progress and take corrective action. Its success requires that management break the project into detailed steps, keep on top of these detailed steps, and eliminate fear. Furthermore, under appropriate management, for most projects little or no schedule slippage should be necessary.

TABLE 17–2
Summary of Scheduling

Phase review—divides project into major phases (macrolevel)
- Structures work into logical tasks
- Provides checkpoints and opportunity to stop project
- Reviews should be done by experienced people
- Facilitates anticipation

Project scheduling for day-to-day work (microlevel)
- Involves staff in planning schedule
- Divides work into small units
- Monitors progress carefully
- Allows management to quickly help staff
- Requires supportive culture without fear

No delays; which requires
- Good project planning, scheduling, and monitoring
- Good research and technology base
- Good contingency analysis and use of backup procedures should problems arise
- Good resources
- Good support

Chapter Appendix

The Phase-Review Process

Robert G. Cooper, jointly with Elko J. Kleinschmidt, both of Mc-Master University, have studied phase review carefully. The following is a generic process based upon their work.[8] Any actual process, of course, must be adapted to the specific product being developed.

REVIEW 0. The initial idea is given a quick, gentle screen to see if it fits the firm's strategic goals. Generally a rough check is made of the following issues:

- size of market
- likely customers
- technical problems
- risk
- fit with the firm's distribution system
- overall potential

No financial criteria are used at this point. To proceed, both marketing and engineering should concur as to the idea's possible viability.

PHASE 1. This is a relatively inexpensive check of the product's market potential and technological feasibility. Focus groups and contacts with key customers might be employed. Estimates are made of:

- market size
- market potential
- competitor response
- possible costs
- software development
- time to develop
- financial returns

A very rough model of the product might be developed.

REVIEW 1. This check of the product's potential is similar to review 0 but somewhat tougher, with the use of checklists and evaluation of the product's financial projections. Typically, a check would be made of:

- marketing plan
- software development plan
- design and manufacturing feasibility
- preliminary product specifications
- business plan
- schedule
- risks
- financial return

PHASE 2. This defines the product and its specifications. This is the final stage prior to heavy spending and full product development. Market research studies will typically be undertaken, and business issues such as distribution, patents, copyrights, and governmental regulation analyzed. Preliminary design and laboratory work will try to validate the technical concepts. This phase comes closest in the Cooper/Kleinschmidt framework to the contract book phase of Chapter 16.

REVIEW 2. This checks the results of the previous phase and makes the decision on whether to spend the funds to develop the product. That decision might be based on:

- final product specifications
- software architecture
- preliminary design work
- outcome of testing of difficult technical or manufacturing issues
- market tests of the product
- detailed user analysis
- regulatory and intellectual property issues
- detailed analysis of competition
- specific manufacturing plan
- specific launch plan
- costs and likely financial return

PHASE 3. This phase develops the product, typically by developing a series of prototypes. During this phase also, manufacturing is designing tooling and getting ready for production. Marketing obtains feedback on the prototypes from customers and is getting ready to launch.

REVIEW 3. This checks the work of the previous phase to ensure that the product developed meets specifications and quality and cost targets. It also reviews manufacturing and marketing.

PHASE 4. This examines the viability of the product with tests of manufacturing, marketing, customer acceptance, and economic feasibility. Typically field tests of the product are conducted. Manufacturing undertakes pilot production.

REVIEW 4. The final decision whether to launch the product is made. All information is reviewed, and the decision is made. Checks are typically be made of:

- software quality, maintainability, documentation, training
- product design
- manufacturing issues, including tooling, equipment, costs, layout, overhead, inventory, labor standards
- quality assurance
- competitor response
- customer acceptance
- marketing launch plan

PHASE 5. The product is launched, and marketing and operational plans are implemented.

REVIEW 5. This is a critical analysis to assess all aspects of the product's development and its market acceptance.

It should be noted that all reviews are to be conducted jointly by marketing, engineering, and manufacturing. Further, complex phases are typically broken down into additional checkpoints of designs and prototypes.

Toward the Future with Several Powerful Techniques and Methods

While the previous chapter described a number of scheduling techniques, this chapter presents several technical approaches that can facilitate concurrent engineering. These methodologies can assist in almost any stage of the product development. In instance after instance, their use has sliced the time or cost in half or more.

A Philosophical Viewpoint

This chapter is more than just a listing of techniques. It proposes the philosophy that in the future, more and more such product-development techniques will be used. Innovation will need powerful ideas—that will never change—but to be successful, innovation will increasingly utilize techniques such as these because they greatly extend the reach of the intellect.

Hundreds of years ago, prior to the Industrial Revolution, virtually all products were manufactured by artisans and by hand. Now machines do the manufacturing, and they do it considerably better, faster, and cheaper. Machines have increased manufacturing efficiency by thousands of percent.

Today much product development and engineering design are still done largely the old artisan way—by the engineer and by hand. Yet in the years ahead, the same revolution that occurred in manufacturing will likely occur in product development. Product development will become considerably better, faster, and cheaper, and as with manufacturing, the increases of efficiency are likely to be thousands of percent. This time, however, the computer will fuel this revolution, and if the rapid increase in computer performance is any indication, these impressive gains probably will not require hundreds of years to attain but only several decades.

A number of techniques are already getting big improvements. Let us now consider some of these potent approaches in more detail.

Concept Selection

Stuart Pugh of Strathclyde University pioneered a novel technique, called concept selection, to systematically enhance the innovativeness of a design.[1] In developing a product, several different competing design approaches must often by evaluated to select the best one. Pugh's approach does not choose one approach out of several, but pools the best properties of the several competing approaches to create a brand-new and even better approach.

Any product has many—often twenty or thirty—important attributes or features like size, ease of repair, performance under heavy load, misuse resistance, and accuracy. Separately for each attribute, each different design approach is rated on how well it does on that attribute. The best design for an attribute is then analyzed to determine which particular property made it win. Finally, the team takes the winning properties and puts together a brand-new design, using the winning properties.

The product shown in the matrix in table 18–1 has five main attributes that are found in three different product designs. The "X" indicates the design that had the best performance on that specific attribute. Under the "Winner" column, the winning design for that attribute is recorded. For the attribute of weight, for example, design B provides the best performance.

Next the team figures out, for each attribute, which crucial property of the design made it win. It learns that design B rated best for weight because of its use of plastics, and that design A rated best for frequency accuracy because of its software. The team then studies the winning properties and tries to create a new design by em-

TABLE 18–1
Concept Selection Matrix

Attribute	Design A	Design B	Design C	Winner
Rust Prevention	X			A
Frequency	X			A
Accuracy			X	C
Weight		X		B
Size			X	C
Leakproof		X		B

ploying these winning properties. Often it is not possible to use all the winning properties in a new design. But the process nonetheless forces innovative thinking that typically leads to major improvements in design.

Value Analysis and Target Costing

Closely aligned to concept selection is the technique of value analysis (see chapter 16 for an example). Repeatedly, value analysis has cut the cost of producing a product by 20, 30, and even 80 percent. Value analysis views a product not as a collection of parts but as a collection of functions. By spotlighting the functions, it determines which systems and parts can provide those functions as inexpensively as possible. A ballpoint pen, for instance, provides not only a writing function but a host of other functions, including being leakproof, retractability, attractiveness, high quality, and pocket clips. The idea is to provide those functions to meet customer approval at the lowest cost.

Each function is analyzed in terms of the parts needed to supply that function. Suppose that making the pen retractable requires five parts, but making those parts constitutes half of the pen's manufacturing cost. That is too expensive for the retractability function. The designers would redesign, trying to cut that cost.

By costing out functionality, value analysis forces a study of the methods, approaches, and material. Would a plastic part be cheaper than a metal part and still provide the same functionality? Would a redesign be cheaper but provide the same functionality?

In complex equipment the functions are broken down into subfunctions. The goal, however, is to deliver each function as well and as inexpensively as possible.

Value Analysis

In this book *Value Analysis,* Theodore Fowler presents a comprehensive approach to implementing value analysis.[2] Here are the crucial steps.

1. IDENTIFY THE WHAT THE CUSTOMER WANTS. Through interviews and focus groups, determine what customers like and dislike about the product and its functionality. In particular, rate how important the different functions are to the customer.

2. BREAK THE PRODUCT DOWN INTO ITS FUNCTIONS AND SUBFUNCTIONS. THEN DETERMINE THE COST OF PROVIDING THOSE FUNCTIONS. To help the creative process, the functions should be stated as generally as possible. For example, a home central air conditioner's main function is not to "cool the air." It is to "provide comfort." That function is then broken down into its subfunctions: cool the air, reduce the humidity, circulate the air, clean the air. Those functions are further broken down into subsubfunctions. The team then estimates the cost of providing each function.

3. ANALYZE COMPETITIVE PRODUCTS FUNCTION BY FUNCTION. Traditional competitive analysis probes the competitor's product part by part. By contrast, value analysis evaluates functions and how the competition provides each function.

4. SELECT THE MOST IMPORTANT EIGHT OR TEN FUNCTIONS. BRAINSTORM HOW TO PROVIDE THOSE FUNCTIONS BETTER AT LOWER COST. On the basis of cost and importance to the customer, determine the functions that the team will analyze in depth. The team then brainstorms how to provide those functions more efficiently. It considers redesign, different materials, different manufacturing processes, and different software.

5. FOR EACH IMPROVEMENT THE TEAM DECIDES TO IMPLEMENT, DETERMINE A CHAMPION—A TEAM MEMBER WHO WILL ENSURE IT IS IMPLEMENTED.

Now consider a very important strategic use of value analysis.

Target Costing

Many firms determine a product's price by adding a markup to its manufacturing cost. In other words, the sales price is set after the cost to manufacture is known. Canon and many other top firms take the opposite approach. They first determine what price will sell in the market. On the basis of that price, they declare what the manufacturing cost must be. The key to making this "backward" approach a success is value analysis (see figure 18–1).

After determining a price that will sell in the market, Canon cal-

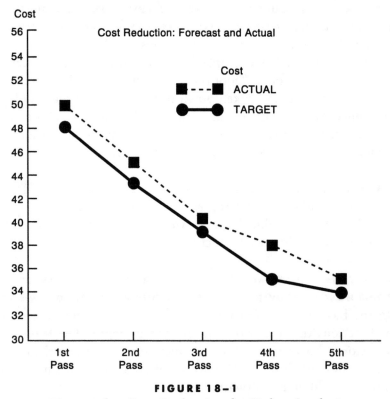

FIGURE 18–1

Targets for Cost Reduction by Value Analysis

culates a target for the product's production cost.[3] Then, over the period of the product's development, Canon subjects the design to repeated value-analysis reviews until it cuts the production cost enough to reach the target. Five or six sessions of value analysis are often needed. Several of these are two- or three-day marathons in a hotel or lodge, with experts invited. To encourage steady progress, Canon establishes goals for the cost reduction expected at each session. In this manner, Canon uses value analysis to provide an excellent product at a highly competitive price.

Suzuki takes a similar approach. Prior to opening its new plant in Hungary, it sent workers to Japan for training. Comments Laszlo Pataki, "They taught me to concentrate on every detail and ask how to do it cheaper. That was not part of the Hungarian culture. We were never taught value engineering. The Communists never did that."[4]

Capability Index

A variety of techniques can help avoid manufacturing problems and ensure that the product can be manufactured inexpensively and with excellent quality. A common difficulty occurs when, to attain high performance, the designers push the tolerances to the limit. A new generation of a product might have tolerances five to ten times tighter than the pervious generation. The problem is, when machines make parts with very exacting tolerances, they often produce many defects. Suppose a design requires a tolerance on a specification to be accurate to plus or minus one millimeter. Assume the machine's output has a standard deviation of plus or minus one-third of a millimeter. That means, after doing the statistical analysis, that the part will be out of spec about 0.3 percent of the time. But in today's world, where defect rates often must be in parts per million, this defect rate is unacceptable.

To solve this problem, William Smith, Motorola vice-president, recommends the use of the capability index, C. More precisely, for any given specification,

$$C = \frac{\text{(tolerance allowed by the design)}}{\text{(normal variation of manufacturing process)}}$$

The tolerance is the maximum allowable range of the specification—that is, plus or minus one millimeter. It is determined by the engineering design. The variation will depend upon the machines doing the manufacturing—that is, plus or minus one-third of a millimeter. The C index should be high, meaning that the tolerance allowed will be much greater than the normal variation of the machine. Having a high C reduces defects.

Smith advocates using the capability index because it encourages cooperation on the cross-functional team. In particular, engineering design determines the numerator, while manufacturing is responsible for the denominator. Achieving a high capability index thus forces engineering and manufacturing to get together to jointly ensure that the product will be of excellent quality.

Design for Manufacturing (DFM)

Because manufacturing issues are so important, an entire field called design for manufacturability and assembly (DFM) has grown up. It has already been mentioned in chapters 2 and 16 because it is so useful. Early in the design phase, as seen in chapter 15, major decisions are made that determine how easy or difficult a product will be to manufacture. DFM tells the designer for almost any design how easy it will be to manufacture and how to make it easier to manufacture.

Using these techniques to build a computer mouse, Digital Equipment Corporation reduced assembly operations from eighty-three to fifty-four, cut assembly time in half, and sliced 47 percent off the cost of materials.[5] Even the cost of packaging was cut from 59 cents to 24 cents. IBM bought its printers from Seiko Epson in Japan, which took thirty minutes to assemble a unit. Using DFM, IBM started making its own and doing it in three minutes.[6]

DFM probes many issues in the design, including:

- Can the number of parts be reduced? Parts reduction is one of the most effective ways to cut manufacturing cost and improve quality. In many cases, DFM techniques have cut the number of parts in half or more.
- If a part must be tested, can it easily be removed for testing?
- Can parts be easily installed by a robot? A robot, for instance, might need a delicate sensing device to pick up parts.

- Can fasteners be eliminated? Fasteners not only add extra steps in assembly, they loosen, causing slippage, rattles, and misalignment. Push-and-snap assembly can often be substituted.
- If parts are stacked upon each other, will there be a drift in alignment that throws off the tolerances?
- Is the sequence of assembly optimal? Usually many choices exist as to which parts should go into what subassemblies, or which parts should be in what locations. Surprising as it might seem, even a relatively simple unit like the front wheel of an automobile can be assembled in hundreds of different ways.
- Can the need for adjustments in the product be eliminated? Screws, springs, pulleys can often be eliminated.
- In assembling the product, must a part be turned over, which wastes effort?
- Can a part be reused (multiple use), minimizing the number of different parts? Many engineers have a tendency to want to design the unique perfect part, when the same part could be used in multiple applications.

Jigs and fixtures, for example, hold parts in place, and often they must be individually designed for each part. When making a variety of parts, the jigs and fixtures typically must be changed for each part—a time-consuming process. Jigless production is much quicker. It either eliminates the jigs and fixtures altogether, or it creates universal jigs that fit all the parts.

DFM works, and by using it for a cash register, Schonberger notes, NCR reduced the number of purchased parts from 115 to 10, in large part by eliminating screws and fasteners and using push-and-snap assembly instead.[7] To promote reuse, NCR made the access doors identical, even though the doors had different purposes, and it used a cathode ray tube and speaker from other products. In fact, the team made the assembly so simple that an engineer could assemble it blindfolded—and Schonberger includes in his account a photograph to prove it. The team also made repair very easy—snap out the old part and snap in the new. Schonberger reports that during the business day of a fast-food store, a repair person replaced a circuit board in the cash register in less than sixty seconds.

In most manufacturing processes, computer programs implement these and other DFM principles, helping designers create a product that can be manufactured inexpensively and with high quality.[8] The programs can even score a design, telling the designer how hard it will be to manufacture.

Time to Market versus Time to Design an Excellent Manufacturing Process

DFM recognizes that developing the most efficient manufacturing process requires time, and that taking that time sometimes delays getting a product to market. In fact, when speed to market is primary, using a decent but not really outstanding design might be better in order to save time. Kodak did that with its Fling 35 (later renamed FunSaver) disposable camera, to rush the product to market against competition from Fuji.

To evaluate the tradeoff between rushing to market and taking the time to develop excellent manufacturing, MIT's Karl Ulrich and his associates have suggested an excellent approach.[9] This approach considers two design alternatives; one fast to market, the other slower to market but cheaper to manufacture. Then it selects the one with superior lifetime costs.

Suppose there are two options to assemble a part: by hand, or by a robot. The robot produces cheaper manufacturing costs, but the by-hand approach is faster to market. The detailed costs of the two alternatives might be examined, as in table 18–2 (adapted from Wheelwright and Clark). The far-right column is the total added cost of option 2 over option 1, where the costs are calculated for the entire life of the product. In this example, the time required to purchase, install, and program the robot delayed entry into the market and caused a loss of sales. That loss exceeded the cost savings the robot provided in assembly. Hand assembly, thus, was the winner.

With the Fling camera, Kodak sacrificed ease of manufacturability in order to get the product to the market faster. It should also be noted that after the initial model got out, Kodak had more time and improved the manufacturability of subsequent models.

Overall, however, and relative to concurrent engineering, DFM helps designers up front—where it can be of significant benefit—to evaluate the manfuacturing issues and create designs that can be easily and cheaply manufactured.

TABLE 18–2

Comparison of Costs: Robot versus Hand Assembly

Cost	Option 1: Human Assembly	Option 2: Robot Assembly	Lifetime Cost Impact of Option 2 versus Option 1 (in thousands of dollars)*
Material cost	Same	Same	−35
Labor cost	Yes	Small, for maintenance	
Capital cost	None	Cost of robot	+15
System cost	None	Program and maintain robot	+10
Cost of later market entry	Shorter lead time, faster to market	Longer lead time: must purchase, install, program, robot	+25
		TOTAL	+15

*A positive number means option 1 is superior.

Design of Experiments (DOE)

Engineers usually have considerable latitude in setting certain parameters. Setting them properly can significantly enhance performance and yield, or cut cost. To make a part, for example, suppose the designers must set three basic parameters; thickness, temperature, and flexibility. Usually these parameters are placed at standard settings. But suppose a more ingenious engineer decides to experiment in order to improve the performance of the part. The first thing he will likely do is to test each parameter separately. That is, he will change one parameter and test its effect, and after that he will change the next parameter and test its effect.

Design of experiments (DOE) methods do something quite different—they change all the parameters at once. This is important not only because it saves time but because it reveals interaction effects that cannot be uncovered with simpler approaches.

The interaction effects are where the "gee whiz" results of DOE methods occur, according to Paul Kantor, CEO of Tantalus. Suppose an engineer changes thickness and obtains a 10 percent improvement; also suppose a change in temperature produces a 10 percent improvement. The "gee whiz" occurs because when both are changed at once, the result might be a 50 percent improvement. The factors may interact in unexpected and unusual ways that are rather astonishing.

It is not easily explained why this occurs because the human brain thinks linearly. Ten percent plus 10 percent does not yield 50 percent. But in a nonlinear system, surprisingly, they sometimes do yield 50 percent. The DOE methods are far stronger than the brain surmises because they exploit these hidden nonlinear interactions, which seem almost magical or paradoxical yet are often rampant in engineering design.

Taguchi Methods

Taguchi methods (introduced in Chapter 16) take DOE one step further.[10] DOE seeks the parameter settings to yield the top performance, and in the above example, DOT set the parameters thickness, temperature, and flexibility. Genichi Taguchi, however, observed that there are other factors—"noise" factors—that are not under the control of the designer, such as the humidity and the stresses the part will undergo.

Taguchi perceived that the success of a product is influenced by two different classes of factors. The first class is the controllable factors—the specific design parameters that the designers can set. The second class is the noise (uncontrollable) factors—the ones that the designer cannot influence, such as external random factors that the product will face in use, uncontrollable aspects of manufacturing, and deterioration.

Taguchi recommends selecting the settings of the controllable factors to be good against the expected range of noise factors. Thus, in our example, the time, temperature, and mix would be selected to yield a good result, even if the humidity varies or the stresses on the part change.

Without Taguchi methods, it is possible for a product to have good performance when the noise factors are at one level, but poor performance when they are at another level. Taguchi methods help the product become effective over the full range of expected noise factors. Moreover, in the Taguchi methods, decisions about the controllable factors are based on providing the best possible performance from the customer's viewpoint.

If a product works effectively over the likely range of random factors (see Chapter 16), it is called robust. Taguchi methods make products robust because they ensure that products perform well not just in the laboratory but even against uncontrollable factors encountered in manufacturing and customer use.

William Golomski, international consultant and lecturer at the University of Chicago, provides the following example. Decorative wheel covers on many automobiles add style and flair and often help sell a car. But their design is more than a fashion statement. An important technical feature is their retention force, or ability to stay on the wheel. The retention force must be strong enough to keep the cover on the wheel despite road shocks and bumps. Yet if that force is too strong, it prevents a person from removing the cover, should a tire need to be changed. The ideal retention force, therefore, must be in a narrow band.

The wheel cover designers are thus confronted with several concerns.

- The cover must be stylish and attractive.
- The retention force must be right.
- The manufacturing cost should as an inexpensive as possible.

Taguchi methods efficiently test a wide variety of cover designs to determine one that correctly balances these three concerns.

Taguchi methods contribute another indispensable advantage. In a product of even minimal complexity—say, a radio—hundreds of design choices must be made. In practice, five to ten percent of these are likely to be poor choices. A poor design choice might cause later problems in manufacturing or customer use and, when discovered, might have to be changed. In many projects, in fact, a great many changes are required, adding considerable delay and expense. Taguchi methods efficiently test the design to uncover poor choices, thereby significantly reducing the need for later changes. In the Fuji-Xerox example mentioned in chapter 16, Taguchi methods helped prevent so many changes that they cut the time and cost of development by more than half.

Barry Bebb, retired vice-president of Xerox, strongly believes that Taguchi methods and the robustness they provide, underlie good product design. They ensure not only that the product performs well from the customer's viewpoint, they also reduce the time and cost of innovation.

Prototyping

Buried in the discussion of scheduling in the previous chapter was a point that problems and fumbles often occur at the interfaces. When items are put together, vast new complexities open up because parts often interact in strange and unusual ways. As more and more parts are put together, the possibility that a problem could occur seems to skyrocket, and many of these problems are quite unexpected. Heat, stress, and vibration occur, and spurious signals and data seem to multiply. Moreover, these problems are often concealed until late in the project because putting parts together often occurs late in the project. Bob Friesen of IBM recalls a project in which each component worked perfectly, but when the team put all the components together, the product would not operate, and months of delay ensued. The same problem is notorious in software.

One quite effective means to tackle this interface issue is called short-interval prototyping—in other words, making prototypes early and frequently. These check what happens when everything is put together. To prototype early when parts are not finished, simulate them. That is exactly what Roger Covey and Jim Franch did with their AS/SET program (see Chapter 12). Also, since the most crucial interface is the one with the customer, check how potential customers react even to very preliminary mockups.

Stereolithography

As Covey and Franch's experience reveals, quick prototyping is very useful in software. But new advances are also making it impressive for hardware. The major development here, called stereolithography, is the ability to very quickly make plastic models of even rather complex objects. Usually a computer-driven laser beam hits a bath of special material, and where the beam hits, a chemical reaction forms the model. Previously, machine shops usually had to make models, which often took weeks. But with stereolithography, models can be ready in hours, often at a savings of thousands of dollars.[11] A study of a number of stereolithography projects, conducted by David Tait of Laserform, reported time savings of 42 to 84 percent and cost savings of 30 to 65 percent.[12]

The products being modeled include jet engine turbines, surgical implants for humans, electrical connectors, car fenders, and a host of other items. The models are not as strong as metal, but they are quite strong and can expose many problems. For example, a twenty-one-inch model was developed of the giant 350-foot Green Bank radiotelescope. If it had been assembled using conventional means, the model would have required 6,500 parts, but stereolithography did it with only twenty-five. The designers were very worried that the telescope could be toppled in a high wind. The model permitted the design to be tested and improved in a wind tunnel.[13]

Prototyping as a Management Approach

Prototypes should be considered not merely as technical tools but, Wheelwright and Clark state, as major management control points in a product's development.[14] Prototyping puts parts together to test what works and to clarify what steps must be taken next. Most products go through several cycles of prototypes. Prototypes require all the key players to come together and check the status of the entire project and thus provide definite review points. In fact, as they did with the Bandit project in the previous chapter, prototype deadlines can form the major milestones in a development effort.

Steven Wheelwright and Dave Ellison of Harvard investigated prototyping at a number of different firms that designed PC boards for work stations. They discovered that slower firms handled the prototype process much differently from the faster firms. The slower firms took four to six weeks between prototypes. When they finished a major phase of the project, they prototyped in order to test their progress. The faster firms did something quite different. They prototyped every two weeks—not when they were ready to prototype but on a fixed and tight schedule, as in the Bandit example.

Interestingly, even though the swiftest firms allotted half the time, they made as much progress between prototypes as the slower firms did. By attacking and eradicating fumbles, they learned to do things faster. The slower firms, by contrast, were still plagued by many easily correctable "goofs"—a dimension on a drawing was incorrect, or the part made did not conform to the specifications.

Further, if the fabrication of the board was done by an outside supplier, the best firms established better and quicker interactions with the supplier. Some of the best firms paid the supplier more for rapid turnaround. Although this might sound costly, time is usually the most crucial aspect of product development. And when the engineers are waiting for the supplier to make the board, they are wasting engineering time, which is costly. In particular, the top firm strove to "leverage" its engineers' time so they could do productive things as much as possible. It got that board back from the supplier quickly.

To further speed their progress, the leading firms made sure their manufacturing people were involved in the prototyping. Manufacturing could then simultaneously work out the production problems.

The very quick prototyping cycles also helped reduce problems that occurred at interfaces. Under the old approach, a person would make a change in a part, but it would be difficult to trace how that change affected other parts. Short-interval prototyping let the person quickly learn the impact of any change and prevented time from being wasted on wrong approaches.

This technique of prototyping on a fast fixed schedule, Wheelwright and Clark call periodic prototyping.[15] They have studied it in a number of industries, seen its effectiveness, and highly recommend it as a powerful method for enhancing the product development process. Periodic prototyping then becomes the means to schedule much of the project.

Honda's Prototyping

Honda prototypes on a fast schedule, according to Scott Whitlock, executive vice-president, and Dave Nelson, vice-president. Particularly when a new car is being developed, it might go through ten to twelve prototypes or trial builds, with a new prototype built every two weeks. That pace might seem extremely tight for automobiles, but Honda has learned how to do it. During the prototyping phase, not only the engineers but the top suppliers almost live at the testing site. For the first couple of prototypes, the parts might not fit, says Nelson, but the team quickly gets them to fit and the car fully operating.

A Caveat

Quick prototyping can be very useful, but like all techniques discussed in this book, can backfire if it is used improperly. One serious concern, as Gerald Hock of General Electric emphasizes, is that management will see an early prototype and then say, "It looks good. Just tidy it up a bit, and get it out fast." Management will take a rough, even experimental prototype and force the developers to rush it out. This locks the developers into what is usually a very inadequate and preliminary design concept. If the management of your firm is like that, disregard everything said here and wait until late in the process before prototyping.

Overall, interfaces—whether they are between components or between the product and the customer—can cause serious fumbles and must be handled astutely. Prototypes provide a means to test interfaces. With adequate regard to the warning just given, management should prototype early, even if some parts must be simulated. Prototypes also provide unmistakable checkpoints on progress. Indeed, for many products, periodic prototyping on a fixed, tight schedule provides an excellent means for management to control and direct the project.

Computer Assistance

In the future, computer-aided design, or CAD (here used generically to subsume any computer-aided activity in design, marketing, engineering, manufacturing, or software) will increasingly be the prime mechanism that cuts the time and cost of product development. Nearly all the techniques that this chapter discusses rely in part upon the computer—whether it is robustness, the "gee whiz" effects of DOE, the DFM, or prototyping. Karl Ulrich of MIT believes that most engineers presently make design decisions using rules of thumb, but that that is inadequate because rules of thumb are likely to be in error. The brain is limited to linear thinking, yet many design decisions are nonlinear. The computer, with its blinding speed, can hunt out even very complex design possibilities, searching for the "gee whiz" effects. Ulrich and his colleagues, for example, are developing programs to design PC boards. This horrendously complex affair involves making decisions about spacing between lines, width of lines, number of layers, materials, and gold plating. The computer helps cut through this thicket of alternatives to root out the right design.

CAD helped Eastman Kodak rush development of its Fling (Fun-Saver) camera when it learned that in just six months Fuji would market a disposable 35-millimeter camera in the United States. As Wheelwright and Clark report, Kodak had to cut its normal product development time of sixty-five to seventy weeks to just forty.[16] Although Kodak had previously used CAD on parts, this time the team used CAD to design the entire camera, even to design the tooling to manufacture the parts. Since CAD is often difficult to learn, the Kodak team made special efforts to employ a very user-friendly system. The system allowed the engineers to easily zoom in or out, from a single part to a subassembly or even to the entire camera, letting them see how all levels of the camera interacted.

Every night, all the work done that day was uploaded into the database. Since a change in one part might influence many other parts, the next day everyone had access to the latest changes throughout the entire product. Changes in the tool and mold designs were also input because CAD was used to help design them. The CAD program was thus accurate and up-to-date, helping engineers to design quickly and find potential difficulties quickly.

CAD also facilitated communications and coordinated the different participating groups, report Wheelwright and Clark. Although CAD required more work up-front, it cut the tooling time from five weeks to one and overall saved significant time. Most important, it helped Kodak successfully counter the threat from Fuji.

Using CAD to design a small disposable camera is one thing. But using it for a large commercial airplane is quite another. Boeing is building its 777 totally on the computer, making it the first commercial airframe design to be "paperless." CAD permits engineers to examine a three-dimensional drawing of a part from any angle, or to see a wing flap unfold on the screen. The computer automatically checks for errors as well, as when one designer tries to run a hydraulic line where another designer wants to run electrical wires. Indeed, CAD has reduced mistakes so much that, unlike previously, Boeing no longer has to build a full-scale mockup.[17]

The computer can also help analyze extremely complex physical phenomena. For instance, automakers typically spend five years and several hundred million dollars developing a car or truck engine.[18] Cray Research has developed software that reveals the gases and explosions inside an engine's combustion chamber in full color and vivid detail on a computer screen. Using the software, the engineer can find the design that, for example, gives peak power while reducing emissions. The software reduces the need to build and test prototypes and should slice a year off of the development time.

Hirsch Cohen, the perceptive senior program officer at the Sloan Foundation, has placed his finger on the future. Customized computer logic chips, he notes, used to be cumbersome and time-consuming to design, involving many stages of effort. Now they are designed quickly and easily by a person sitting in front of a computer. The computer calculates the exact specifications for the foundry to make the chip.

In the years ahead much of product development, Cohen believes, will come from a person at a computer rapidly designing almost any features wanted. The computer will not be operating alone, of course, but will be coupled to a host of other methods

TABLE 18–3

Summary of Innovation Techniques

1. Concept selection
   - Pools the best features of several designs
2. Value analysis
   - Provides the product's functions at lowest cost
3. Target costing
   - Uses value analysis repeatedly to ensure the final design is manufacturable at the targeted cost.
4. Capability index
   - Improves product quality
   - Promotes coordination of design and engineering
5. Design for manufacturing and assembly
   - Simplifies manufacturing of product
6. Time to market versus time in design
   - Evaluates benefits of shorter time to market versus better design
7. Design of experiments
   - Tests several parameters of the product at once
8. Taguchi methods
   - Account for uncontrollable factors
   - Provide robustness
9. Prototyping
   - Tests interfaces between components and between product and customer
   - Provides schedule and control points for project management
10. Computer support
    - Facilitates rapid design

and techniques, such as those described in this chapter. Indeed, these trends portend the future—a deluge of new techniques, usually computer-related, to make product development faster, cheaper, and better, perhaps by thousands of percentage points.

Summary

A number of techniques can impressively cut the speed and cost of product development (see table 18–3). Design for manufacturing and assembly can reduce the cost and improve the quality of manufacturing. DOE and Taguchi methods can uncover hidden nonlinearities and boost performance and quality. Using prototypes permits early testing and validation, thereby avoiding later headaches. Moreover, the computer will pilot and control the implementation of nearly all of these concepts. Techniques such as these can help reduce fumbles and enhance product development. More important, they extend the reach of the mind to yield great improvements in innovation.

Improve Continuously

Implementing Continuous Improvement

Whatever process is used to develop a product today, it will be wrong tomorrow, because the world is improving. But in today's furiously competitive environment, where everyone is trying to improve, success demands that a firm improve faster than its competitors. This means that improvement must be systematic and structured, with goals, measures, and procedures. This chapter presents how to stay ahead by considering the concept of continuous improvement. Specifically, it explores metrics, post-mortems, and a number of other potent procedures, including a different way to look at planning.

Planning as a Means for Improvement

Traditionally, the purpose of planning a project is to plan the project. That sounds reasonable, but it is not—it disregards the fact that many other projects will be planned in the future and that planning the present project should also improve future projects. Incorporated into a plan should be clear criteria and measures to help the firm do better in the future. General Motors executive Al Jordan mentions that GM is now developing two thousand such measures. Discovering that 50 percent of engineering documents are late or that a supplier is slow, for example, can provide much information that can be used to improve.

Continuous Improvement Paradigm

To include continuous improvement in their planning, many firms start by implementing the following two steps:

1. Determine improvement goals and objectives.
2. Establish metrics (performance measures) to monitor whether progress toward the improvement goals is being made.

The first step establishes explicit goals for improvement, but it generally has little value without a definite procedure to monitor progress. Hence the second step. Consider now how several top firms implement these steps.

3M, as we saw in chapter 1, has the overall goal of improving product innovation. To encourage that, it requires its divisions to have 25 percent of sales come from products developed in the last five years. This 25 percent of sales is the metric that monitors success in meeting the overall goal.

Motorola established the following goals and metrics for improving quality and cutting cycle time.[1]

1. Quality is to be improved by a factor of ten every two years (68 percent per year).
2. Cycle time is to be cut by 50 percent each year.

Interestingly, these two goals apply not just to manufacturing but to all areas of the firm, including office work, sales, finance, distribution, and administration.

To monitor quality, Motorola employs the metric of total defects per unit—defects per item manufactured, errors made in a sales order, or errors made in an invoice. Cycle time is the time required to complete a process—the time it takes to manufacture a product, the time it takes to respond to a customer request, the time it takes to close the books each month, or the time it takes to file a patent application.

Even though these goals are very ambitious, according to Bill Smith and Paul Noakes, vice-presidents, Motorola is meeting them. The quality of many products is now measured in terms of a few parts per million defects. Cycle time improvement is also on target. One of the most important cycle-time metrics is the time from when a customer places an order until the product is shipped. In its communications sector, Motorola cut the average from fifty-four days to fewer than fourteen in a couple of years, and it is still cutting. For some products the time from order to shipment is just a few hours, and that includes making the product.

Anticipation

Anticipation, as this book has emphasized, is a vital goal for continuous improvement. At every phase of the development process, the team should formally anticipate what problems might arise in later phases. A metric to monitor that goal might seem difficult to conceive, but NEC has found the following one to be of great value.[2]

$$\text{Percent problems anticipated} = \frac{\text{total number of problems anticipated}}{\text{total number of problems that occurred}} \times 100\%$$

The total number of problems that occurred includes both those anticipated and those not anticipated.

At the end of each phase NEC records the problems that actually did occur. Then the team takes steps to prevent similar problems from arising in the future. To facilitate this analysis, they classify the problems by cause, such as:

- incomplete design review
- inadequate understanding of customer
- inadequate training of personnel
- failure to coordinate.

Problems are also classified by the aspect of the project in which they occurred, such as

- circuit design
- mask design
- prototype.

By systematically taking steps to prevent the occurrence of unanticipated events in the future, NEC has seen a steady rise in the metric—that is, in the percent of problems anticipated.

Satisfying the Customer

In innovation the must crucial goal is satisfying the customer, and NEC even uses a metric to check this: the design sample hit rate, or the percent of design samples accepted by a customer without any modification. Suppose a company wants NEC to design certain microchips. NEC would show early design samples of the chips to the customer. NEC would then calculate the percent of design samples that the customer liked. For the samples that are not fully acceptable to the customer, the NEC team would identify and attack the causes of the problem. The most frequent problem NEC found, for example, was inadequate understanding of what the customer wanted in the first place. By working on this and other problems, NEC has boosted this metric and satisfied its customers better.

Other Goals and Metrics

In obtaining continuous improvement, goals and metrics are essential. For most applications, however, it is necessary to state only the metric, as the goal will then be obvious. Here are several examples of useful metrics. Motorola, as mentioned in chapter 16, uses metrics to predict how many staff hours will be required to do the steps of a project. Motorola also employs metrics to measure:

- how long it will take to obtain a part from a supplier
- how far a project is ahead of or behind schedule
- how many of the design reviews initially scheduled are actually held
- how many changes are made in the product definition.

For example, if the number of changes in the product definition is too high, the reasons for that are investigated and corrected.

Metrics can be applied to almost any area of innovation, including:

- interaction between designers and customers
- staffing levels
- accuracy of cost estimation
- extent of reuse (of designs, of systems, of parts, of manufacturing processes)

- revisions of design (number revisions per project, number of layouts changed)
- cycle time (the time to complete a specific type of design task)
- quality (warranty costs, bugs, defects).

Also, since support activities can cause severe delays in product development, as noted in chapter 9, management should establish improvement metrics for the time and quality of obtaining approvals, scheduling reviews, getting models made, and processing purchase orders. Several specific examples of metrics are provided in this chapter's appendix.

Obtaining the Improvement

A warning must be issued here. Establishing metrics does not by itself do much good. Even worse, it might do harm. In a classic example, a firm put in a metric to monitor quality and reduce defects. Defects were indeed reduced. But the production employees did this by throwing away parts that were not perfect, and the scrap rate skyrocketed. To make one measure better, they made another measure worse.

Root-Cause Analysis

Certainly, trading one problem for another is not helpful; we want to actually improve. The key to doing that is to eliminate the original root cause of a problem. Indeed, root-cause removal is perhaps the most important concept in continuous improvement. Rather than improving quality by increasing scrap, the company should have eliminated the original causes of the defects. Possibly machines drifted out of alignment, or dirt got into the process, or parts were being damaged in storage. Problems like these are the underlying sources of the bad quality, and they should be ferreted out and corrected.

Eliminating original root causes prevents the problems from recurring in the future and obtains true improvement. Taiichi Ohno pioneered this idea in the 1950s at Toyota. When a machine was leaking a bit of oil, the suggested solution was to add more oil to the crank case. But Ohno said that that did not get rid of the cause of the problem. He asked why the oil was leaking in the first place. The engineers found a pipe with a tiny hairline crack in it and wanted to replace the pipe. But Ohno said that that did not get rid of the cause. He asked why the pipe had split in the first place. The engineers found excessive vibration of the machine and wanted to replace the machine. But Ohno said that that still did not isolate the cause of the problem, which might occur again in the new machine. Finally, the engineers determined that the pipe did not have enough support, so they added two brackets, and the problem was finally eliminated.

In this example, none of the suggested solutions except the last would have prevented the problem from recurring. Rather, the original root cause of the problem had to be searched out and eliminated. Eliminating the root causes is what makes continuous improvement so useful—it assures true improvement.

Post-Mortems

One of the most widespread techniques in continuous improvement is the post-mortem, a careful and formal review of how well a project has proceeded (see table 19–1). It is typically done at the end of a development project, although a smaller post-mortem might be done after each phase. Its purpose is to identify the errors, delays, and other problems in the project. Then, by isolating their root causes, the team implements steps to ensure that in the future the problems do not recur (or at least occur considerably less often). The post-mortems prevent important knowledge gained during the

TABLE 19–1
Post-Mortems

Conduct a major post-mortem at end of project, and a minor one at end of each phase.

- Identify what went right and wrong, and how to improve.
- Implement findings with a special action team.
- Create a database repository of what was learned.
- Review past findings at the start of new projects.
- Train teams in how to search for original root causes.

project from being lost. Top companies like Motorola, Honda, IBM, and Xerox employ post-mortems. At Xerox, for projects of any magnitude, the post-mortem is called the presidential review because the president personally attends.

IBM, according to executives Robert Mays and Don Studinski, uses a formal post-mortem process for its software development. At the end of a project, the team discusses any problem that took place and how it might be prevented in the future. The central concepts of the post-mortem are:

1. Every individual should learn from his or her own errors.
2. Every individual should learn from other people's errors.

IBM, however, discovered long ago that it could not expect a development team to implement the ideas they conceived in the post-mortem meeting themselves. It has formed a special action group of people to do that. Depending upon the problem found in the post-mortem, the action group might provide training on how to avoid it or publish information on it. The action group, in particular, maintains a database repository of the problems that the post-mortems found, coded by key words for easy retrieval. Whenever software engineers are tackling a particular type of issue, by accessing the database they can discover what problems occurred in similar situations in the past and how to avoid them.

One of the best times to learn how to avoid problems, Mays and Studinski note, is right at the start of developing a new product. The senior people on a project team check the database about potential problems that might occur, and they present that information to the team at the initial kickoff meeting.

Results

Mays and Studinski report excellent results from their post-mortems, the technique chopping error rates by 50 percent. With fewer errors injected into the system, inspection and rework costs and time have dropped. In one project, they said that due to the time savings, "We finished sixteen weeks ahead of schedule."

Motorola's experience has been similar. According to Ron Akers, his group instituted post-mortems after his boss proclaimed, "I'm tired of getting so many systems errors." The post-mortems involved not just the development team but everyone associated with the project, including sales and marketing personnel. The ideas generated not only cut errors but enhanced performance and improved customer satisfaction. Akers says that from this Motorola got seven-figure savings.

Training

Just throwing the development team together to conduct a post-mortem, however, might not work. John Milford of Northern Telecom describes what generally happens then. A specific bug is brought up for discussion, and the ways to prevent the bug in the future are considered. People will say, "Just give me more time. If I had had more time, I could have detected the bug."

The problem, he notes, is training. People need training in how to search for and eliminate root causes. They must learn to think about the actions that will prevent a problem from re-occurring at all. In the IBM case, many errors were traced to a lack of clear understanding of what the customer wanted, or to not taking the time to clarify interfaces with other parts or modules. To help post-mortems proceed properly, IBM often has an experienced facilitator sit in.

At Mentor Graphics a special person assists with post-mortems. At the end of each phase, it is his job to go around to the team members and interview them about what happened during that phase. In this way he records not just the problems but the successes.

Other Improvement Techniques

Teams

For another powerful approach to improvement, assign a team to attack a specific problem. Motorola, according to Frank Lloyd, vice-president, has teams analyze key aspects of the development process. One team might study prototypes in order to figure out how to reduce the number of prototypes needed or to cut the time between prototypes. Another team might consider the issue of reuse and how to increase the reuse of designs and parts. Additional teams are assigned to improve support processes, such as the processing of purchase orders.

Data Beget More Data

After a firm gains experience with these concepts, something curious is often revealed: the need for more detailed data on the specifics of the processes. Randy Young, vice-president of Intel, notes that teams there collect data on just about everything: problems, delays, quality, costs, and yields. Much of these data are captured automatically in a computer. The information is immediately fed back into the process to improve it. Similarly, Motorola is developing a computerized system to automatically record bugs in software. Indeed, the more data are collected, the more their value will be revealed and the more data will be wanted.

A Caveat

Consider now a deep and ominous issue concerning continuous improvement—one that we have encountered before: fear. Metrics, post-mortems, and many other continuous-improvement techniques require the identification and examination of errors and mistakes. If people are afraid that management will hold an error against them, fear is the result. That fear, real or imagined, will kill the improvement process.

Incontrovertible safeguards must be established to ensure that this situation does not occur. Even a rumor of this can kill an improvement effort, say Robert Mays and Don Studinski of IBM. There, top management at one point actually had to come in and promise that no errors would be associated with individuals and that the purpose of examining errors was solely to manage projects better.

Summary

Traditionally, the purpose of planning was to plan, but planning now has an additional purpose: to facilitate continuous improve-

TABLE 19–2

Summary of Continuous Improvement

- Establish goals and objectives for improvement.
- Use metrics to monitor progress.
- Eliminate root causes.
- Use post-mortems and teams to conduct continuous improvement.
- Eliminate fear.

ment (see table 19–2). Improvement goals, metrics, and post-mortems should be built directly into the plan. All these procedures have one cardinal aim—to pinpoint and eradicate the root causes of problems. For them to work, however, it is crucial to eliminate fear. If people are afraid they will be blamed for mistakes, they will resist coming forward with problems, and improvement will cease.

Appendix
Improvement Metrics

Here are several specific examples of metrics, adapted from Hewlett-Packard.[3]

Designer-Customer Interaction

To promote more interaction between designers and customers, the firm might monitor the metric:

$$\text{understanding customer needs} = \frac{\text{visits to customers}}{\text{number of designers}}$$

This metric quantifies the amount of contact that designers or engineers have with customers.

Overall Effectiveness of Product Development

To measure the overall effectiveness of a product development program, the following metrics might be helpful:

$$\text{Staffing level effectivness} = \frac{\text{staff initially forecast as needed for a project}}{\text{staff actually needed by the project}} \times 100\%$$

The above metric monitors how close the projections for the staff needed on a project matched the actual staffing required by the project.

$$\text{Stability of the design} = \frac{\text{number of design changes in a project}}{\text{total cost of project}} \times 100\%$$

The above metric tracks the number of design changes made. As larger projects might need more changes simply because they are larger, this metric, by dividing by the project's cost, adjusts for the size of the project.

Overall Effectiveness of the Innovation Process

The following metric evaluates the overall effectiveness of the innovation process:

$$\text{Innovation effectiveness} = \frac{\text{number of projects finishing development}}{\text{number of projects started development}} \times 100\%$$

Other Metrics

Other metrics can also be useful in monitoring the project, such as:

$$\text{Progress rate of project} = \frac{\text{months late}}{\text{total months initially scheduled for project}}$$

$$\text{Cost estimation} = \frac{\text{actual cost of phase}}{\text{projected cost of phase}}$$

$$\text{Milestone progress rate} = \frac{\text{number of milestones reached during month}}{\text{number of milestones scheduled that month}} \times 100\%$$

Action Plan

Lightning Strategy for Innovation can dramatically improve innovation, reducing time and cost and enhancing effectiveness. To help top management strive for these improvements, this chapter outlines a step-by-step action plan to implement LSFI. It also reviews some of the central concepts and spotlights how LSFI ideas are significantly different from traditional approaches to innovation. Finally, the chapter appendix suggests an outline of how to audit the product innovation process. (The appendix also serves as a detailed review of LSFI.)

Action Plan for LSFI

The following action plan presents steps that top management might take to implement the LSFI concepts. The action plan itself is a composite of the best approaches used by General Electric, Ford, and Canon.

I. Organizational and Management Structure of the Task Force Team

1. FORM A TASK FORCE TO ANALYZE THE PROCESS. Select a core team of the "best and brightest" people to analyze the innovation process. The team members should have an excellent understanding of product development and be personally highly regarded. The core team will usually include representatives from marketing, engineering, software, manufacturing, and quality, with other experts as needed. The exact size and composition of the team, of course, will depend upon the firm.

2. THE TEAM MEMBERS SHOULD WORK FULL TIME ON THE TASK FORCE.

The core team members should be relieved of all other duties and work full time for the task force. Chapter 15 discussed the need for total concentration. The same applies here as well, because piecemeal efforts get piecemeal results. Certainly the thought of removing several of the very best people from the firing line where they are crucially needed is unpleasant. But at least for a period of time, the higher priority should be improving the innovation process itself.

3. THE TASK FORCE SHOULD REPORT DIRECTLY TO THE CEO.

The task force should be viewed not as just another study group, but as a team with the authority of the chief executive. When the task force requests information from a person, that individual should understand that the task force speaks for the highest executive in the company.

4. THE TASK FORCE SHOULD HAVE WEEKLY MEETINGS OF AT LEAST ONE HOUR WITH THE CEO TO DISCUSS PROGRESS.

Task force members might often want to wait and involve the CEO only when the task force has something to say. On the contrary, the CEO should be directly involved in the deliberations and understand the nuances. Moreover, the CEO's direct interaction signals to everyone that this project is important.

Another frequent objection is that the CEO is an accountant or lawyer and so does not understand innovation. Therefore he or she cannot be helpful and need not participate in weekly meetings. That reasoning is flawed. Especially a CEO who is not knowledgeable in innovation should be involved. His or her lack of knowledge about innovation is probably causing problems now. In that case, twice-weekly meetings might be advisable.

5. THE TASK FORCE SHOULD QUICKLY MAKE AN EXPLICIT RECOMMENDATION TO THE CEO FOR IMPROVEMENT, EVEN IF THE IMPROVEMENT IS SMALL.

Some people may believe the task force should wait until thoroughly analyzing the situation before it makes any recommendations. However, that might take so long that while people are waiting, the task force's credibility is impaired. Getting a quick hit is important. Within several weeks, the task force should suggest some change, even a small one, that clearly improves the situation. Doing that establishes believability, gains support throughout the organization, and eases the remainder of the task force's work.

6. THE TASK FORCE SHOULD SPEAK WITH AND INVOLVE AS MANY PEOPLE AS POSSIBLE AT ALL LEVELS OF THE ORGANIZATION. The task force members may have a tendency to go off by themselves and consider what should be done. Instead, both to gain organizational support and to gather facts, the task force should speak to people in all relevant areas of the organization. It is crucial to have input from the worker level, where much of the action takes place and where many of the real problems are uncovered. In chapter 15 we saw that GM's involvement of assembly-line workers produced major improvements.

II. Functional Duties of the Task Force

With the organizational issues considered, the task force should start to dig out the facts. Its major task is to gather data on the causes of fumbles, delays, and unanticipated changes, as that will reveal where to make improvements. Recall from chapter 9 how the Canon team obtained data and found significant wastes of time. Based upon that information, Canon cut its product development time in half.

To collect the data, the task force might examine the innovation activity from two different perspectives. First, it might audit the overall innovation process itself—the sequence of steps and events that occur when a product is developed. Second, it might study the individual staff-level activities—what individuals who work on an innovation project do during the day. Some specifics on implementing these two actions are presented next.

1. THE TASK FORCE MIGHT AUDIT THE PRODUCT DEVELOPMENT PROCESS TO IDENTIFY WHERE IMPROVEMENTS CAN BE MADE. A more detailed audit program based upon the seven steps of LSFI is contained in the chapter appendix. Here, however, are some of the key areas that the task force might investigate:

- inadequate funding of projects, causing engineers to work on several projects at once or shift around to different projects;

- inadequate understanding of the customer, which forces the project to be changed and revised in midstream;
- failure to adequately fund and plan the research base, requiring the engineers to invent during product development;
- management that is not on top of day-to-day activities, so they are not immediately aware when slips or delays start and do not quickly take corrective action;
- slow support and approval activities;
- a negative culture of conflict that gives rise to politicking and game playing;
- fears of discussing mistakes and problems;
- failure to do the up-front analysis;
- failure of groups to fully cooperate and help each other.

This list is brief, and more specifics are found in the chapter appendix. Nevertheless, however, the task force should identify the major reasons why delays and changes occur and how to improve the innovation process.

2. THE TASK FORCE MIGHT ANALYZE WHAT PEOPLE DO DURING THE DAY. When the task force analyzes the actual activities of the innovation staff, they likely will discover that very little value-added work is going on (see chapter 8). They might learn, as Canon did, that 25 percent of the time is spent on administration. Or they might learn, as Perry Gluckman of Process Plus did, that most of the time is spent in meetings. Or they might learn, as Tim Fuller of the University of Chicago did, that everything is revised or changed an average of 1.3 times.

An efficient way to gather this information, used by Gluckman and Fuller, is to give each person an electronic watch that is set to beep every forty-seven minutes. These watches are cheap and available at any drugstore. Whenever the watch beeps, people write down what they are doing. The forty-seven-minute interval falls at irregular times and is sufficiently long. (Twenty-three minutes also works well. A thirty-minute or sixty-minute interval seems to be too predictable.)

At the sound of the beep, the people jot down in a log the activity they are doing at that precise instant. Here are some examples from a software engineer:

- on a break
- on the phone with Jane to find out where information on the CAD is
- on the phone checking why a program module has not arrived
- getting blueprints
- completing travel expense voucher

None of these, notice, is actual design work.

Collecting a few hundred data points for any given activity is usually sufficient. When the task force examines the logs of data, they will typically find patterns. For example, people may spend a lot of time obtaining purchase orders or answering customer questions about products already developed. Indeed, the data usually reveal that surprisingly little actual design work is going on, or that what design work is being done is changed several times.

3. THE TASK FORCE MIGHT BENCHMARK. Once the task force has obtained this information, they will be in a position to benchmark the innovation process. If the firm does a lot of molding of plastics, for instance, the team should visit a top firm that molds plastic. If flexibility of design is a major concern, they should visit a firm that excels in that. This might require travel abroad or extensive phone calls. (The steps presented in chapter 5 can be helpful.)

It is important to stress the crucial role of benchmarking, since too many firms give it short shrift. They somehow feel they can learn things for themselves and do not need outside information. But that reasoning is imperfect. First, it is not clear that they can learn by themselves what the top firms know. Second, discovering things themselves takes time, since a lot of trial and error is involved. Third, if the firm wants to be best, it must learn the best ideas of others and then do even better.

4. THE TASK FORCE SHOULD SUGGEST CHANGES TO THE PROCESS AND INSTITUTE CONTINUOUS IMPROVEMENT WITH METRICS. Armed with data on their own innovation process and with information on what the top firms do, the task force should be able to suggest changes and improvements. Moreover, it should institute continuous-improvement techniques, including metrics, post-mortems, special teams assigned to improve key aspects of the process, and annual benchmarking.

The task force should develop an action plan to implement these recommendations. It is often helpful for the task force to present its findings to senior executives on a retreat devoted to restructuring the innovation activity, like the GE workout discussed in chapter 9.

Why LSFI Gets Such Big Improvements

What is so different about Lightning Strategy for Innovation? Although traditional approaches get five to ten percent gains, the approaches suggested herein are targeted at improvements of several hundred percent. The reasons that can occur are perhaps best demonstrated by contrasting the LSFI view of innovation against the conventional viewpoint.

1. Strategy
   - *Conventional viewpoint:* Strategy is the province primarily of finance and marketing.
   - *LSFI viewpoint:* New product innovation often dominates strategic success. In fact, rapid innovation revises the old strategic concepts of market share, mature markets, and even how acquisitions and divestitures should be handled.

2. Innovation
   - *Conventional viewpoint:* Innovation is a random and largely uncontrollable phenomenon.
   - *LSFI viewpoint:* The innovation process is complex, requiring careful coordination of marketing, engineering, and manufacturing. It requires a strategy and management and should not be left to chance.

3. Staff
   - *Conventional viewpoint:* In a division of labor, the work is organized into portions and people are hired to do the portions.
   - *LSFI viewpoint:* The quality and interaction of the people are almost everything. People must be trained and nurtured—their expertise determines success.

4. Risk
   - *Conventional viewpoint:* Certainty is surety. Risk is dangerous.
   - *LSFI viewpoint:* Even though the future is highly indeterminate, uncertainty does not mean unprofitability. Using a flexible and modular product design can help reduce risk in many cases. Risk can be managed, and doing so creates competitive advantages.

5. Goals

- *Conventional viewpoint:* Product development is driven by many goals, including time, budget, and the customer.
- *LSFI viewpoint:* The customer comes first, and the firm strives not just to satisfy the customer but to create delight. Engineers should have contact with customers. Formal techniques as in chapter 11 can help marketing and engineering interact and develop a product more likely to sell.

6. Changes

- *Conventional viewpoint:* Making changes later in a project is permissible.
- *LSFI viewpoint:* Changes get exorbitantly costly the later in a project they are made. Few things are as important to a project's success as the up-front planning to conceive the product right and prevent later changes. Cross-functional teams provide an excellent vehicle to accomplish this.

7. Foundations

- *Conventional viewpoint:* A product development project is a fairly independent activity needing only a good idea and some dedicated people.
- *LSFI viewpoint:* Product development requires solid technological foundations. Trying to invent during the product development process is too costly and too late and delays the product's market entry.

8. Efficiency

- *Conventional viewpoint:* The product development process is fairly efficient and needs only a little fine tuning.
- *LSFI viewpoint:* Fumbles—delays, changes, and waste—tend to be rampant, and most of them are hidden. But with some data collection and analysis, they can be slashed, making the product development process dramatically more efficient.

9. New Knowledge

- *Conventional viewpoint:* Most of the knowledge we need is internally available. Anything NIH—not invented here—is irrelevant to us in our circumstances because we are unique and different. Further, anything really important we will think of ourselves.
- *LSFI viewpoint:* Throughout the world, new techniques, tools, and ideas are constantly being developed. A firm must continually benchmark and keep up to date. To be the best, the company must learn what is best and go beyond that.

10. Improvement
   - *Conventional viewpoint:* People in a firm will naturally keep improving. After all, is that not what the firm pays for?
   - *LSFI viewpoint:* To lead, a firm must improve faster than its competitors. This means implementing an organized approach to continuous improvement.

These principles demonstrate how LSFI differs from other views of innovation. It is these differences that produce the significant improvements.

An Overall Perspective: Go for Big Improvements

A widespread belief is that innovation is largely unplanned and occurs almost by happenstance, as if struck by lightning. This book suggests the opposite—that innovation can be planned, structured, and greatly increased. On a recent trip to Philadelphia, I toured the wonderful historical site devoted to that extraordinary figure, Ben Franklin. Prior to his experiments, people did not understand lightning and felt it occurred in a random, uncontrollable way. With his kite flying high on a stormy day, Franklin channeled that lightning down the cord and proved that lightning could be controlled, managed, and directed. The lightning flashes of innovative ideas, this book contends, can also be controlled, managed, and directed.

Gerald Hock and Len Morgan (prior to his retirement) were part of GE's special team that helps GE divisions improve their product development. They fully concur that innovation can be managed. Morgan notes that the initial impetus is often a competitive threat, but with the right leadership people can be astonishingly creative.

Reconceptualize the Process for Big Improvements

Many companies hope to make improvements of a few percent a year. But they should switch their thinking and instead seek improvements of hundreds of percent. Fujitsu helped Kawasaki put in a new programming regimen that improved its software productivity by 250 percent.[1] According to Hiroshi Harafu of Fujitsu, "What we brought them was standardization, reusability, and a whole production approach."

Motorola has been one of the most sophisticated firms in seeking large gains, and it has corporate goals for improvement that have produced remarkable results:

- a factor-of-ten improvement in quality every two years, and
- a 50 percent reduction in cycle time each year. (Cycle time is the time it takes to complete a process or project.)

According to Bill Smith and Paul Noakes, both vice-presidents of Motorola, these impressive results cannot be obtained by enhancing the present way of conducting business. The key is for people to totally reconceive what they are going—in their words, "to reconceptualize the process."

Hewlett-Packard is also dramatically improving its innovation and product development. According to HP vice-president Joel Birnbaum, HP has a corporate goal of cutting product development time by half in five years. HP vice-president Harold Edmonson emphasizes the need not to go for a 20 percent or 30 percent improvement but to strive for the big gains. He urges his colleagues to "go for a factor-of-three improvement in sales, profits, performance, and quality." In response, one HP division decided to improve a product that was adequate but not great in reliability. The team proceeded to improve the reliability by a factor of six, pushing reliability to unprecedented levels. The team had so much fun doing this that they developed a new generation of product and improved reliability by another factor of three.

Innovation is not a random occurrence that happens simply by chance. Under proper leadership, the Lightning Strategy for Innovation can quickly produce impressive improvements. Reconceptualize. Go for the really big gains. Let the lightning strike.

Appendix
Auditing the Product Innovation Process

The following is an outline of issues that a team auditing a product development process might examine. The issues are based upon the seven steps of LSFI. This outline is only suggestive, as a firm's actual audit would be tailored to its products and markets.

1. Senior Management
   - Realizes the strong correlation between effective innovation and the success of the firm.
   - Is aware of the percent of sales from newly developed products, both for its own firm and for its competitors.
   - Knows the life-cycle of its products and the speed of innovation required to stay ahead competitively.
   - Realizes that the time and cost of innovation can often be slashed dramatically.
   - Discerns how innovation changes strategy including marketing, acquisitions, and finance.
   - Understands how innovation can often rejuvenate declining or dead markets.
   - Comprehends, at least in general terms, the trends in the relevant technologies.
   - Requires all sections of the firm to be world class and to annually benchmark.
   - Gives very fast (twenty-four hour) response to issues that reach its attention about innovation.
   - Supports personnel policies that provide for outstanding expertise in innovation.
   - Visits labs and development centers.
   - Keeps in contact with customers—and not just the management of a customer's firm, but the actual users of the company's products.
   - Is involved in key reviews of products and in strategic decisions about innovation. Avoids meddling in aspects where its expertise is not up to date.
   - Insures adequate funding of innovation.
   - Has goals for innovation, such as percent of sales from new products.
   - Establishes an open culture, without fear, where innovation can flourish.
   - Ensures that innovation is rewarded and recognized.
   - Understands that design governs most of the cost of manufacturing a product.
   - Highlights innovation in speeches.
   - Knows the importance of speed in product development and the high cost of being late to the market.
   - Knows the importance of fast delivery to customers and, in general, of fast response to customers.
   - Stresses quality and cycle-time issues throughout the organization.
   - Promotes close coordination and interaction between marketing, R&D, and manufacturing and has effective incentives to promote that.

- Stamps out the "not invented here" syndrome.
- Supports innovation and the variety of suggestions listed below.

2. Strategic Planning
    - Uses technological road maps.
    - Ensures that core competencies and key success factors are well considered, funded, and managed.
    - Uses the portfolio concept, in which the products being innovated are balanced for timing, for market, and for risk in market, technology, and manufacturing.
    - Ensures joint planning between R&D and marketing.
    - Uses the anticipation concept to estimate future products and learn how to anticipate better.
    - Builds a solid research base so that little innovation needs to be done during actual product development.
    - Estimates trends in the market, technology, government, and relevant issues.
    - Builds flexibility and responsiveness into the system so that the company can respond rapidly to an uncertain future.
    - Uses functional maps.
    - Ensures adequate funding of innovation, and especially that no aspect of innovation is overloaded or jammed up.
    - Uses early warning teams to monitor markets and trends.
    - Gathers competitor intelligence.
    - Uses computer models.

3. Corporate Culture
    - Uses *waigaya*.
    - Has open culture, without fear.
    - Requires that customers come first in innovation.
    - Ensures that no new product idea is blocked.
    - Provides multiple funding sources for new product ideas.
    - Stresses trust and being trustworthy with open discussion, no game playing, and full disclosure of information.
    - Expects all problems to be revealed immediately.
    - Expects that others will be supportive of a person with a problem.
    - Does not allow blame or finger-pointing.
    - Expects everyone to be mutually supportive.
    - Surveys staff to find out their true feelings about innovation and the management.

4. Fumble Elimination
    - Understands that fumbles—delays, changes, unnecessary work—can waste over half of development's time and money.

- Has formal procedures to eliminate waste using such techniques as tiger teams, workouts, work sampling, bottleneck breaking, and use of theoretical limits.
- Understands that fumbles in almost any part of the firm—including suppliers, support services, and senior management—can harm and delay innovation.
- Realizes that fumbles should be eliminated before capital investment.

5. Customer First
   - Stresses the Customer First Questions.
   - Highlights giving customers delight.
   - Realizes the importance of cooperation between marketing and engineering, and has procedures to have engineering join marketing in obtaining information about customers.
   - Understands that many conflicts between marketing and engineering can be resolved with more accurate information about what customers want.
   - Gets information about customers that engineers need.
   - Knows the value of having engineers and managers in personal contact with customers.
   - Uses techniques like quality function deployment, conjoint analysis, cultural anthropology, and kansei analysis to better comprehend the customer.
   - Ties all aspects of the innovation process, including manufacturing and quality assurance, to the customer's needs.
   - Discerns the importance of speaking not just to one's own customers but to the customers of competitors and to noncustomers.
   - Stresses the importance of understanding the customer's needs and wants, and how not only the firm's products but also competitive products satisfy those needs and wants.
   - Understands that revolutionary products need different customer analysis procedures from evolutionary ones.

6. Flexibility and Rapid-Cycle Learning
   - Realizes that in many markets traditional customer research is not worth the time and cost.
   - Understands that flexibility permits adaption of the product to actual customer buying patterns.
   - Uses rapid-cycle learning to quickly respond to the market and quickly add improvements to the product.

7. Business Strategy
   - Understands the importance of having experts from marketing, engineering, and other key areas jointly think through the big picture of the business issues.

- Employs a checklist of criteria, such as Edith Wilson's points, NewProd, or other evaluation system.
- Thinks through the business strategy of the product before starting actual product development.
- Evaluates risks in technology, marketing, manufacturing, and other relevant areas. Has backup procedures for any likely risks, and permits "no surprises."
- Considers time to break even and cost of being late to market.

8. Platform, Reuse, and Modularity
   - Perceives that for many products, PRM is the crucial strategy for success.
   - Plans for product families, for multiple generations of families, and for modularity.
   - Employs reuse for low cost, high-speed product introductions, and for improvements.
   - Considers product development in terms of modules that are re-used, where the modules subsume designs, parts, and processes.
   - Stresses reuse of software to cut costs and bugs.
   - Implements PRM strategies in product development. Specifically, shortly after the development of one model is launched, the development of the subsequent model is started. Early in the development of a model the specifications are frozen, and any improvements are fed into the subsequent model. The models are highly modular, permitting model variety and rapid improvements. Innovations and technical advancements are done off line by research so that minimal invention is done during the actual product development.

9. Actual Product Development (Concurrent Engineering)
   - Understands the high cost of changes later in the product development process.
   - Understands the value of parallel processing.
   - Understands that the old sequential way of product development was faulty and led to conflict and delays.
   - Uses a cross-functional team to manage the project and to correctly conceptualize the development effort up front.
   - Has the cross-functional team avoid later changes by using robustness, Taguchi methods, design reviews, involvement of customers and suppliers, and other relevant approaches.
   - Gives the team leader authority to finish the project without meddling from senior management.
   - Has a godfather oversee and facilitate progress.
   - Uses co-location, isolation, dedication, and concentration to promote creativity.

10. Contract Book
    - Plans out the development project to avoid problems.
    - Freezes specifications to avoid later changes.
    - Ensures that any aspect that cannot be frozen is carefully considered and has appropriate backup and contingency plans.
    - Uses PRM strategies, if appropriate.
    - Provides goals for the product specifications and for all aspects of the development, manufacturing, and marketing process.
    - Uses staffing level metrics based upon historical data to estimate the cost and time of development.

11. Scheduling
    - Uses the phase-review process (with phases overlapped). But ensures that the reviews are not excessively stringent, that the reviews are held expeditiously, that the reviews are conducted by experts, and that top management participates only if they can make a positive contribution and not meddle.
    - Uses anticipation to forecast problems and learns to anticipate problems better.
    - Does good day-to-day scheduling and monitoring of that schedule.
    - Involves all staff in an up-front, several-day-long session to carefully think through the development process and each phase.
    - Eliminates fear, so that staff feels free to discuss problems.
    - Establishes procedures to ensure a project keeps on schedule, including: research done ahead of time, good up-front planning, problems revealed and attacked quickly, good funding, careful monitoring of progress, no delays from support or other activities, and good coordination.

12. Technical Approaches
    - Uses concept design approaches.
    - Ensures low-cost, high-quality manufacturing through the use of value analysis, capability index, and design for manufacturing and assembly.
    - Employs target costing to ensure that manufacturing cost is low enough to be successful in the market.
    - Uses design of experiments and Taguchi methods to ensure product robustness and avoid later engineering changes.
    - Employs rapid prototyping to test out development.
    - Uses periodic prototyping as the milestones to schedule the project.
    - Uses CAD extensively.

13. Continuous Improvement
    - Employs goals and a variety of metrics for all aspects of the development process, including quality, cycle time, anticipation, customer satisfaction, and delay reduction.

- Does root-cause analysis to obtain improvements.
- Uses post-mortems to improve the innovation process.
- Ensures that errors and mistakes are used not to penalize anyone but solely to improve the development process.

14. Action Plan

- Utilizes a task force of top experts to improve the product development process.
- Has the task force report to the CEO and get a quick hit.
- Understands that massive improvements are possible by "reconceptualizing the process."

Notes

Chapter 1

1. Lawrence M. Fisher, "A World Boom in Mountain Bikes Revives American Manufacturers," *New York Times,* 1 April 1991, p. A1, col. 1.
2. Quoted in Janice Castro, "Sporting Goods: Rock and Roll," *Time,* August 19, 1991, p. 44.
3. Doron P. Levin, "Where Car Makers Fear to Cut," *New York Times,* May 16, 1991, p. C1, col. 3.
4. "Market Place: Reebok Rebounds With the Pump," *New York Times,* June 7, 1991, p. C6, col. 3.
5. Quoted in G. Pascal Zachary, "Apple's Sculley Looks for a Breakthrough," *Wall Street Journal,* March 15, 1991, p. B1, col. 4.
6. Noel Capon, John U. Farley, Donald R. Lehmann, and James M. Hulbert, "Profiles of Innovators among Large U.S. Manufacturers," *Management Science* 38 (February 1992), pp. 157–69.
7. Albert Page, presentation to Product Development and Management Association, Chicago, November 13, 1991.
8. John Hauser, presentation to ORSA/TIMS conference, Philadelphia October 29, 1990.
9. Preston G. Smith and Donald G. Reinertsen, *Developing Products in Half the Time* (New York: Van Nostrand Reinhold, 1991).
10. Robert I. Winner, presentation to "Time Based Competition: Speeding New Product Development" conference, Vanderbilt University, May 16–17, 1991.
11. N. R. Spies, "How 'Strykeforce' Beat the Clock," *New York Times,* March 25, 1990, sec. 3, p. 1.

Chapter 2

1. William M. Bulkeley, "Changed Industry," *Wall Street Journal,* September 5, 1991, p. 1. col. 6.
2. "New Japanese Winner: A Mazda Convertible," *New York Times,* July 8, 1989, p. 15.
3. "Ringing in Saturn," *U.S. News and World Report,* October 22, 1990, pp. 51–54.

4. Ralph Gomory, "From the Ladder of Science to the Product Development Cycle," *Harvard Business Review* (November–December 1989), pp. 99–105.

5. G. Pascal Zachary, "Hewlett-Packard Revises Its Game Plan," *Wall Street Journal,* October 12, 1990, p. A4, col. 1.

6. Rebecca Henderson, *Underinvestment and Incompetence as Responses to Radical Innovation,* working paper no. 3163-90-BPS, MIT Sloan School of Management, May 1990.

7. Quoted in George Stalk, Jr. and Thomas M. Hour, *Competing Against Time* (New York: Free Press, 1990), p. 146.

8. "Japanese Portables Threaten American Lead in Computers," *New York Times,* November 24, 1990, p. 1.

9. *Our Story So Far: Notes from the First 75 Years of 3M Company* (St. Paul, Minn.: Minnesota Mining and Manufacturing, 1977), p. 74.

10. Karl T. Ulrich and Charles H. Fine, "Cost Estimation Tools to Support Product Design," presentation to ASME Manufacturing International Conference, Atlanta, March 1990.

11. Dan Dimancescu, *The Seamless Enterprise* (New York: Harper Business, 1992).

12. Ralph Gomory, "From the Ladder of Science to the Product Development Cycle," pp. 99–105.

13. "Cadillac Celebrates Quality Turnaround," *Chicago Tribune,* November 18, 1990, sec. 17, p. 5.

14. Geoffrey Boothroyd and Peter Dewhurst, *Product Design for Assembly* (Wakefield, R.I.: Boothroyd and Dewhurst, 1987).

15. Quoted in Robert Wrubel, "GM Finally Fights Back," *Financial World* 160 (November 1991) pp. 22–26.

16. *Hewlett-Packard and Engineering Productivity* (Hewlett-Packard Design Center, May 1988); *Electronic Business* (July 1983), p. 86.

Chapter 3

1. Barry W. Boehm, *Software Engineering Economics,* (Englewood Cliffs, N.J.: Prentice-Hall, 1981), p. 446.

2. See Barry W. Boehm and Philip N. Papaccio, "Understanding and Controlling Software Costs," *IEEE Transactions on Software Engineering* 14 (October 1988), pp. 1462–77.

3. "Microsoft to Pitch a New Hardball," *New York Times,* November 12, 1990, p. C1.

4. "Japanese Labs in U.S. Luring America's Computer Experts," *New York Times,* November 11, 1990, p. 1.

5. Lance Ealey and Leif G. Soderberg, "How Honda Cures Design Amnesia," *McKinsey Quarterly* (Spring 1990), p. 3.

6. Michael W. Miller, "Giant IBM Stumbles Over Minuscule Chip," *Wall Street Journal,* March 21, 1989, p. B4, col. 1.

7. T. R. Reid and Brit Hume, "On Computers: Transplant May Be in Store for PC's Brain," *Chicago Tribune,* August 11, 1991, sec. 7, p. 8, col. 3.

8. Jim Carlton, "U.S. Construction Firms Trail Japanese in Research," *Asian Wall Street Journal,* August 12, 1991, p. 10, col. 1.

9. C. K. Prahalad and Gary Hamel, "The Core Competence of the Corporation," *Harvard Business Review* (May–June 1990), pp. 79–91.

10. Ibid.

11. Ibid.

12. John Markoff, *New York Times,* October 6, 1991, sec. 3, p. 1.

13. Robert H. Schaffer, *The Breakthrough Strategy* (Ballinger Publishing, 1988), p. 186.

14. Alan M. Webber, "An Interview with Compaq's Rod Canion," *Harvard Business Review* (July–August 1990), pp. 115–23.

15. Markoff, *op. cit.*

16. Gene Bylinsky, "Turning R&D into Real Products," *Fortune,* July 2, 1990, pp. 72–77.

17. Amal Kumar Naj, "GE's Latest Invention: A Way to Move Ideas From Lab to Market," *Wall Street Journal,* June 14, 1990, p. 1, col. 6.

18. Ealey and Soderberg, "How Honda Cures Design Amnesia," p. 3.

Chapter 4

1. Deborah Dougherty and Trudy Heller, "The Illegitimacy of Product Innovation in Large Firms," working paper, The Wharton School, Philadelphia, Pa. (November 1990).

Chapter 5

1. Cuneyt Oge, "Achieving World Class Performance in Product Development: The Organizational Challenge," *EIU International Motor Business* (April 1990), pp. 95–123.

2. David Altany, "Copycats," *Industry Week,* November 5, 1990.

3. Quoted in ibid.

4. Cyril Charney, *Time to Market: Reducing Product Lead Time* (Dearborn, Mich.: Society of Manufacturing Engineers, 1991).

5. Tom Inglesby, "How They Brought Home the Prize," *Manufacturing Systems* (April 1989), pp. 26–32.

Chapter 6

1. Robert D. Hershey, Jr., "Weak Economy Takes Toll on Its Experts," *New York Times,* September 26, 1991, p. 17, col. 3.

2. Quoted in Milt Fredenheim, "Cashing In on Health Care's Troubles," *New York Times,* July 21, 1991, sec. 3, p. 1, col. 3.

3. Christopher Knowlton, "Shell Gets Rich by Beating Risk," *Fortune* 24 (August 26, 1991), pp. 79–82.

4. Steven C. Wheelwright and Kim B. Clark, "Creating Project Plans to Focus Product Development," *Harvard Business Review* (April 1992), pp. 70–82.

5. Abe Reichenthal, presentation at "Speeding New Products to Market: Best Practices and Teamwork" conference, jointly sponsored by the Marketing Institute and the Product Development Management Association, Chicago, March 23–24, 1992.

6. Robert W. Hallman, presentation at "Speeding New Products to Market: Best Practices and Teamwork" conference, jointly sponsored by the Marketing Institute and the Product Development Management Association, Chicago, March 23–24, 1992.

7. Thomas D. Kuczmarski, presentation at "Speeding New Products to Market: Best Practices and Teamwork" conference, jointly sponsored by the Marketing Institute and the Product Development Management Association, Chicago, March 23–24, 1992.

8. Wheelwright and Clark, "Creating Project Plans to Focus Product Development."

9. Albert Page, presentation at "Speeding New Products to Market: Best Practices and Teamwork" conference, jointly sponsored by the Marketing Institute and the Product Development Management Association, Chicago, March 23–24, 1992.

10. Steven C. Wheelwright and Kim B. Clark, *Revolutionizing Product Development: Quantum Leaps in Speed, Efficiency, and Quality* (New York: Free Press, 1992).

Chapter 7

1. Robert Winner, presentation at "Time Based Competition" conference, Vanderbilt University, May 16–17, 1991.

2. Claudia H. Deutsch, "007 It's Not. But Intelligence Is In," *New York Times,* December 23, 1990, col. 3, p. 24.

3. Vincent A. Mabert, John F. Muth, and Roger W. Schmenner, "Collapsing New Product Development Times," discussion paper no. 487, School of Business, Indiana University.

Chapter 8

1. *The Mythical Man Month* (Reading, Mass.: Addison-Wesley, 1979).

2. Richard J. Schonberger, *Building a Chain of Customers* (New York: Free Press, 1990), p. 290.

3. Michael Hammer, "Reengineer Work: Don't Automate, Obliterate," *Harvard Business Review* (July–August 1990), pp. 104–12.
4. David Sartorius, Sloan School of Management, MIT, May 1990.
5. George Stalk, Jr., and Thomas M. Hout, *Competing Against Time,* (New York: The Free Press, 1990), p. 123.
6. "Questing for the Best," *Business Week,* October 25, 1991, p. 11.
7. Dan Dimancescu, *The Seamless Enterprise* (New York: Harper Business, 1992).
8. Stalk and Hout, *Competing Against Time,* p. 177; Joseph D. Blackburn, ed., *Time-Based Competition,* (Homewood, Ill.: Business One Irwin, 1991).

Chapter 9

1. *Wall Street Journal,* May 1, 1984, p. 38.
2. Jerry Flint, "Banzai with a Georgia Accent," *Forbes* 147 (February 4, 1991), pp. 58–60.
3. Michael Hammer, "Reengineer Work: Don't Automate, Obliterate," *Harvard Business Review* (July–August 1990), pp. 104–12.
4. "Getting Everybody Into the Act," *Business Week,* October 25, 1991, p. 152.
5. Daniel E. Whitney, "Manufacturing by Design," *Harvard Business Review* (July–August 1988), pp. 83–91.
6. Richard J. Schonberger, *World Class Manufacturing Casebook* (New York: Free Press, 1987).
7. Ibid.

Chapter 10

1. "New Products Clog Groceries," *New York Times,* May 29, 1990, p. C1.
2. Glen Urban and John Hauser, *Design and Marketing of New Products,* (Englewood Cliffs, N.J.: Prentice-Hall,).
3. *New Product Management for the 1980's* (Booz Allen and Hamilton, 1982).
4. Albert Page, presentation to Product Development and Management Association, Chicago, November 13, 1991.

Chapter 11

1. "New Products Clog Groceries," *New York Times,* May 29, 1990, p. C1.
2. Eric Weiner, "New Boeing Airliner Shaped by Airlines," *New York Times,* December 19, 1990, p. C1, col. 4.
3. Lawrence M. Fisher, "British Air Chooses Boeing and Orders G.E. Engines," *New York Times,* August 22, 1991, p. C3, col. 3.
4. Edwin McDowell, "Slow Book Sales? Off to the Front," *New York Times,* July 30, 1990, p. C1, col. 3.

5. Robert G. Cooper, *Winning at New Products* (Reading, Mass.: Addison-Wesley, 1986).
6. Quoted in Kim Foltz, "New Species for Study: Customers in Action," *New York Times,* December 18, 1989, p. 1, col. 1.
7. Quoted in ibid.
8. "In Search of New Products," *New York Times,* February 24, 1991, p. 25, col. 3.
9. Michael Lev, "Nissan Sued by U.S. Couple; Was Boarder Really a Spy?" *New York Times,* December 9, 1989, p. 10, col. 6.
10. Paul Galloway, "The Culture Club," *Chicago Tribune,* November 27, 1991, see. 5, p. 1.
11. Louis P. Sullivan, "Quality Function Deployment," *Quality Progress* (June 1986), pp. 39–50.
12. "No. 1—And Trying Harder," *Business Week* October 25, 1991, p. 22.
13. Quoted in Adam Bryant, "It's Flash, It's Dash, and It's Out of Detroit," *New York Times,* February 23, 1992, sec. 3, p. 5, col. 1.

Chapter 12

1. Susan Walsh Sanderson, and Vic Uzumeri, "Strategies for New Product Development and Renewal: Design-Based Incrementalism," Center for Science and Technology Policy, Rensselaer Polytechnic Institute (n.d.).
2. David E. Sanger, "Sony's Norio Ohga: Building Smaller, Buying Bigger," *New York Times Magazine,* February 18, 1990, p. 22.
3. Ralph Gomory, "From the Ladder of Science to the Product Development Cycle," *Harvard Business Review* (November–December 1989), p. 99–105.

Chapter 13

1. Tom Inglesby, "How They Brought Home the Prize," *Manufacturing Systems* (April 1989), pp. 26–32.
2. Edith Wilson, *Product Definition Factors for Successful Design* thesis, Stanford University (December 1990). See also Edith Wilson, "Product Definition: Assorted Techniques and Their Marketplace Impact," *1990 IEEE International Engineering Management Conference Proceedings,* pp. 64–68.
3. Quoted in Marshall Schuon, "In the Doldrums, a New Lease on Life," *New York Times,* July 7, 1991, p. 18, col. 3.
4. Quoted in Eduardo Lachica, "Surge In Japanese Competition Expected As U.S. Lifts Tariff on Laptop Computers," *Wall Street Journal,* August 5, 1991, p. B6, col. 3.
5. Robert G. Cooper, "The NewProd Systems: The Industry Experience," *Journal of Product Innovation Management 9* (June 1992), pp. 112–13.
6. *World News Tonight,* ABC Network Television, September 25, 1991.

7. Sunder Kekre, presentation at "Time Based Competition: Speeding New Product Development" conference, Vanderbilt University, May 16–17, 1991.
8. Chris Kemerer, "An Empirical Validation of Software Cost Estimation Models, *Communications of the ACM* 30 (May 1987).
9. "Hewlett-Packard and Engineering Productivity," brochure (Hewlett-Packard Design Center, May 1988).

Chapter 14

1. Daniel E. Whitney, "Manufacturing by Design," *Harvard Business Review* (July–August 1988), p. 87.
2. Gary Reiner, "It Takes Planning to Put Plans into Action," *New York Times,* March 12, 1989, sec. 3, p. 3.
3. Susan Walsh Sanderson and Vic Uzumeri, "Strategies for New Product Development and Renewal: Design Based Incrementalism," Center for Science and Technology Policy, School of Management, Rensselaer Polytechnic Institute (n.d.).
4. Robert H. Yacobellis, "White Paper on U.S. and Japanese Software Engineering" (Motorola Corporate Software Resources Development, January 1990).

Chapter 15

1. "A Smarter Way to Manufacture," *Business Week,* April 30, 1990, pp. 110–17.
2. IBM, *The Quality Journal Continues* (December 1990), p. 10. Order Number G325-6015-00. IBM Rochester, Malcolm Baldrige Office, Department 802, Highway 52 and NW 37 St., Rochester MN.
3. Barry Boehm, *Software Engineering Economics* (Englewood Cliffs, N.J.: Prentice-Hall, 1981), p. 40.
4. Robert I. Winner, presentation at "Time Based Competition: Speeding New Product Design and Development" conference, Vanderbilt University, May 16, 1991.
5. Daniel E. Whitney, "Manufacturing by Design," *Harvard Business Review* (July–August 1988), p. 83.
6. James L. Nevins and Daniel E. Whitney, ed., *Concurrent Design of Products and Processes* (New York; McGraw-Hill), p. 3.
7. Dan Dimancescu, *The Seamless Enterprise* (New York: Harper Business, 1992).
8. Jon Turino, "Making It Work," *IEEE Spectrum* 28 (July 1991), p. 31.
9. "A Smarter Way to Manufacture," *Business Week,* April 30, 1990, pp. 110–17.
10. Doron P. Levin, "The Nation: Where 'Buy American' Is More Than a Slogan," *New York Times,* January 26, 1992, sec. 4, p. 2, col. 1.

11. Tom Inglesby, "How They Brought Home the Prize," *Manufacturing Systems* (April 1989), pp. 26–32.

12. Edward O. Welles, "The Shape of Things to Come," *Inc.* 14 (February 1992), p. 74.

13. Robert Wrubel, "GM Finally Fights Back," *Financial World* 160 (November 26, 1991), pp. 22–26.

14. Doron P. Levin, "A Bet Chrysler Can't Afford to Lose," *New York Times,* August 26, 1991, p. C1, col. 3.

15. Hirotak Takeuchi and Ikujiro Nonaka, "The New New Product Development Game," *Harvard Business Review* 64 (January–February 1986), pp. 137–46.

16. Quoted in Inglesby, "How They Brought Home the Prize," p. 27.

17. "A Smarter Way to Manufacture," *Business Week,* April 30, 1990, p. 110.

18. Clarence L. Johnson, "Kelly", with Maggie Smith, Kelly, *More Than My Share of It All,* (Washington, D.C.: Smithsonian Institution Press, 1987).

19. John Markoff, "Abe Peled's Secret Start-Up at I.B.M.," *New York Times,* December 8, 1991, sec. 3, p. 1, col. 2.

20. William J. Spencer, "Research to Product: A Major U.S. Challenge," *California Management Review* 32 (Winter 1990), pp. 45–53.

21. Barbara Berke, presentation at "Time-Based Competition: Speeding New Product Design and Development" conference, Vanderbilt University, May 16–17, 1991.

22. Robert Wrubel, "GM Finally Fights Back," *Financial World* 160 (November 26, 1991), pp. 22–26.

Chapter 16

1. K. Uchimaru and S. Okamoto, *NEC's Total Quality Program for Design Engineering,* Product Development Consulting, 19 Perry Street, Cambridge Mass., 02139 (617) 661-1470.

2. "A Design Master's End Run Around Trial and Error," *Business Week,* October 25, 1991, p. 25.

3. Robert Wrubel, "GM Finally Fights Back," *Financial World* 160 (November 26, 1991), pp. 22–26.

4. Uchimaru and Okamoto, *NEC's Total Quality Program.*

5. "Miles Traveled, More to Go," *Business Week,* October 25, 1991, p. 70.

6. Daniel E. Whitney, "Manufacturing by Design," *Harvard Business Review* (July–August 1988), pp. 83–91.

7. Doron P. Levin, "G.M. Woes Add to Pressure on Saturn," *New York Times,* December 17, 1991, p. C1, col. 2.

8. Joseph B. White, "Foreign Aid: Japanese Auto Makers Help U.S. Suppliers Become More Efficient," *Wall Street Journal,* September 9, 1991, p. A1, col. 1.

Chapter 17

1. Robert G. Cooper, "Stage-Gate Systems: A New Tool for Managing New Products," *Business Horizons* 33 (May–June 1990), pp. 44–54.

2. Ibid.
3. Ibid.·
4. Quoted in Fred Moody, "Mr. Software," *New York Times Magazine,* August 28, 1991, p. 26.
5. Steven D. Eppinger, Daniel E. Whitney, Robert P. Smith, and David A. Gebala, "Organizing the Tasks in Complex Design Projects," Alfred P. Sloan School of Management, MIT, working paper no. 3083-89-MS revised (June 1990).
6. Tom Inglesby, "How They Brought Home the Prize," *Manufacturing Systems* (April, 1989), pp. 26–32.
7. Steven C. Wheelwright and Kim B. Clark, *Revolutionizing Product Development: Quantum Leaps in Speed, Efficiency, and Quality* (New York: Free Press, 1992).
8. Cooper, "Stage-Gate Systems." See also Robert G. Cooper and E. J. Kleinschmidt, *Formal Processes for Managing New Products: The Industrial Experience* (Hamilton, Ont.: McMaster University, n.d.)

Chapter 18

1. Stuart Pugh, *Total Design* (Reading, Mass.: Addison-Wesley, 1990).
2. Theodore C. Fowler, *Value Analysis* (New York: Van Nostrand Reinhold, 1990).
3. Japan Management Association, *Canon Production System,* (Cambridge, Mass.: Productivity Press, 1987).
4. Roger Cohen, "Suzuki in Hungary: Team Spirit Sags," *New York Times,* May 16, 1992, p. 17, col. 3.
5. "Digital Builds a Better Mousetrap," *DFMA Insight* 1 (Wakefield, R.I.: Boothroyd Dewhurst).
6. "Pssst! Want a Secret for Making Superproducts?" *Business Week,* October 2, 1989, p. 106.
7. Richard J. Schonberger, *Building a Chain of Customers* (New York: Free Press, 1990), p. 221.
8. G. Boothroyd and P. Dewhurst, *Product Design for Assembly,* (Wakefield, R.I.: Boothroyd and Dewhurst, 1987).
9. Karl Ulrich et al., "A Framework for Including the Value of Time in Design-for-Manufacturing Decision Making," working paper no. 3243-9-MSA, MIT (February 1991).
10. G. Taguchi and M. S. Phadke, "Quality Engineering Through Design Optimization," *Conference Record,* vol. 3, *IEEE Globecon* (November 1984), pp. 1106–13.
11. Barnaby J. Feder, "Making a Model, and Doing it Fast," *New York Times,* September 23, 1990, sec. F, p. 9, col. 1.
12. David Tait, *Rapid Prototyping Report* (June 1991), p. 4. Published by F Cubed, 10717 Wilshire Blvd., Suite 802, Los Angeles CA 90024, (213) 470-4320.

13. Ibid.
14. Steven C. Wheelwright and Kim B. Clark, *Revolutionizing Product Development: Quantum Leaps in Speed, Efficiency, and Quality* (New York: Free Press, 1992).
15. Ibid.
16. Ibid.
17. John Holusha, "Pushing the Envelope at Boeing," *New York Times,* November 10, 1991, sec. 3, p. 1, col. 2.
18. Adam Bryant, "Engine-Testing Software Built for Speed," *New York Times,* February 5, 1992, p. C5, col. 1.

Chapter 19

1. Bill Smith and Willard I. Zangwill, *Total Customer Satisfaction: The Motorola System,* report, Graduate School of Business, University of Chicago, 1988.
2. K. Uchimaru and S. Okamoto, *NEC's Total Quality Program For Design Engineering* (March 1990). Product Development Consulting, 19 Perry St., Cambridge, MA 02139, (617) 661-1470.
3. "Hewlett-Packard and Engineering Productivity," booklet, Hewlett-Packard (May 1988).

Chapter 20

1. "Now Software Isn't Safe From Japan," *Business Week,* February 11, 1991, p. 84.

Index